Holy ~~~~~ The Hill

C000182613

LOOK W~~
THE LORD
HAS DONE!

An Exploration of
Black Christian Faith in Britain

LOOK WHAT THE LORD HAS DONE!

An Exploration of Black Christian Faith in Britain

Mark Sturge

Published by Scripture Union, 207–209 Queensway, Bletchley, MK2 2EB, England, UK

Email: info@scriptureunion.org.uk
Website: www.scriptureunion.org.uk

Scripture Union Australia
Locked Bag 2, Central Coast Business Centre, NSW 2252
www.su.org.au

© Mark Sturge

First published 2005

ISBN 1 85999 680 9

British Library Cataloguing-in-Publication Data
A catalogue record for this book is available from the British Library

Cover design by Leigh Jones Limited of London
Internal design and typesetting by Servis Filmsetting Limited of Manchester

Printed and bound in Great Britain by Creative Print and Design (Wales) Ebbw Vale

& Scripture Union is an international Christian charity working with churches in more than 130 countries, providing resources to bring the good news about Jesus Christ to children, young people and families, and to encourage them to develop spiritually through the Bible and prayer.

As well as our network of volunteers, staff and associates who run holidays, church-based events and school Christian groups, we produce a wide range of publications and support those who use our resources through training programmes.

Dedication

This book is partly inspired by my conviction that Black Christians have an important role to play in transforming British society and a significant contribution to make to church life in Britain. It is also a mark of the love and respect I hold for two men who have nurtured, shaped and left a lasting impact on my life.

From the age of six months until I was twenty-one years old, my grandfather Henry Hubert Sturge was, to all intents and purposes, my 'father'. He taught me that strength of character was one of the most important qualities I could develop. 'Ask questions and you will know things!' was his mantra. He also showed me what it takes to be a man, the discipline of hard work and commitment, and what it means to dedicate one's life to serving others.

As a Christian, my grandfather created the environment for me to learn about God, encouraged me to attend Sunday school and to sing in church (though he was not above resorting to the occasional bribe!). There were additional incentives and punishment in equal measure to ensure that I did not waste my life on youthful follies. In the end, Grandfather became my confidant on the big questions of life and the big decisions I wanted to make. Thanks, Dad, for investing so much of your time and energy into my life. You have laid the foundations for all that I have done and hope to become. You are a large part of me, and I love you dearly.

I found a second father in Philip Mohabir, a founder and father of the African and Caribbean Evangelical Alliance. Philip embodied the spirit of seeking unity and reconciliation in the church in the UK. He was a missionary, a pioneer, an ambassador, a mentor and a father to many leaders. He lived his life for the cause of the gospel.

Philip went to be with the Lord on 26 November 2004. Although he did not have the opportunity to read this book, I am sure that he would have been proud of its content, the challenges it poses and the contribution it will make to Black Christian faith in Britain. I feel extremely privileged to dedicate this book to his memory and to his inspiration, courage and tenacity to go against public opinion and do whatever it took to honour God. My thanks also to his wife Muriel and to his daughters and their families for sharing him with us. Well done, good and faithful servant!

Mark Sturge

What church leaders think of this book

The unfolding history of the Black Christian community in this country is a truly powerful testimony of how God works among and through minority communities to demonstrate the impact of the gospel. In his book, Mark takes us further on our journey of understanding the nature and purpose of Black Majority Churches and Black Christianity. This is a highly significant contribution to the growing literary genre that seeks to locate the Black Christian experience within the wider church and society. Read it and marvel at what God has done, and as a sign of what God will do in the future.

Bishop Dr Joe Aldred, Churches Together in Britain and Ireland

Mark has provided us with a considerable compendium of information on Black Majority Churches, embracing important facts and trenchantly argued personal opinion. My hope is that this book will take us beyond the superficial understanding that characterises much well-meaning inter-church liaison and generate new levels of respect. Such an outcome would serve us all well for the future.

Rev Hugh Osgood, Senior Minster, Cornerstone Christian Centre and member of the ACEA Board.

Mark Sturge has drawn an audacious line that connects our heritage with our destiny. He has skilfully delivered to us an understanding of the times, so that we can know what we ought to do for the future. A 'must read' for any Black Christian who wants to make a significant impact in the twenty-first century.

Dr Tayo Adeyemi, Senior Minister, New Wine Church, London

The relevance and contributions of the Black Majority Churches in Britain needed to be spelt out. As a person who was converted in Britain and spent my formation years in British churches, both as member and minister, I needed convincing about the need for the BMC. However, the needs of people who wish to integrate without being assimilated helped me to appreciate the pivotal role that BMCs can play.

Reverend Dr Paul Jinadu, General Overseer, New Covenant Church

I commend Mark for his well-researched and timely book which helps us to better understand the contribution of Black people to British Church life in particular. This book is a much needed resource and should prove useful to those in education, religion, social and political life.

**Eric A Brown, FRSA, Administrative Bishop,
New Testament Church of God, England and Wales**

Perhaps the Lord has sent people from across the seas to participate in carrying the Ark of God. The Ark always represents God's glory. Mark Sturge has appropriately and accurately represented the Black Majority Church in the UK.

Dr Albert Odulele, Glory House, UK

Mark Sturge's book makes for an uncomfortable read but that doesn't mean we should avoid it; rather the reverse. Mark tells the British church a few home truths. Given his own experience and his standing as a church leader, we should listen carefully and then act.

Dr Derek Tidball, Principal, London School of Theology

Considering the role that the Black Majority Churches have played in this nation in recent years, it is amazing there are so few books about them. With his wealth of experience, Mark Sturge is arguably the best-suited person to fill this vacuum. His book is a 'must read' for Christians, Black or White, and for anyone wanting to understand the phenomenon of the Black Majority Churches.

Dr Agu Irukwu, Jesus House for All Nations

Mark Sturge has done the British church an invaluable service. He has not only helped clarify the ethos and identity of Black Majority Churches, he has also demonstrated the outstanding contribution that Black Christians have made to British church life. His work is a positive contribution towards unity and understanding.

**Pastor Colin Dye, Senior Minister,
Kensington Temple, London City Church**

Contents

Acknowledgements

Before I knew that God loved me, I knew that my wife Sharon did. I feel extremely blessed that they are both still in love with me! The time taken to write this book has meant time away from Sharon and Mark Anthony, our son. Thank you both for your patience and for giving me that time to research and pen this work. Without your support, it would not have been possible. I love and cherish you both.

My thanks to all those churches – including both leaders and members – who have supported me and the work of ACEA over the years. This book is about your story, your success, your challenges and your future. It is my hope that you will feel able to embrace it and use it to inform your current thinking and the furtherance of your ministry.

I am grateful to my wider family and friends whose continual queries about how the book was going gave me the courage to complete it. Equally, to Ailish Eves and Deryck Sheriffs, who made a significant contribution to my spiritual and theological development. Thank you so much.

I would like to thank my colleagues, Bishop Dr Joe Aldred, Reverend Wale Babatunde, Reverend Joel Edwards, Reverend Dr Jonathan Oleyede and Dr Anthony Reddie, who have taken the time to read the draft of this manuscript and to offer their helpful comments and support for this project. My thanks to Andrew Clark, my Commissioning Editor, for his patience, his confidence in me and his cooperation throughout; and to Josephine Campbell, the book's Desk Editor, for her hard work and thorough scrutiny of the text throughout the editing process.

Finally, to you the reader: thank you for taking the time to engage with the content of this book. I wanted to take this opportunity to write something that you will cherish for years to come. I hope that it inspires you as much as it has me.

Preface:
A brief summary of 'Black, Black-led or What?' by Arlington Trotman

When I was aged about nine or ten, my stepmother came to Guyana on a visit with my younger brother Andrew and my sister Alison. My father had not accompanied them, so the thought of meeting them for the first time was a very nervous one for me. The biggest challenge that my brother and I had was what to call her. 'Mum' did not seem appropriate at the time, so as a family we tried to work out the various scenarios. Should it be 'Aunty', or 'Mrs Sturge'? Certainly using her first name was out of the question, as this would be seen as rude and ill mannered. My aunts decided that, since she was their sister-in-law they would call her 'Sister Myrna', and it felt right for us children to do the same. Our careful preparation and consideration of all the options allowed us to choose a name that is held with fondness to this day.

In a similar way, before we look in greater detail at the faith of Black Christian congregations in Britain, we need to consider what to call them. Choosing a name is fraught with many difficulties, not least because of Arlington Trotman's contribution to the debate in his article 'Black, Black-led or What?', in which he attempts to summarise briefly the issues relating to the labels ascribed to minority ethnic churches. 'Black, Black-led or What?' was written in 1992 as a contribution to an anthology entitled *Let's Praise Him Again* (edited by Joel Edwards). It is the most comprehensive argument to date on the matter of finding an appropriate term to define Black churches which they can also accept. With his permission, I have reproduced Trotman's chapter here (as an Appendix to this book) in the hope that readers will come to appreciate more fully the wider issues in the debate. You will find reading it through at this point extremely beneficial, as it provides the context for discussion in the rest of the book.

Central to Trotman's thesis is that there is something fundamentally wrong with Black Christians calling themselves 'Black', 'Black-led', 'West Indian' or 'Pentecostal' churches; by deduction, he would have also objected to the term 'African church'. He argues that disharmony between Black and White Christians has prevented Black Christians from taking their rightful place and making a full contribution to British church life. In his view, race alone has been the determining factor that has placed the Black community within a 'second class or marginal context'. Even more, their race has been used to determine their social, political, economic and religious status and to lock them into a distinct 'caste' in Britain. Whites, he argues, have created tensions in the minds of Black people about their identity, and are therefore not qualified to label Black Christian congregations as 'Black church', 'Black-led church' or even 'Pentecostal church' (often used as a synonym for 'Black church').

Trotman makes the case that the attributes associated with Black-led churches were in fact inherited from their historic denominations, who were White, as the result of the latter's missionary work in the Caribbean and Africa. In his view, therefore, it would not be unreasonable for these churches to want to identify with their historic and theological heritage and experience, and to avoid any description which bears negative connotations. Nonetheless, Trotman concedes that it is extremely difficult to construct an all-embracing and accurate description. Given that the 'mainstream' denominations have emerged primarily out of theological and biblical interpretations, the so-called 'Black-led' churches should really be identified by their common theological roots.

In his quest for an appropriate name, Trotman sets out the parameters for an all-embracing term that would 'satisfy diversity, ecclesiology and theology, culture and spirituality in the kingdom of God'. He concludes with the proposition that the name should include the words 'Holiness', 'Pentecostal' and 'Church', for the reason that a 'non-nationalistic or non-racial title may be used with great effectiveness'.

Introduction

My inspiration for this book has come through the knowledge that not enough is written or understood about what seems to me one of the most dynamic aspects of church life in Britain today.

The churches formed by early pioneers migrating from the Caribbean to Britain between 1940 and 1960, and, more recently (from the 1980s onward), by pioneers from the African continent, have been characterised by the wider society in a number of ways: 'happy clappy', 'fundamentalist', 'West Indian', 'African', 'Black' or 'Black-led', to name a few of the labels. Each of these terms has met with significant resistance from within the churches themselves, primarily because it was felt that these were labels which marginalised, devalued and promoted division. The pioneers merely wanted to be identified as 'the church' or as part of the 'body of Christ'.

In 1992, the African and Caribbean Evangelical Alliance (ACEA) published one of the most significant pieces of work on the churches established by the West Indian diaspora. The book's title, *Let's Praise Him Again*,[1] was drawn from the 'call and response' practices of many Caribbean churches: the speaker would say, 'Shall we praise the Lord?', and the congregation would respond, 'Praise the Lord!' Then, to aid further worship, the speaker would reply, 'Let's praise him again!', and on it goes. In the book, Arlington Trotman posed the question, 'Black, Black-led or What?' His seminal chapter was written in response to the categorisation, outlined above, of the churches emerging from the Caribbean during the late forties to early sixties.

In this book I have picked up the story where Arlington left off, as it seemed that many of the issues he highlights are of relevance here. I have therefore reproduced his contribution in full in the Appendix, as I believe it will add an important historical dimension to the discussion and give readers a better understanding of the concerns raised. In fact it would benefit readers greatly to read through the whole of Trotman's chapter before going on to engage with the rest of this book. In Chapter 2, I provide a critical response to Trotman's ideas. Without a doubt, I thoroughly appreciate the journey he has taken in presenting his case: at the time of writing it remains one of the more serious critiques to come from a Black Christian regarding the thoughts and practices of those in the established and historic churches. In fact, in Chapter 1 I chart my own journey from being somewhat sceptical, someone who left a Black Majority Church to go into a multicultural situation, to becoming a keen exponent for the recognition of the role and contribution of Black Christian faith in Britain.

However, let me assure you that, in presenting my arguments, I have not just been putting ticks against the things I agree with, or crosses where I disagree. The way to view my response is to see it as the work of someone wrestling with a map in order to arrive at an agreed destination: I have merely highlighted those points that may need clarification or further analysis to help me get there. I will admit, however, that I do not concur with Trotman's conclusion and the alternative solutions he has suggested. Instead, I would like to take up his generous offer 'to discover to what extent these terms – "Black-led" in particular – have correctly described our Christian community'.[2] My main focus here is to try to uncover the real essence of churches with majority ethnic congregations from African or Caribbean backgrounds, and to arrive at a suitable term which both epitomises that essence and which the churches themselves feel is most appropriate for defining who they are.

In Chapter 3, I propose the term 'Black Majority Church' (BMC) as 'a more excellent name' (Hebrews 1:4) for churches emerging from the African and Caribbean diaspora. Most readers would now recognise that the term 'Black-led church' has been superseded by this term. Its origin is not known, but it may have originated from Bishop Oswald Williams, a former National Overseer of the Church of God of Prophecy (COGOP). The first time I came across the term was during the spring of 1996, when I applied for the post of General Director of ACEA. Immediately, I recognised its potential and the fact that it provided a new way in which minority ethnic congregations from African or Caribbean backgrounds could view and affirm themselves without feeling that they were betraying the essence of unity present in the gospel. Since then, no one has done more than ACEA to promote this change: it is now viewed as correct to use the term as the normative or 'household' name for these churches, not only in British church life but also in the media and the political arena. However, like anything else in public life, events and editorials tend to take on lives of their own, and the user of a term tends to make it fit a need even if this betrays its author's original intent. Variations in use then cause greater confusion, and the term becomes less helpful. This certainly seems to be true for the term 'Black Majority Church'. To my mind, however, the term is not loaded with disruptive, divisive and isolationist tendencies in the way that other imposed labels have been, nor does it maintain the unintentional exclusivity of Trotman's suggestions. I believe that the 'BMC' label offers greater freedom and clarity of purpose to those Christians whose sincere desire to be Christ to *all* people has prevented them from fully embracing and developing the ministry to which they are called.

Chapter 4 asks the question, does God accept a church that focuses solely on one people group? Here I take a look at the homogeneous church from within looking outwards, and introduce the concepts of open and closed homogeneous churches. I also critique the lack of understanding and inefficient pastoral care that comes with a mind that is closed to the reality that people's social and spiritual needs are often best met within the context of their culture and life experience. I also pose a tough proposition: why do we expect people, whose abuse, disenfranchisement and marginalisation the church ignores from Monday to Friday, to then sit at its feet on Saturday and Sunday?

Chapter 5 identifies five segments that could be said to fall within the category of 'Black Majority Church'. Using historical associations and cultural heritage as the primary basis for their classification, I have sought to highlight the distinctiveness of churches from the African and Caribbean diaspora, churches within both the White Pentecostal denominations and the historic denominations, and the African and Caribbean Spiritual churches. By highlighting their distinctiveness, I hope to avoid the pitfall of seeing them as homogeneous in every way. This also provides my point of departure from Trotman's proposition. To a large extent, this book focuses on churches from the African and Caribbean diaspora, although there will be many features that cut across all the various segments.

Chapter 6 presents an historical account of the huge contribution of Black Christians throughout the ages. The key point to bear in mind when reading this chapter is that the church today is not the beginning of the Black Christian story or history in Britain. Black Christians were missionaries to and from Britain for centuries. There are some familiar names and many new ones too. If anything, I hope that encountering men like Quobna Ottobah Cugoano, Ignatius Sancho, Joseph Jackson Fuller and Daniel Ekarte will challenge your commitment to God and your understanding of the issues that stirred their passions, so that you too will be inspired to engage in the transformation of British society.

Chapter 7 takes up the story from 1948 onwards, and charts the growth and development of the churches from the beginning of post-war migration up to the present day. The challenge here was what to include and what to leave out. I have tried to avoid being too detailed a storyteller or favouring one church over another. Instead, I have tried to create the context and to paint a broad canvas in which the specific histories of each denomination and independent church could be included. Therefore, I have talked about phases of development that often overlapped because they were experienced by different groups at different times. Looking at the contribution of the churches, it is arguable that I have over-censored their contributions; nonetheless, I hope that I have provided enough information to enable readers to explore, in greater detail, those areas of interest to them.

Chapter 8 looks at the theologies and doctrines of the BMCs. Here I have chosen to look at core doctrines in the churches, and to highlight their reasons for emphasising certain aspects and the rationale that governs their world view on a number of issues. I also explore diversity in the church which in the past has led to division, accusations of heresy and the branding of others as either 'unsaved' or 'cults'. What is very evident in this chapter is that these churches may well have much more in common than they think.

Chapter 9 is concerned with the themes of race, reconciliation and partnership. I remain unconvinced that Christians, both Black and White, have set society a sufficiently positive example as to have the moral mandate to lead on this fundamental issue. Often the wider church pays lip service to the problem of racism, but in fact uses cosy terms like 'unity' and 'reconciliation' to conceal its indifference. A large proportion of the BMCs has also avoided raising this issue in the public domain, yet it is the daily experience of their members and communities. The goal of this chapter is to ensure that Christians are more engaged with the reality of racism. I have used the relationship between Black and White Christians as a basis for the discussion, but this is not to say that here is where our dilemma starts and ends. I go on to talk about partnerships and to use the relationship between the African and Caribbean Evangelical Alliance (a Black Majority organisation) and the Evangelical Alliance (a White Majority organisation) as a model of what partnership working can achieve.

In Chapter 10, I present some of the unmet challenges in the BMCs, in the hope that these churches will face up to them and seek to tackle them. Why is it that, despite the enormous achievements of the BMCs, these churches are still seen as 'sleeping' or in a comatose state? What might this sleeping giant do if he would only awake? Here I explore some of the issues which I feel would add an authentic and credible focus to the work of BMCs. In any other walk of life, such a mass group of people, with shared aspirations, a common purpose and collective human and financial resources, would be exercising economic, social and political influence. But the lack of ambassadorial purpose, of understanding the implications of being a diaspora and of a coherent policy on social justice, and the presence of an independent and competitive spirit, are just some of the causal factors. Moreover, the absence of theological debate and dialogue has prevented BMCs from exploring new issues or coming to a common mind on other important concerns. I also attempt to unpack the stereotyping, suspicion, distrust and worries over status that constitute the main factors behind the continual tension that exists in the relationship between the African and the Caribbean churches. As a way forward, I have used the relationship between Joseph and his brothers (Genesis chs 37,39–45) as a model for African and Caribbean Christians to offer each other a genuine embrace and to achieve true reconciliation.

Chapter II sets out a biblical approach to unity. If Christians (and ultimately society) are to coexist with mutual recognition and respect, then there must be a basis or common values that we can share. I passionately believe that there are some boundaries which, if crossed, can exclude individual Christians from fellowship with God and disqualify us from being people of integrity. Each of us must take personal responsibility for our attitudes and actions. Using Paul's first epistle to the Corinthians as a framework, I identify ten principles, all of which are necessary to promote healthy and productive relationships, especially across cultures.

The final chapter probes the future. What will BMCs be like then? Are they merely White Majority Churches in transition? To cast a vision for the future, I propose that we look in three directions: upwards, to understand what God may yet do; outwards, to understand how events in society and the wider church will impact on BMCs; and inwards, to examine our own confidence in the future. How will the churches meet the changing aspirations of their members? Will they have the vision to inspire a new generation? Ultimately, it will be about the way in which the BMCs consolidate to use public space in order to get their message across.

Writing this book has allowed me to crystallise my thoughts on many issues. I embarked on the task with the sole motive of bringing clarity to what we (ACEA) mean by the term 'Black Majority Church'. I wanted to identify their distinctive characteristics and to resist the temptation of seeing these churches as homogeneous units. I have tried to highlight some of the political and sociological factors associated with them. Most significantly, I desire to promote greater understanding in the hope that the true value and contribution of BMCs will be properly appreciated. I also want to take the debate further: to offer some reflection on the current state of BMCs; to look at their strengths, weaknesses, hopes and aspirations; and to explore some of the future challenges they are likely to face. I want to take the liberty of going beyond merely reporting what is obvious to Black Christians (or perhaps not so obvious, as the case may be). I want to be a voice from within, posing challenges and offering personal insights as to how BMCs should be organising themselves as a cohesive force in order to maximise their impact on British society.

Finally, I am grateful to Jane Vicarage from Dean Close Junior School, Cheltenham, Gloucestershire, whose curious question – 'What on earth is a Black Majority Church?' – made me see the importance of penning this book. I trust that you will enjoy reading it as much as I enjoyed writing it. May God be praised for any change of heart or mind that it generates in the process.

Endnotes

1 Joel Edwards (ed.), *Let's Praise Him Again: An African Caribbean Perspective on Worship*, Kingsway, 1992.
2 Arlington Trotman, 'Black, Black-led or What?' in Edwards, *Let's Praise Him Again*, p18.

Part 1
In search of a name

I

Learning to belong: my story

I became a Christian in a multicultural Assemblies of God church in Guyana, South America. Our church, which worshipped on the ground floor of a house, consisted of Indians, Amerindians, Portuguese and Blacks. I did not know I was an 'Afro' or 'African Caribbean' until I returned to live in Britain. To discover that there were churches for specific ethnic groups was a shocking and alien concept to me.

I returned to the UK in 1986, after living in Guyana for over twenty years. It was an emotionally difficult time for me. I had left so many relatives and friends behind. No one knew anything about me and, at best, most conversations seemed like series of long interviews in which everyone had their questions answered. I often left those dialogues not knowing the name of my interrogators and embarrassed at having constantly to ask them to repeat themselves as I wrestled with their accent. It was like starting life all over again with a new identity, and I had to learn fast. I made up my mind early on that the most important thing for me was my studies: that way I could return to Guyana, get a good job and make a contribution to the development of that country. I would also be able to marry Sharon, the fiancée I had left behind. Church was to become a secondary part of my life: I would attend but not get too involved, and would certainly ensure that it did not take over my life. However, I needed to find one first.

My older brother, Colin, had arrived in the UK three months before I did. Together, we consulted the *Yellow Pages* to find an Assemblies of God church. I cannot remember how many we visited or never found. What I do know is that we were disappointed with the churches we attended. Congregations suffered a lack of young people, did not have the vibrancy of our 'bottom house' church in Guyana, or we just felt we did not fit in. Finally, we arrived at the New Testament Church of God on Willesden High Road, north-west London – a place my brother had attended with my aunt on several occasions before, and had thought was not for him. Worship was already in full flow when we arrived. I peered through the glass panes of the inner door separating the sanctuary from the foyer. Although this is difficult for me to explain, what I saw there led me to believe that this was 'a confusion' in which I wanted no part. However, just as I was about to retreat, I felt a witness in my spirit and heard a voice saying, 'Stay and clean up this mess.' After all these years I still feel rather uncomfortable repeating these words. I did not understand what they meant at the time, neither am I convinced that I really know what they mean now. It was inconceivable to me that I could make a difference to anyone's life, much less the kingdom of God.

It has only recently dawned on me (as a matter of fact, it has 'hit' me) that the only plausible explanation for what I felt and heard at that moment of epiphany was the context of my role as General Director of ACEA. It only made sense if God was speaking to me not about the church in Willesden High Road but about churches from the African and Caribbean diaspora generally. In the UK these churches are very 'young' by every standard, yet they have great expectations, legislative responsibilities and requirements as regards theological orthodoxy to fulfil. There is also the huge challenge of transcending culture and being relevant to every generation and people group. While some may be overwhelmed by or ignore these challenges, others have risen to them.

Seen from this perspective, my calling to Christian ministry was altogether more profound than I realised at the time. Nevertheless, it was sufficient to stop me turning away and returning home after seeing the 'conflicting spirits' that 'flashed across my face' when I first peered through the church's door! It also reversed my priorities, placing my Christian life back on the top and forming the basis for my commitment to Willesden NTCOG, the church of which I eventually became a member.

I never saw the church in the same light as I did on that first encounter. Like any other church, it had its challenges and I had my preferences. In particular, I felt that we lacked discipline and leadership regarding the way that the gifts of the Spirit should be administered in the church. The generosity and openness of participation, while being a strength, sometimes became the gateway to abuse and woolly theology, though it also provided unexpected and unwarranted entertainment for us all! However, I became an active member of the church, and underwent a spiritual transformation there. Under the guidance of the older members, I learned to fast and pray, to intercede and see God intervene and change lives. I had a profound interest in young people, although I was keenly aware that my cultural upbringing would not always enable me to identify with their concerns. But it was here that I preached my first full-length sermon and honed my preaching skills in 'exhorting the brethren' at various church meetings.

Soon afterwards, as part of the University and Colleges Christian Fellowship (UCCF), I took up a prominent role in the Christian Unions of three different institutions. In each situation I was in the minority. The songs we sang from the *Songs of Fellowship* songbook were all alien to me – after all, Bill Drake, Chris Bowater, Noel Richards and Graham Kendrick did not contribute to *Sacred Songs and Solos* or the *Redemption Hymnal* used in the NTCOG at the time! And yes, I got into the routine of living a dual Christian life. At college I took on a different personality to the one I used in my church. No one demanded this duality, but there seemed to be no way of reconciling these two worlds: each viewed the other with suspicion, and certainly, from my church's standpoint, there was a question mark over whether there were indeed any Christians at all in the historic denominations. Navigating between these two worlds demanded a steep learning curve from me, and I was determined to be a good student.

During this time I was also attending one of the four Sunday services at Kensington Temple, in west London, which kept intact my desire for the church to make an impact on society. For about five years, I went to their nine o'clock service before rushing off to my own church or to teach Sunday school at our satellite outpost on the infamous Chalk Hill Estate, located about four to five miles from the church. I was (well, almost) always happy in my local church, but I was never proud. Often the fluidity and unpredictably of services made me uncomfortable and worried about what was going to happen next. Would it be a joyous moment or would I have to cringe? Many people with whom I shared my faith wanted to go to my church, yet I would always find a way of referring them to one that was more multicultural or which I perceived would deal with their development in a structured way while not destroying the essence of their personality.

I finished studies in January 1992, my engineering degree course lasting one term longer than other courses at that time. I was in a serious dilemma. Should I abandon all I had learnt and come to appreciate in the wider church, in order to resume 'normality' in my local church? What should I do about my 'church-hopping'? I had already agonised over these decisions for months prior to completing my course, and was becoming unhappy with the situation in which I found myself. To stay would almost certainly mean abandoning my 'freedom' and confining myself to the rules and regulations imposed on so many young people and friends. Yet I was becoming increasingly uncomfortable with the division that existed between the young people and the older members. I was dissatisfied with the lack of progress and the unwillingness to deal positively with the issues and challenges that young people were facing. I was envisaging what my church would look like in ten years time and coming to the conclusion that it would be no different from what it was now. I was concerned, too, about the sense of alienation I might feel were I to lose contact with the multicultural world I had come to know and appreciate. Most of all, I pondered the virtue of forfeiting the ability to cross into new frontiers if I remained in an 'all Black' church. In my agonising, my prayer life became intense. I did not want to be a hypocrite, to develop a criticising spirit and always wear a frown to assert my disapproval: I had seen these attributes in others and had found it ugly and discouraging if not disrespectful and rude. I wanted to maintain a tender heart towards God and fought very hard to do so. I would almost always rather exit a situation before losing my 'what you see is what you get' demeanour!

After receiving some prophetic reassurances from people who could not have had a clue what was in my heart, my wife Sharon and I came to the conclusion that it was right to leave Willesden High Road, but we would remain open to God about what he might yet say in the future. There was no easy way of doing this: many people would be disappointed with us; another fear was that other young people would follow our 'bad' example. We dealt with the situation the best way we knew how: we decided that we would only speak to my pastor and leave it to him to manage the best way of communicating our decision to the church. Our plan was that I would pursue a career in electrical engineering for five more years before taking time off to go to Bible college.

As soon as we settled into Kensington Temple, I felt God challenging me about my numerous pledges to make myself available for full-time ministry. Over the years, many people whom I respected had pointed out to me that God had called me to be in Christian service. I often thought about this, but my own fears, including my perceived lack of ability, prevented me from doing anything about it; and so my response to these challenges, whenever I was in a context that demanded such a commitment, would be always to make it crystal-clear to God that I was available whenever *he* was ready. This made me what I call a 'frequent affirmer'; but these affirmations gave me confidence that I was not ignoring my future 'calling' and it certainly bought me time, as I did not have to pursue ministry there and then. Therefore, the unequivocal challenge to attend Bible college came as a shock to Sharon and me, and left our five-year plan in tatters after only a few months. Nevertheless, we were not overwhelmed by this, and began to explore how we should respond. In the end, it was one of our easiest decisions.

Having left a 'Black-led' church, I was determined to attend a theological institution that was part of the 'mainstream'. I applied to attend London Bible College (LBC) – now the London School of Theology – in Northwood, Middlesex. At the same time, I challenged God to confirm his call and to convince me that I was not acting selfishly. I wanted Sharon to be confident in the decisions we were making and to understand the implications of challenges we were likely to face – this was not just about my future, but *ours*. I knew that if I was to expect her support in the future, then I needed to have her 100 per cent agreement from the beginning. We felt that God was pointing us in the direction of three Christian leaders who had no reason to agree with us on our future plans, and we made arrangements to meet with them in turn. We were returning from our second appointment when Sharon turned to me and said, 'At the end of the day the decision will be ours, and I think attending Bible college is the right one.' As if to confirm her statement, my acceptance into LBC was a breeze. I had only ever visited the college informally, and was concerned that I had not been invited for interview. Soon afterwards, however, I received a letter which (surprisingly!) offered me an unconditional place – except that I would need to pay my own fees, of course!

This was not the first time I had wanted to attend Bible college. In 1987, I had spoken to my pastor, Issachar Lewinson, about attending Overstone Theological College, the NTCOG college then based in Northampton. He felt at the time that it was more important for me to continue my studies in electrical engineering, seeing that I was engaged to be married and that most theological graduates, including himself, needed a second career to support themselves financially. At the time I was a little disappointed with his counsel, since I had much more faith than 'a grain of mustard seed'. However, over the years I have grown to appreciate, with fondness, his wisdom.

When I started at LBC in October 1992, I was determined to learn as much as I could. I aspired to be different from other Black preachers I had encountered: I wanted my study to enable me to pass the integrity test. I was going to master how to preach sermons that did not depend solely on stirring up emotions, as was the practice in many Black churches where often, I believed, sermons lacked the desired characteristics or effect of transforming and empowering people to change their lives. As a learner, I wanted to build on the world view I had developed while leading the UCCF Christian Unions. I wanted to be as equal to the task as any vicar in the Church of England or Baptist Church. I did not want to be found wanting in understanding or to compromise my faith through error. It was all or nothing, as far as I was concerned.

My first jolt came when God challenged me to recognise that I was not at LBC merely to learn but to be, and I was to make a contribution to the life of the college community. It was important to God that my fellow students saw me not merely as Mark, but Mark who was a Christian, Pentecostal and Black, with convictions of my own. My second and most significant challenge came during the time when my wife and I were spending weekends travelling to various independent and Baptist churches on the college's preaching circuit. Often, I did not have a clue where I was, but Sharon and I enjoyed the hospitality afterwards and the opportunity to see other aspects of British life. The homes we visited were a far cry from the one bedroom we were renting in Harrow, Middlesex. Without fail, there was a genuine interest in my future on the part of our hosts. Almost everyone commented favourably on my sermons and acknowledged my gifting. The leadership teams were always interested in what I was planning to do after LBC. Sharon and I agreed that we would explore whether I should become a pastor of one Baptist church in particular which had been without a pastor for at least six years. However, as I turned over the possibility in my mind, as clear as can be I heard God speak to me: 'Mark, these people do not need a pastor, and they surely don't need you. Your people need you. If you walk away, who is going to stay?'

I was shocked, horrified and disappointed! Only a year before I had walked away from a Black church. And what did God mean by 'my people'? I had spent the last six years emphasising how different I was from other Black British people. I wanted nothing to do with the scandals surrounding African Caribbeans, the level of crime in the community, their underachievement in education, lack of opportunities in employment, constant complaint about racism and lack of progress within British socio-economic life. For these and other reasons, I had dissociated myself from even being called a West Indian or, worse, a Jamaican – I had even forgotten that my mother was a Jamaican. I was a

Guyanese from South America and, no, I did not belong to an island, much less a 'small island': I came from a *country*.

The Lord's new challenge provoked deep questions in my mind and revealed aspects about myself that I had not considered before. For the first time, I had to understand what it meant to be a Black Christian. I had to learn not only about 'my people' but to identify with them and their needs. This challenge also revealed something about God which, until now, I had been very uncomfortable with – that he cares profoundly about the way that Black people in Britain feel and behave, and about the circumstances in which they live. He is not concerned only with the universal church: he is also interested in the future of the Black church here in Britain. I was astonished to know that, far from being ashamed of them, God was *for* them and wanted the Black churches and their communities to succeed. This encounter changed the nature of my time at LBC. I often describe my three years there as one of *conscientisation*, a time when I both learned about and found my people and myself.

Within months of this challenge, I was offered the opportunity of leading the Caribbean Fellowship at Kensington Temple. I recognised that, over the years, weekly prayer groups had been established at the college for all the regions of the world except the Caribbean, so we started one. I persuaded LBC to buy *The Voice* newspaper and the *Weekly Journal* as part of its weekly reading. It was at this point I took an interest in ACEA, and spent two weeks learning about its role and function. I also spent a week researching the areas of Notting Hill and Ladbroke Grove, looking for 'my people'. I was desperate to understand their plight as it was reflected in the news media and on television. What I discovered was that a large amount of social engineering was taking place. As a result of the Notting Hill riots, the Black community had all but disappeared, with people being offered large sums of money by housing associations to relocate in the east and north-west of London. Yet the news media were presenting them as though they were a thriving community just waiting for the first opportunity to start a riot! Equally, the community services had disappeared, leaving only the Pepper Pot Club for the elderly, the Ebony Steel Band and a bookshop that sold more drugs than books. These experiences paved the way for me to begin a new journey with God, and gave me an understanding of issues such as those relating to the homogeneous church. They challenged and changed my political ideology and convictions. From here on, it was a case of learning to belong.

Endnote

1 'Small island' or 'smallie' is a derogatory term used by Jamaicans to refer to other Caribbean islands. It is their way of saying that they are superior or better. In the past this was so prevalent that it was not widely acceptable for a Jamaican to marry someone from a 'smallie'.

2

Has anything changed?
A response to 'Black, Black-led or What?'

What has changed

I was sitting with two prominent White leaders and a Black leader of international renown. Our conversation centred on the divide that existed between Black and White Christians, and possible solutions to bridge this gap. As we talked, it occurred to me that the catalyst for our conversation was not the realisation that a radical reassessment was needed of the way that structures within the Christian church are managed and expressed; nor was there a sense that this was an urgent issue that we needed to prioritise for future change and transformation. It was simply a matter of uneasiness that 'these Black-led churches are growing so fast and so big, and if we do not respond now we will be in trouble later'.

Later, I asked some senior evangelical leaders, 'What has changed?' Had there been any recent theological reflection or written apologetics? Why had the 'Black-led' churches become acceptable to evangelicals? Why were they no longer looked upon as merely 'fundamentalist' or 'sects'? One response surprised me: 'I suppose it's convenient – we are in crisis!' Unfortunately, such a response tends only to encourage greater scepticism. At best, it brings to any discourse that tinge of patronage; at worst, it portrays the attitude of the opportunist seeking to co-opt into his ranks what may seem good for the cause. Whatever the case, it explains, in part, why there remains a large chasm between Black and White Christians in Britain today.

However, much has changed since the penning of *Let's Praise Him Again*. Arlington Trotman rightfully points out that 'to a large degree the black church has been placed in a second-class and marginal context', and that race has a major part to play in this demotion and exclusion.[1] I would argue that, whatever the size of the chasm between Black and White, it is smaller today than it was more than a decade ago.

One change can be seen in the effort made by 'established denominations' to appoint racial justice advisors and workers to raise issues affecting minority ethnic groups. There is also the increasing involvement, representation and consultation with 'Black or Black-led' churches in critical decision-making processes. I will discuss the effectiveness of these strategies later, but they are a significant enough development to gain a mention here.

Much credit must also be given to institutions that have made themselves vulnerable by 'swimming against the tide' and appointing sons and daughters of 'Black or Black-led' churches as their leaders. Evidence of this is easy to substantiate:

- in 1996, Angela Sarkis, from the NTCOG was appointed by the Church of England as the Chief Executive of the Church Urban Fund (the Fund expends grants of almost £3 million per annum);
- also in 1996, Bishop Joe Aldred, from the Church of God of Prophecy (COGOP), became Director of the Centre for Black and White Christian Partnership;
- Joel Edwards, from the NTCOG, was appointed as General Director of the Evangelical Alliance (EA) in 1997;
- that same year Beverly Thomas, also with roots in the NTCOG, took up directorship of the Evangelical Christians for Racial Justice (ECRJ).

The litmus test becomes even more conclusive: Arlington Trotman, who hails from a Wesleyan Holiness Church background, is now the Secretary for the Churches' Commission for Racial Justice (CCRJ), a commission set up by the Churches Together in Britain and Ireland (CTBI). In 1991, Reverend Cecil Perry became the first Black President of the British Union Conference of Seventh-day Adventists. This move coincided with Reverend Donald McFarlane becoming President of the South England Conference, a position vacated by Reverend Perry. The picture was completed in 1994 when Reverend Edgerton Francis became president of the North England Conference, placing the top leadership of SDA in the UK firmly in the hands of Black Christians.

From an African perspective, there were at least two key appointments. Emmanuel Olidapo, of Nigerian origin, was appointed General Secretary of Scripture Union International in 1992, a post he held until his retirement at the end of February 2005. Prior to his appointment, Emmanuel was Scripture Union's Africa Regional Secretary based in Kenya. Then in September 2001, Joe Kapolyo, Principal of the Theological College of Central Africa in Ndola, Zambia, was appointed Principal of All Nations Christian College in Ware, Hertfordshire. The appointment of two Asians to similar positions should also be viewed as significant: Frederick George became President of the Baptist Union in 1998; and, in June 2000, Inderjit Bhogal became President of the Methodist Church in the UK.

To suggest that these appointments are mere tokenism or acts of political correctness would be to devalue the ability of those concerned, and to question their integrity and that of the institutions who appointed them. It would also place in the dock the grace, favour and gifts of God. The evidence so far has shown that all these individuals have brought significant and diverse perspectives to the life of the church. Their elevation has opened new ways for 'Black or Black-led' churches to view ministry and has provided greater aspirations for young and emerging leaders. Most significantly, they have all responded to the call to serve the wider body of Christ and society as a whole.

By far one of the most crucial developments in recent years has been the increased self-confidence among the 'Black or Black-led' churches themselves. They have less of an inferiority complex, and many feel that they can succeed despite the lack of support or help from external sources. There is less restlessness among leaders, and a more firmly entrenched sense of permanence. There is also a greater political will: 'Black or Black-led' churches appear more alert to the importance of ensuring that their voices are heard on matters of faith and national issues. They understand that they are now the most cohesive representatives of their community. All this means that they must broaden their agenda to deal with the challenges that face the wider Black community. What is most encouraging is that these areas of responsibility are already being extended to communities of other ethnic groups. There is the realisation that everyone in the community should enjoy the support given by the churches.

From rejection to acceptance

Nevertheless, the overriding question remains: is it possible to redeem a label that has been used to objectify, discriminate, exclude or promote segregation? Trotman takes offence at the fact that Black people, who are created in the image of God, should collude with the inventors of terms like 'Black church' or 'Black-led church' by also defining themselves as such. He points out that 'there is no logical or ethical reason for Black people to justify our heritage by using defensive or polemic language given to us by others in an attempt to define our religious experience.'[2] Further, he argues that those Whites who are responsible for imposing a 'secondary or marginal status' on Black people, and who have caused 'tension' in Black people's minds as to their identity, are 'less than qualified to determine that identity [as] "black-led" '.[3]

In my view, Trotman is justified in his objection. It seems to me a legitimate protest when the purpose for labelling a group or individual is to objectify, ascribe shame or promote discrimination and any other form of prejudice. Indeed, the church itself has been guilty of using labels to identify, categorise, engage in adverse social engineering, marginalise and even manipulate others. One of the problems with the 'Black-led' label is that, when used to describe churches, it so often isolates Christians from each other – both within the established and historic churches, and within churches initiated by minority ethnic communities – and it generates a negative reaction to the separatist connotation it is inferring. More significantly, it oversimplifies the diversity that exists within churches.

Yet there is another way of looking at this issue. While one may recognise the deficiencies of a particular label, and may be able to discredit its source, this does not mean that with time some good may not come out of it. It is possible to argue that most inventions are treated with scepticism until their true value is established. During the 1980s, those on the right-wing of the Conservative Party derided the far-left of the Labour Party as the 'loony-left'. The Conservatives' campaign was so successful that no one in their right mind wanted to be tarnished with that brush by belonging to such a group. But two landslide victories by the Labour Party, in 1997 and 2001, the arrival of devolved government and directly elected mayors – especially the election of a left-wing Mayor of London, Ken Livingstone – has ensured that many of the issues raised by the 'loony-left' are firmly back on the agenda.

The same could be said for the eco-warriors who managed to embarrass the then Conservative government into rethinking their road-building schemes. These eco-warriors were viewed as social misfits, work-shy and anti-establishment. They protested by building and living in tunnels within designated construction areas such as the Newbury bypass. They erected tree-houses and chained themselves to them, and arranged for mass-occupation of prospective road-building sites, increasing constructions costs by millions of pounds. They grabbed the media's attention, and managed to raise the nation's consciousness as to the potential damage to the environment and countryside. A few like Swampy (real name Daniel Hooper), one of the 'human moles' who stayed underground for a number of days, became instant celebrities.

On the face of it, these eco-warriors were not natural allies with middle England, but common concerns and objectives, motivated by past successes, made their partnership seem inevitable rather than outrageous. It is important that we make room for unlikely associations if doing so furthers the objectives of the marginalised. Therefore, I would diverge slightly from Trotman and maintain that including the word 'Black' in any future identification should remain an option for churches from the African and Caribbean diaspora: I believe there are still healthy tensions to be explored in retaining this designation rather than agreeing to its outright rejection.

The importance of names

There is no doubt that there is evidence in Scripture to affirm a divine purpose in choosing the correct name. In fact, it could be said that a name can be a receptacle for theology. Often biblical names foreground their bearers' identity, mission or character, or the context or circumstances in which they live. God himself instigated the change of Abram's name to 'Abraham', or 'father of a multitude', as tangible proof of his promise to him (Genesis 17:3-5). Similarly, he changed the name of Abraham's wife from 'Sarai' (meaning 'contentious') to 'Sarah' ('princess'), in acknowledgement of the transformation of her personal character and outlook on life, from shame and frustration at being infertile, to her new association with royalty and privilege: her new name epitomised the her significance to God's plan and the respect she had come to deserve (Genesis 17:15,16).

There are several other instances in Scripture where God initiated or requested that people's names be changed: Jacob became 'Israel' (Genesis 32:28), and Jesus gave Simon the name 'Peter' (Mark 3:16). From birth, children were given names that reflected their life's mission: no other name could be conferred on the Christ except 'Jesus'; neither could Elizabeth and Zechariah bow to pressure from neighbours and relatives, and name their son anything other than 'John' because 'the hand of the Lord was with him' (Luke 1:57-66). Personal circumstances or national tragedy were also marked in the names of individuals. Deeply hurt and grieving over the death of her husband and two sons,

Naomi insisted of her family, 'Do not call me Naomi [meaning 'my pleasantness' or 'delight']; call me Mara ['bitter'], for the Almighty has dealt very bitterly with me' (Ruth 1:20). Similarly, following the death of the prophet Eli, the murder of both Eli's sons and the capture of the Ark of the Covenant by the Philistines, Eli's daughter-in-law named her newborn son 'Ichabod' ('no glory'), before she herself died as a result of her strenuous labour. There is no glory! There is no need to celebrate because today 'the glory has departed from Israel' (1 Samuel 4:19–22).

It may be useful here to examine the origins of the name 'Christian', as it offers additional insights into the way that a name can evolve, and may help us in determining whether to retain the word 'Black' in any label we might attach to churches from the African and Caribbean diaspora. AF Walls makes a strong case for the word 'Christian' having a Latin source. Plural nouns in Latin end with the suffix '-iani' and were usually used when referring to the soldiers under the authority of a particular general.[4] So, for example, Caesar's slaves and clients were known as 'Caesariani', while those of King Herod were called 'Herodianoi'.[5]

The word 'Christian' is mentioned three times in the New Testament (Acts 11:26; 26:28; 1 Peter 4:16), all within a public context. The most popular understanding of Acts 11:26, which describes the term's first use in Antioch, is that very likely the opponents of Christ's followers originally employed it as a slanderous and insulting label. It was only time, however, before new non-Jewish converts saw their faith as more than just a sect within Judaism, and they adopted the name because they saw its original meaning and felt it to be appropriate.[6] By the time of Agrippa's interview with Paul, in Acts 26:28, it is still possible that the king intended his remark to be sarcastic; but, with the passing of time, it became accepted that the church would identify themselves with Christ in this way, and the name gradually filtered into the language of the establishment (1 Peter 4:16).

'Black', the dirty word

I remember objecting acutely to a banner being present in our church hall which said 'Proud to be Black': I felt that such notions had no place within a church. Although it was explained to me that this was an essential part of affirming young people at the summer play scheme, I did not understand why it was necessary. I was equally disturbed when I discovered, from BBC television, that the preacher we had invited to lead our Sunday morning worship service was the Reverend Al Sharpton, the

Black civil rights activist from the United States of America. I thought our church would be marginalised, and feared that it was politically incorrect, offensive – indeed, suicidal – action for the church to take. My pastor was also surprised at the news as, in making the invitation, he had trusted a good friend's recommendation. I protested in my own way by asking the Reverend to take off his gold chain and huge medallion because it would damage our new clip-on microphone. (That pendant seemed larger than Goliath's shield!) My religious zealousness and youthful ignorance prevailed.

My point in narrating these events is that a label's journey from rejection to acceptance depends acutely on the way that an individual is impacted by it and on the stage of his or her personal development. This is not intended to suggest that those objecting to a term are merely ill informed or lacking understanding. However, there does seem to be much mileage in the colloquial adage, 'Pig ask he mama "Wa mek yo mouth so long?" "Yo time go come! Yo time go come!" ' ('The piglet asked its mother, "Why is your mouth so long?" She replied, "Your time will come! Your time will come!" ') It is not surprising that there is now a greater level of acceptance by Black people themselves that they are created in the image of God. And if Blackness were a sin they would have 'moulted' when they became Christians, either through the washing of the water or the blood! Yet is it highly entertaining to see some Black Christians hop, skip and jump, and engage in all forms of saintly acrobatics, to convey a very clear message, 'Don't even think about it! Don't mention that word! Don't you dare mess up my party or ruin my life!' The depth of embarrassment they feel when any issue relating to the perspectives or dignity of Black people is raised seems disproportionate to any possible rewards or benefits they are likely to gain from being silent or an 'insider'. Further, it disqualifies one from being either an advocate or ambassador for minority ethnic people. I echo the sentiment of a White colleague when she said, 'I am proud to be White. I am God's gift to my parents and I am grateful for that.' Black Christians should feel no less proud, and should resist any attempt to make them ungrateful for the gift they have become. In my view, Ian MacRobert is correct in saying that the term 'Black' 'constitutes an essential aspect of our identity'.[7]

Towards an adequate terminology

Trotman acknowledged that, though there were inescapable difficulties with the terms 'Black church' or 'Black-led church', it was 'equally problematic to construct an all-embracing and accurate description'.[8] It should not be surprising, therefore, that even his suggestions are fraught with difficulties. In particular, it is difficult to comprehend why, despite the historical and cultural difficulties that Trotman so ably identified with the Holiness-Pentecostal traditions and practices, he is still able to recommend them. It may well take a miracle to find a definition that satisfies the diversity, ecclesiological and theological, cultural and spiritual experiences and expressions of the churches initiated by minority ethnic groups. On the other hand, the criteria that Trotman sets out may be too large for any single definition to encompass.

First, he invites us to consider a theological basis for a name rather than one based on the colour of our skin. While this is a noble aspiration, not even God chose it when dealing with the people of Israel. The faith that God created 'to be a light to the nations' was nationalistic to its core. The Jewish people were identified, and either affirmed or despised, because of their culture, rites, ceremonies, laws and practices. If an individual wanted to be regarded as one of the people of God, he or she had to take on these very traits. During his life, Jesus lived and embodied most of them, arguing that he had not come to abolish the law and its demands but to fulfil them (Matthew 5:17). The early Christians carried over many Jewish cultural practices into their churches.

Trotman also posits the term 'Holiness' as a potential solution to the problem. I once asked Bishop Ron Brown, the former National Overseer of the NTCOG, how he would respond to an article entitled, 'Holiness, the enemy of the "Black churches"!' His response was, 'I would be offended.' He preferred instead to see it as a question to be explored – 'Holiness: the enemy of the "Black churches"?' The reason for my original query was that I had already concluded that the Black churches tended to wrap cultural preferences into biblical requirements: on the one hand, they had a high view of the Scriptures, the Holy Spirit and his work; on the other, there seemed to be an active distrust that the same Holy Spirit was able to convict Christians and non-Christians alike about right living and practice. They compensated for this dilemma by instituting a generous set of rules and regulations which did nothing but stifle creativity, kill joy, 'embalm the living' and exclude those with a tender heart towards God. Granted that holiness was at the heart of the faith received from White missionaries, it in no way makes right the admonitions and excommunications that were administered for deviating from the strict codes. Let me stress, I believe in the doctrine of holiness and see it as the standard for the church, but this does not mean that we should ignore the harmful way in which that standard has been enforced in the past. Equally, the very churches for whom holiness is the primary doctrine are not at the forefront of church growth today. If anything, they are fast declining and in grave danger of extinction in just over a decade. Moreover, I do not recall many of the churches outside the denominations choosing to include the term 'Holiness' in their titles.

As a teenager living in Guyana, I decided to join my local theatre company, The Theatre Guild. This was a big step for me – I wanted my future to be different from what I saw in the ghetto area where I lived. Kingston was a rather intriguing place: one half of a street was a ghetto, while along the other lined with the most prestigious homes, embassies, government buildings and a tourist hotel. Joining the best, and probably the only proper, theatre company in the country was my way of crossing the street. I was only the second person in the area to do so.

When I became a Christian, I understood that there were issues related to values and codes of conduct which would be challenging. But when I returned to Britain, I was unprepared for the news that becoming a member of the NTCOG meant *going* to the theatre or cinema would become a sin, much less acting in plays or films. I always knew, and still maintain, that this doctrine is wrong, but at the time I thought it was a small price to pay if God was going to be glorified by my being in the church. (I believe that this teaching has now been repealed in the NTCOG, but no doubt many denominations have similar regulations intact.) Nevertheless, it put an end to one of my most enjoyable social pursuits. This is my first reason for arguing that we should not include the word 'Holiness' in naming churches from the African and Caribbean diaspora.

My second reason for rejecting 'Holiness' as a possible candidate for inclusion can be found in the story that has yet to be told by the Windrush generation. During the late forties and the early sixties, when many West Indians answered to the call, 'Your mother country needs you', the majority of the migrants were young people, many of them only teenagers. Listening in on the reflections (and sometimes the boasts) of some of that generation, one can't help but wonder what life must have been like, from a moral standpoint, when so many young people were left to fend for themselves with little or no adult supervision or guidance. Many looked forward to the weekend house parties where the main drink was Stones Ginger Wine or Ruby Wine. In those days, men arriving from the Caribbean far outweighed women and there were generous 'meshing' (liaisons) with the locals. One of the new arrivals boasted, 'They use to call me King Dick!' Samuel Allen, who came over in 1959 from Montserrat, recalls, 'They [British women] were on the street. They were like that, they were calling you, it was like that. Even where you were working in the day, they would come there asking for money . . . if you wanted to get to meet one they were on the street.'[9] So many lost their faith to the point where coming to England was seen as going to the burial ground.

This is part of the context in which the Black churches started, and I strongly believe that it resulted in holiness assuming an importance and taking far deeper roots than it would have under different circumstances. It may be for this reason that 'maintaining the old landmarks' came to regarded as so crucial to the churches established by the Caribbean community, and that being a Christian was not merely an encounter with God – there was the demand for you to look like one, too. And to look like one meant that a women, for example, could not wear trousers, cosmetics or jewellery, while the minimum length for clothing was a prescribed length. Looking back, I wonder how much of God's goodness has been lost because of poor theology. For this reason, I feel unable to include the word 'Holiness' in any future definition of 'Black or Black-led' churches – unless, of course, it is redefined and can be seen only in the light of God's holiness.

Similar difficulties can be found for the terms 'Pentecostal' or 'Pentecostalism'. While they may represent a large section of the constituent churches, they exclude those churches Trotman identifies in his chapter, such as the Wesleyan Holiness Church. It also excludes the African Methodists Episcopal (AME) churches, the AME Zion churches and Lutheran churches. More significantly, it does not include the independent churches, which may be more akin to the Charismatic Movement. Nor does it take into account the additional diversity I will propose later.

My final reason for rejecting Trotman's suggestions is that they, whether naively or intentionally, compromise both himself and the churches from the African and Caribbean diaspora. It is astonishing that Trotman, a student of the Holiness Movement, seems to have forgotten the existence of the denomination of International Pentecostal Holiness Church (IPCH) based in the USA.[10] The Pentecostal Holiness Church (PHC), as its name suggests, amalgamates two major revival movements: the Holiness revival of the late nineteenth century, and the Pentecostal revival of the twentieth century. Equally, Trotman would be aware that the denomination's first world conference met in September of 1990 in Jerusalem, most probably at the time when he was writing his piece. At the conference they adopted 'The Jerusalem Proclamation', which has since become a 'global battle cry' for PHC members, exhorting them to become 'a kingdom of worshipping priests', 'an army of witnesses who live to share the good news' and 'a unique instrument of world evangelisation'. It would be unacceptable to expect the spectrum of denominations in the UK to embrace the tenets of a single denomination. I am sure that the Wesleyan Holiness Church in the USA would reject any notion which sees its 'satellite missionary outpost' in the UK pledging allegiance to another denomination. Imagine the outcry if I were to suggest that the Church of England assume the name 'Catholic' so as to remove any uncertainty about the universality of the Christian faith.

That said, I have benefited significantly from the passing of time! Churches initiated by the African and Caribbean diaspora have now 'developed arms and legs', a vantage point was denied to Trotman in 1992. Now in my sixth reading of *Let's Praise Him Again*, I am as convinced as I was on the first reading that, more than any other work, it has allowed me to better understand the minority ethnic churches in Britain. I am thoroughly grateful to Arlington Trotman for his diligence in guiding my thoughts and pointing the way for future discussion.

In the final chapter of this part of the book, I offer my own preferred definition for churches from the African and Caribbean diaspora, which I hope will transcend historical, theological and denominational boundaries.

Endnotes

1 Arlington Trotman, 'Black, Black-led or What?', in Joel Edwards (ed.), *Let's Praise Him Again: An African Caribbean Perspective on Worship*, Kingsway, 1992, p12.

2 Trotman, p19.

3 Trotman, p21.

4 A F Walls, 'Christians', in *The Illustrated Bible Dictionary*, InterVarsity Press, 1998, p266.

5 Walls, p266.

6 Walls, p266.

7 Iain MacRobert, Lecture sponsored by ACEA's Youth Network, Birmingham,1991, cited in Trotman, p19.

8 Trotman, p28.
9 Z Nia Reynolds, *When I came to England: An Oral History of Life in 1950s and 1960s Britain*, Macmillan, 2001, p50.
10 For details and the historic background of the International Pentecostal Holiness Church, visit their website on **www.iphc.org**

3

A more excellent name

In the previous chapter, I argued that names are important to God and should be important to us too; furthermore, whatever their source or intent, names can be redeemed and worn with pride, as a badge of honour, once their true value has been ascertained. I also set aside the suggestion made by Arlington Trotman, that any suitable definition for churches from the African and Caribbean diaspora should include the words 'Holiness' and 'Pentecostal', since the premise underpinning those terms render them untenable at the outset.[1] Similarly, we should reject the terms 'Black church' or 'Black-led church' because, as Selwyn Arnold comments in his book *From Scepticism to Hope*:[2]

> The term was a nomenclature ascribed to churches with black leadership and a majority black membership by the indigenous churches when they accepted the fact that the churches were not cultic ghettos for the practice of the supposed 'black religion', but were legitimate branches of Protestant orthodoxy led by black clergy. Several years elapsed before the acceptance of this fact. However, for some indigenous white people, there are other elements that make up the black-led church, such as spontaneous loud congregational praying, vibrant, if not emotional, singing and hand clapping, and in such cases, ecstatic worship and speaking with unknown tongues. Some have even believed that this type of worship is peculiar to black people, and that the average white British person regards the church to be the black people's church.

The Black Majority Church

It is no secret that the term 'Black Majority Church' has superseded the terms 'Black church' and 'Black-led church': it is now the standard nomenclature used by the press and the media, politicians, statutory organisations and the wider church. This has not occurred by accident or chance but, rather, has been a deliberate and strategic process. It was deliberate in the sense that we at ACEA, which instigated the use of the term, did so because we wanted to be rid of a badge that churches were not comfortable with and which, at worst, was patronising and disrespectful to Black Christians. It was also a matter of self-identity. We wanted to offer a lens through which to view Black Christians in order to recognise their true and proper value and role. All in all, it was about making a strong statement about the need to search for a preferred title.

From a strategic point of view, a new name was warranted because the churches were changing. The evidence of their growth was clearly a striking factor: their congregations were becoming some of the largest in many inner cities and in the nation as a whole. The new kind of church emerging was one that took seriously the issues raised by and affecting young people in wider society. It was preparing to engage holistically in its social responsibilities – not that it had not been doing so already, but what was different was the emergence of younger leaders who were either born or brought up in British society. They brought with them a new linguistic dynamic, and were able to transcend generations and cultures. It was a church ready to stand up and be counted.

At the same time, the contributions of Christians from the African diaspora changed not only the composition but also the very notion of 'Black-led' churches. Many of the leaders who started these churches in the UK were graduates or missionaries sent by their denominations to support their brothers and sisters in Christ overseas. Equally, the entrepreneurial fervour of the economic boom years in the 1980s (the Thatcher years) generated individualistic, prosperity-orientated, 'can do' attitudes in church, just as it did in the rest of society. This climate became the motor driving the development of many new churches.

The church members themselves were also changing. Many were now stakeholders in the wider society, their success in education paying dividends at their places of work. Not only was it inaccurate to refer to 'Black-led' churches as though they were 'simple folks', it was now rude and disrespectful. Society was changing so fast, many members in the older Caribbean churches, I included, felt that they were going to be left stranded in an irrelevant church if they missed the opportunities that such change was presenting. Many Christians were willing to deal with the issues of race and inequalities that existed within church and society. These factors among others meant that a concerted effort was needed to change the image that had been foisted on these churches. For this to happen, it was essential that they had a better understanding of who they were and what they about.

Proposed definition of a 'Black Majority Church'

A Black Majority Church is a worshipping Christian community whose composition is made up of more than 50 per cent of people from an African or African Caribbean heritage.

This definition is careful not to use the term 'Black' in the political sense of 'anyone who is not White'. It has also chosen not to include churches in which, though Black Christians make up the largest ethnic grouping, they are, overall, in the minority. It could be argued that almost every church is already multicultural, including those with 100 per cent Black membership (I will develop this idea further in Part 2); but for now it is enough to say that while a BMC may well be a multi-ethnic church, it does not follow that every multiethnic church is a BMC. While recognising, therefore, that this definition is strict in its parameters – namely, it is the preserve of the orthodox Christian religion and reflects numerical and sociological realities – we now go on to examine what it offers to Black Christians and the wider church.

Positive aspects of the definition

One of the most significant attributes of this definition of a 'Black Majority Church' is that it shifts the focal point, taking the spotlight away from the leadership and firmly placing it on the members: in other words, no longer is the flock to be identified by whoever happens to be the shepherd at any given time, but, rather, by their distinctive composition. Furthermore, it provides a convergence for unity, crossing the denominational and theological barriers, and reconnecting friends and families whom previous labels had wrongly led to believe that they had nothing in common: consequently, it presents huge opportunities for better pastoral support and local cooperation. The definition removes the monolithic view that lumps Black people and Black Christians into one homogeneous unit in worship, lifestyle, thinking and behaviour. Moreover, the old adage holds true: 'In unity there is strength'! BMCs are able to provide another perspective on community life for Black people in Britain.

This definition also has a positive psychological effect on those within these churches, helping to restore the often tarnished image of God in Black people. It offers a redemptive wholeness that restores a sense of pride where it is neither scandalous nor arrogant to be Black. It is important that we all recognise the profound effect on both individuals and communities when, in every area of their lives, they must continually plot a course through the issues and circumstances of being a minority. This continual pressure can cause minority communities to develop an inferiority complex, lose their sense of belonging and see themselves as outsiders forced to navigate a gruelling obstacle course before they will be accepted or retain permanence. The name 'Black Majority Church' challenges those notions and offer opportunities for them to be, and feel, at one with themselves. It elevates adherents from outsiders to insiders, from visitors to hosts, from followers to leaders, from the nervous to the bold, from 'nobodies' to 'somebodies'.

Negative aspects of the definition

This characterisation of a 'Black Majority Church' will always be challenged in the same way that critics have helpfully pointed out that the term 'ethnic minority' is in fact a misnomer, since *everyone* is an ethnic person – Black, Asian and White. This difficulty has led to the use of the term 'minority ethnic' as opposed to 'ethnic minority'. A similar debate rambles on regarding the use of the label 'Black and Minority Ethnic' (BME) groups – Black people are themselves part of the minority ethnic community, so why should terminology separate them?

One suggestion mooted to me was to consider rearranging the word order to 'Majority Black Church': that way it would be in line with the term 'minority ethnic group'. While accepting the premise of this argument, I believe that it does not take the debate any further in terms of the term's conceptual relevance and practical outworking. Neither do I believe that the name 'Black Majority Church' carries within it the fallacy that only 'non-Whites' are an ethnic people group; on the contrary, it gives us the opportunity to reflect on the realities of a given congregation at a particular point and time in their history.

Another difficulty with the definition could be the contention that if we create a new majority, by inference we are also guilty of creating a new minority with all the flaws that such a status brings. My objection to this proposition is that it seems to suggests that to offer dignity to one group in society is tantamount to removing it from another. A 'Mugabian principle' would be at work – such as when, to redress an historic imbalance and injustice of his nation and people, Zimbabwean President Robert Mugabe was accused of resorting to the forcible eviction of White farmers from their farms. Such lunacy must be treated with the disdain it deserves. The use of the term 'Black Majority Church' is not merely about relegating or promoting people within their context; it is about clarifying the realities in which we live so that we can come to new and different understandings. Equally, it is about providing a rationale to guide our thoughts and actions. And yes, people should change after being enlightened – of course they should change course, to use a pun. Nevertheless, this will involve the whole church and society recognising the priceless gifts we are to each other.

Some critics might argue that to use such an all-encompassing term will make it difficult to identify the various segments within a group, thereby losing its distinctiveness. The assumption here is that we must be able to separate the UK historic churches (Anglicans, Methodist, etc) from the newer churches emerging from the African and Caribbean diaspora. However, I see no difficulty with this, as it is possible to include prefixes when separating out the particular identities: so it would be as reasonable to talk about an 'Anglican BMC' as it is an 'African or Caribbean BMC'.

What if some Black Christians refuse to be identified with this definition? My simple response is, 'No problem!' This name has already taken so much root that it may well be impossible now to rid ourselves of it, unless it is for a very good and plausible reason – for example, because it is demeaning to all Black people, which in my view it is not. Looking at the issue from a faith perspective, the process of the term's acceptance will probably be like the process of conversion (Matthew 13:3–8,18–23): for some, acceptance will be instantaneous; some will take more persuasion; some will accept it in their own time and on their own terms; and some will opt in and out, depending upon the personal and corporate benefits and opportunities it brings. Sadly, some may never be convinced. However, those who may choose to stand on the fringe are already in the minority, and anyway, it would be inappropriate to label them as 'enemies of the cause'.

Assuming a new identity

Ironically, a few Black Christians, having understood their identity in this way, have become quietly uncomfortable or have rejected the name 'Black Majority Church' outright. Yet this rejection is not sufficient to suggest that no badge should be placed on Black Christians. As a matter of fact, it is naive to take the view that somehow 'Black churches' and Black Christians will be viewed in an acceptable and positive light anyway, and so there is no need to call attention to their strengths, value and contribution to Christianity in Britain and society as a whole. Moreover, Black Christians must rid themselves of what is essentially an inferiority complex that makes them feel dissatisfied and uncomfortable unless their spirituality and practices are approved by their White Christian brothers and sisters.

There should be no debate that our identity should be, and is, founded in Christ. The earth is different from the other planets, the moon, the sun and the stars; yet it makes up the same solar system, and only a fool would argue there is no merit in trying to understand that system in its unique parts. In the same way, people are different, depending on their geographical locations, ethnicity and culture; but to deny their uniqueness would be like saying to a husband, 'There is no good reason in seeking to understand your wife', and visa versa; or like ruling out the possibility that each child in a family is different and should be nurtured in a way befitting his or her character. The church and society will be poorer if we fail to explore the distinctive dynamics and nature of Black Christians as worshipping communities. Those within the churches who reject this possibility are no better than someone who hides his or her light under a container:

> 'No one, when he has lit a lamp, puts it in a secret place or under a basket, but on a lampstand, that those who come in may see the light.'
>
> (Luke 11:33)

As Jesus is pointing out here, it makes no sense to scupper the very purpose of the light's existence, nor should it be part of anyone's 'tradition' to do so. On the other hand, those outside the BMCs who reject the possibility of exploring Black Christian uniqueness are like one who discovers treasure hidden in a field but, through laziness, personal preference, prejudice or busyness, never bothers to enjoy them (Matthew 13:44). The kingdom of God resides within and among us, and finds its expression in the local church, whatever its ethnicity.

The challenge is clear: let us get to know each other and ourselves better. Living within the kingdom of God demands that we not only pursue the purposes of God, but also treat each other with the dignity given to us by Christ. More than that, it is about ensuring that our perceptions of each other are undergirded with grace and love, not malice and rivalry. Knowing that we belong to one another should spur us on to reclaim our common heritage in Christ. This is my desire, and why I embarked upon writing this book. And this is why I think it is essential that, as a starting point, we take seriously how we may greet each other as his people. I am proposing that we embrace 'a more excellent name' (Hebrews 1:4), and call ourselves 'Black Majority Churches'.

Endnotes

1 Arlington Trotman, 'Black, Black-led or What?' in Joel Edwards (ed.), *Let's Praise Him Again: An African Caribbean Perspective on Worship*, Kingsway, 1992, p33.

2 Selwyn E Arnold Snr, *From Scepticism to Hope: One Black-led Church's Response to Social Responsibility*, Grove Books, 1992, p11.

Part 2

Understanding Black Majority Churches

4

The homogeneous church

At the heart of the debate over finding an appropriate name that best describes the churches emerging from Black immigrants to the UK, with all their distinctiveness, lies psychological and theological struggles with identity. There are some huge questions to be resolved. Does God accept, agree with or value churches that are centred predominantly on one people group? Is it not a new type of apartheid for Black Christians to barricade themselves in ghettos of their own making? What will White people and other Christians think? Will it not restrict the potential for churches to grow and develop if the focus is on the minority rather than the majority community? For the new arrivals to Britain the question might be that if God has called them to witness only to their own people, would it not be more effective to do this in their country of origin? Most significantly, what do the Scriptures have to say about all this?

Homogeneous versus heterogeneous churches

There has been much discussion regarding the merits of homogeneous churches (one congregation made up of one people group) over hetero-geneous churches (one congregation containing several people groups). The chief proponent of the homogeneous church model has been Donald McGavran, who defines the 'homogeneous unit' as 'a section of society in which all the members have some characteristic in common'.[1] Such a unit could be a group of people from the same tribe, ethnicity or nation, who share a common language, culture, or social or economic background, or some other characteristic that makes them distinct from other groups. Central to McGavran's argument is that under-standing and then reaching people within the context of their homoge-neous group is the best way to disciple and retain them during and after missionary and evangelistic activities, because they do not then have to learn a new language, or abandon their culture or family, as a conse-quence of their conversion. McGavran argues powerfully that Christians often ask the wrong questions:[2]

They think exclusively about, 'What should Christians do?' rather than 'How do non-Christians accept Christ?' They are particularly critical of allowing one kind of people (one subculture) to form congregations of its own. They erroneously call it segregation, and say that Christian mission should never promote or condone it. It is better, they think, to have a slow-growing or non-growing church that is really brotherly, integrated and hence 'really Christian,' than a rapidly growing one-people church.

The noble call of every Christian is to make disciples of all nations (Matthew 28:19). Some may smirk at my analysis of the situation, which is that we are in the 'smash-and-grab' business – we must be able snatch people out of the grip of sin and the hands of the evil one. We are not on a debating team; this is not just about winning intellectual arguments. We are engaging in territorial warfare for the souls of humankind, striving to persuade people to surrender their opposition to Christ and his gospel, and to cross the battle lines – not to go home but to resume the battle as active combatants.

During my years at Bible college, I once asked fellow students in my year, 'If you saw two people walking on the road, one Black and the other White, who would you approach to tell about Jesus?' Without fail, they all said, 'The White one.' Their reasons for this ranged from not having ever talked to a Black person about matters of faith before, to being afraid that a Black person might respond aggressively or violently – a perception created by the media. The discussion brought home to me the shocking realisation that, as a Black person living in Britain, I stood far less of a chance of hearing the good news of the gospel if I had to depend on White Christians. McGavran is correct when he argues that 'it is a self-defeating policy, and in rare exception, contrary to the will of God,' if churches insist on planting heterogeneous churches in homogeneous areas without concern for 'whether the church grows or not'.[3] It is a crying shame that the consequences for people living and dying without Christ are also often overlooked and allowed to fade into insignificance because of the petty preferences and political indulgence that dominate some church vestries.

Furthermore, would it ever really be acceptable for a church to devote all its energies to appealing to many people groups to join their fellowship, but succeed in persuading only two per cent of those groups to attend while the remaining 98 per cent baulk at crossing barriers of class or race to become disciples of Christ?[4] No wonder those outside the church tend to see Christians as uncaring or unconcerned about their real needs – and this disinterest is actively preventing people from becoming Christians. All the evidence suggests that churches in the UK which are experiencing significant numerical growth are those that adopt some form of homogeneity as part of their mission and evangelism strategy.

A disappointing aspect of the 'homogenous vs. heterogeneous' church debate is that it is quickly degenerates into making distinctions between Black, White, Asian, Chinese and other minority ethnic groups – proof, in my view, that its main concern is race and not diversity. It is also the case that many African and Caribbean churches do not pay sufficient attention to the diversity that exists within themselves, except when it relates to White people. Indeed, many Caribbean churches such as the NTCOG, the COGOP and the Calvary Church of God in Christ (COGIC) are dominated by Jamaican culture: in all my visits to those churches, I have never heard a song sung that originated from another Caribbean island. Similarly, African churches tend to attract people from the culture to which the leader belongs. Therefore, any conversation about 'multicultural' churches must be careful to acknowledge that most African and Caribbean churches are in fact already multicultural, though this may not be overtly expressed in their church life. The honest question to consider, therefore, is whether, in order to adequately represent the cross of Christ, a church should actively reflect greater diversity, or a representative sample of the people groups living or working within its vicinity?

Open versus closed homogeneous churches

Any argument about the merits of homogeneous churches, which does not take seriously the circumstances under which they emerge, is at best flawed and at worst mischievous. There must be a clear distinction between 'the separatists' and 'the excluded'; between the racially motivated rejectors and the 'rejectees' who are simply reacting to the treatment meted out to them. Equally, we must respect the choices made by those who, because they have observed unrighteous behaviour or heretical theology in the life of a church, make a conscious decision to leave. When the young Edwin Mayers first arrived in Britain, he found himself facing just such a dilemma:[5]

When I came here I wanted to go to Good Friday service, because as a young man in the West Indies I used to go whether I wanted to or not. So I asked the landlady where the nearest church was and she told me, 'Just go down the road and ask the vicar if you can attend church', which was strange to me because in Jamaica I would just walk into any church once the door was open. So I asked the vicar and he said to me 'Personally sir, I don't mind, but I don't know what my parishioners would say.'

I said, 'I beg your pardon, I don't understand that.'

And he said, 'You see, the congregation might not want to accept you in church.'

So I said to him, 'Are they God-serving people?'

He said, 'Oh yes, oh yes.'

I said, 'Then why wouldn't they accept me in the church?'

And he said, 'Because you are a Black person.'

I said, 'Then what god do they serve?'

He said, 'Very good question. Sorry I can't answer that one.' So he said, 'If you want to come to church, just come in.' And I went. There were no Black-led churches at that time that I knew of, and then I heard of one in Dalston, east London and then I start attending that until they open up a branch in Tottenham. So, church for me was all right. I take what I want. I wasn't a partygoer. Church was my main entertainment.

Historically, both in the USA and in Britain, Black people were excluded from the main churches, thereby leading them to establish their own. Segregated societies produced segregated churches; and segregated churches were, by definition, a form of homogeneous church, but they are what I would call 'closed' homogeneous churches.

In South Africa, the Dutch Reformed Church at one time took the position that it was incompatible with the Scriptures to say that Black people and White people were equal in the sight of God, and they unreservedly gave their support to apartheid. The churches that emerged in the townships, as a result of Black South Africans' express desire to serve and worship God, can hardly therefore be seen as illegitimate. Instead, these churches ought to be looked on as one of the best representations of God's kingdom on earth, if only because they came into existence as a protest at a sinful barrier that was put up to separate Christian from Christian. They refused to accept that they were unworthy or less worthy of the grace of God, and they created new opportunities for God to work within their communities. They have 'received the Spirit of sonship' (Romans 8:15, New International Version) who confirms their status as 'heirs of God and co-heirs with Christ' because they 'share in his sufferings in order that [they] may also share in his glory' (v 17, NIV). I call churches like these 'open' homogeneous churches. I see them as instigated by God, his intervention being necessary in order that his righteousness and justice should be properly reflected to the world. Moreover, these churches should be cherished because they did not turn away to serve other gods in times of crisis and persecution.

However, if as Christians we are to be faithful to our conscience, to God and to the Scriptures, we should view closed homogeneous churches as a betrayal of the cross of Christ and sinful to the core. At times the members of such churches have seen themselves as racially superior and distinctive from other ethnic groups; they have also tended to consider themselves morally and intellectually superior. As a result, they have excluded others, primarily on the basis of race, and some have even gone as far as to actively discourage interracial marriages, since 'the products of such unions were not what God intended for humanity'. They have usually been more economically enfranchised than those whom they reject. Finally, they have usually proclaimed a biblical imperative to be the way they are.

Open homogeneous churches, on the other hand, are often born out of specific need or circumstances. Their members may be from a particular ethnic group, country or region, or speak a distinctive language; they are often immigrants seeking to find their role in a new country or to form new communities. Their worshipping lives are often the only opportunities they have to 'sing the Lord's song in a foreign land' (Psalm 137:4) in a way that affirms all that they are and hope to be. Viewed in this way, what they need is support and encouragement from the wider church. We ought to celebrate their contribution to the Christian family, since 'God, who knows the heart, showed that he accepted them by giving the Holy Spirit to them, just as he did to us' (Acts 15:8, NIV). This is the litmus test for any church, whatever the nature or make up of its congregation. And if God has generously given them his Spirit, then we 'should not make it difficult for [those] who are turning to God' (Acts 15:19, NIV).

Concession or inclusive diversity

Many Christians concede that a limited amount of homogeneity is necessary within existing churches in order to meet the needs of the congregation. However, the perception of these 'concessionists' is often limited to the recognition that language can be a barrier between communities, and they do not see that social and cultural differences might also be important issues. Furthermore, they fail to value the skills and knowledge required to work with other cultures. In the past, many church leaders have failed to acknowledge their lack of 'cultural competence' and, as a result, minority ethnic Christians received little or inadequate pastoral care and attention, were poorly advised in the areas of family life and relationships, and found that their concerns either bore no relevance or made no sense to their uninformed listeners. This failure was reflected in the exposition of Scripture. Black Christians often felt that 'the sermon did not touch me'. I would argue that these were the main factors contributing to the existence of minority ethnic congregations. What the 'concessionists' do not always seem to recognise is that, by and large, they themselves are operating homogeneous units when they establish women's, men's, youth, children's, singles', single parents' or mums-and-toddlers groups in their churches. It is ironic that while recognising the needs and particularities of each of those groups, they fail to see the merit in people of a particular culture or ethnicity celebrating or dealing with their challenges together.

One of the best models for the homogeneous principle in action can be found Kensington Temple in west London. Although KT is an Elim Pentecostal Church, in the 1980s it identified itself as London's International Charismatic Church. Within six years the church had multiplied from 300 to 2,000 members. I can remember being turned away on several occasions because services were too full. A key reason for this growth was the adoption of the Antioch church model, which meant being a church that:[6]

- was open to the moving of the Holy Spirit;
- was willing to engage in outreach;
- fasted and prayed;
- had a world vision;
- had a training programme;
- was aware of the need for multiple ministries;
- had a commitment to people;
- allowed nothing to stop its progress.

A primary aspect of the Antioch model was its international dimension and diversity of cultures. KT recognised that many nations come to

London either as students, diplomats, refugees or asylum seekers. It was on this basis that the leadership actively encouraged the establishment of homogeneous groups to support, win and disciple the various nationalities. Wynne Lewis, then the senior pastor, recalls: 'I felt the Lord saying, "You are to build a multi-racial church. One church where you will be a demonstration to the world, with all its cultural differences, with all its prejudices, that the Gospel enables us to accept each other's foibles and understand each other."'⁷ Very soon Filipino, Ethiopian, Chinese, African and Caribbean fellowship groups were started, and the growth of the church was ramping up to 5,000. However, the level of membership often dipped in the summer as students, around 26 per cent of the congregation, returned to their various homes in the UK or to their home country. I often felt that the church operated like a 'petrol station': people came to get filled and then went on their merry way. No wonder its congregation was often described as 'nomadic', with 75 per cent of the congregation changing every three years in 1991, and 71 per cent in 1993. By 1991 minority ethnic groups had become the majority in Kensington Temple (see Table 1).

Table 1   Percentage of minority ethnic groups in Kensington Temple, 1991–1997

Year	Member-ship	African %	Caribbean %	Caucasian %	Chinese %	Asians %	Latin America %
1991	3,700	58		26	11	5	—
1993	4,500	55	12	20	6	6	—
1995		54	13	20	4.2	6.2	—
1996	5,000	47.6	9.7	22	9.7	5.3	9
1997		46.8	11.9	19.1	4.2	6.9	—

Source: Insight and London City Church annual reports 1993–1999. No figures are available after this period.

Kensington Temple adopted its London City Church identity in 1993: its mission was now to win London, and the world, for Christ. The church recognised that minority ethnic people were here to stay, and that many more churches were needed to reflect the cosmopolitan and European city of London. KT had more than 2,500 people worshipping in 100 satellite churches, and many of these churches and their leaders were emerging from the homogeneous groups. For me, this is a true model of inclusive diversity, and not a mere concession.

To my mind, there are many more merits for homogeneous churches than points against them. We have already established that it is the best way to multiply the church and stimulate growth. The majority of people, 60 to 90 per cent, were introduced to church by their friends or relatives.[8] Homogenous units provide fertile ground for developing leadership skills and personal gifts within the groups in a way that is often difficult or impossible within a larger 'melting pot'. Equally, group members are most fulfilled in their worship of God when they can use their first language or cultural norms, and receive teaching that is relevant to their context. If this is true, then it infers that minority ethnic people are best evangelised by members of their own community. As Wynne Lewis comments:[9]

> Some people have difficulty in understanding that ethnic groups in a church should have the opportunity of meeting separately. To them this speaks of segregation. However, that is not the case at KT. When ethnic groups conduct their own meetings and in the style more familiar to them, the new arrivals from their home countries can immediately identify with them.

What KT has succeeded in doing is to provide an opportunity for the various streams can meet separately to worship, support each other and be discipled in an appropriate way; they can then come together to celebrate their faith and worship God with boldness, confidence and trust, knowing that they belong to the whole family of God. I call this 'inclusive diversity'.

Attempts to break out

In the 1980s, the NTCOG in Britain attempted to transform their denomination from being one that was predominantly African Caribbean into something more multicultural. The church went about this by targeting other minority ethnic groups and the White population, and establishing what they called 'metro churches' – new church plants along the lines of McGavran's homogeneous unit principle. They succeeded in establishing an Asian congregation in Southall, and a Tamil congregation in north London. The denomination has now created a multicultural district of thirteen congregations, including its largest in the whole country, the Faith Church of God, which has 1,000 members. The ideal of a truly multicultural church failed, however, because they did not make any headway with the White population. They also failed to expand their understanding of 'multicultural' to include Africans and other new immigrant communities – for example, those from eastern Europe or fleeing the volcanic eruption on Montserrat. As a matter of fact, they finally gave up on the idea because the churches established to attract White members did not succeed.

The first COGOP congregation in the UK was a White Majority Church in Bedford. However, when Black Christians joined the church, the White members left in what is now known as 'White flight'. Nevertheless, the denomination has successfully reached the Spanish and Greek speaking communities, and protests vigorously when it is called a 'Black Majority Church'. More recently, the Kingsway International Christian Centre – an independent church based in east London, with a congregation of 7,000 – has embarked on a campaign, targeted at White people, to encourage them to be part of the church: KICC wants to create 'a church without walls'. It is still too early to evaluate the effect of this drive, but the church has certainly changed from meeting as one central congregation to forming over a dozen chapels (satellite churches). They have also started a French-speaking congregation. Their primary objective, however, does not seem to have succeeded. For one thing, it is difficult to target a specific people group if you are unable to meet them either through geography, language or shared interests or aspirations. In addition, the 'crusade' or 'tent meeting' methodology is now being heavily debated within White Christian circles, who seem to be moving towards a 'discovery' model promoted chiefly through Alpha courses. Only time will tell whether such initiatives will change one of the largest Black Majority Churches into a 'rainbow' church.

Much can be said about the merits and weaknesses of these churches' individual strategies for establishing homogeneous units within their fellowships, but in every case there was a desire on the part of Black Christians to ensure that the mosaic pattern of the universal church was represented in their own. More significantly, these aspirations are shared by many other churches from the African and Caribbean diaspora. But it is my observation that, in Britain, the reason multicultural churches exist is not because White Christians have joined African and Caribbean churches; on the contrary, it is most often because Black Christians have made themselves vulnerable, and have determined in their own hearts and minds that God demands unity, forgiveness and reconciliation. They are the ones who, despite 'White flight' from congregations, have committed themselves to the task of transforming church structures from within. They have chosen to suffer loss in the hope that the kingdom of God will be better enriched and reflected than if they abandoned the quest for mutual acceptance and respect. But it is unfair to place the burden of establishing 'multicolour' churches on Black Christians only: there must be a critique as to why White Christians still tend to see belonging to an African or Caribbean church as retrograde or incompatible with their social status and with their aspirations for their children.

Are homogeneous churches compatible with Scripture?

> I planted the seed, Apollos watered it, but God made it grow. So neither he who plants nor he who waters is anything, but only God, who makes things grow.
>
> (1 Corinthians 3:6,7, NIV)

The verses above are Paul's analysis of church growth. It is clear that, in his view, unless God and the Holy Spirit are active in the life of a church, there will be no growth worthy of heaven. How easy it is to forget that we are not the ones setting God's agenda, that we are the servants, his workers, facilitating his priorities and his programme. It would be futile, then, for us even to attempt to force an agenda that is contrary to God's purpose and plan. This is why it is important to ensure that whatever strategies we use to add people to the church are in line with Scripture and guided by the Holy Spirit.

One of the first questions to consider when planning for church growth is this: are we concerned enough about those who deserve compassion and care, who are on the fringes of society'? One of Jesus' passions was to bring those on the margins to the centre stage so that they could experience the God's grace. He did not allow himself to be hampered by the expectations of religious people or by the desires of one people group. Sadly, many of those objecting to the homogenous church principle have no idea of what it means to be on the margins of society; they have never joined the chorus for justice, or to plead for better treatment for vulnerable minority groups.

> 'No one puts a piece of unshrunk cloth on an old garment; for the patch pulls away from the garment, and the tear is made worse.

'Nor do they put new wine into old wineskins; or else the wineskins break, the wine is spilled, and the wineskins are ruined. But they put new wine into new wineskins, and both are preserved.'

(Matthew 9:16,17)

These verses from Matthew offer an insight into Jesus' perspective on church growth. It is clear from both his words and actions that 'old cloth' and 'old wineskins' represent the existing, untransformed religious people, structures and practices. The new scheme of things required new thinking and action; merely adopting a patchwork solution, by grafting in the 'new cloth' to sustain the old order of things, was unacceptable. Such a piecemeal approach could not sustain the 'new wine', the metaphor for those who have been transformed by Christ. It is clear that the so-called 'tax collectors and sinners' who were coming to Jesus were never going to be acceptable to the scribes and Pharisees who were even questioning the legitimacy of their eating and drinking with Jesus (Matthew 9:10,11). Similarly, the woman who had suffered from bleeding for twelve years would find it strange that she should have no other choice than to worship in the synagogue that had rejected her for all those years in the belief that they were upholding the Law (vs 20–22).

Jesus desires from us 'mercy and not sacrifice' (v 13). His greatest challenge to the religious people of his day was that they face up to the needs of the new breed of believers, those who were 'filled with awe and glorified God, who had given such authority to men' (v 8, NIV). He wanted to transform the synagogues in every village and town. His radical message, his good news of God's kingdom and his acts of healing should all have been enough to stir the religious leaders into changing their teaching and practices. They could have become 'new wineskins' and received the benefits of the work of Christ. Instead, they left it to Jesus and his disciples to deal with the 'distressed and downcast' crowds who were 'like sheep without a shepherd', and to pray to 'the Lord of the harvest to send out workers into his harvest' (vs 36,38). By implication, he had discounted the 'old cloth' and 'old wineskins'. If Jesus thought it irresponsible to place new converts into an environment that would be unhelpful for nurturing their newfound faith, then so should we! If God is still 'the Lord of the harvest', we should respond like Jesus and realise the scandal and wastefulness of an unharvested crop. It is my contention that homogeneous units are in fact a way to preserve the unity of the church. Jesus saw that the only way to preserve old wineskins was to protect them from new wine, and visa versa. We ignore this at our peril. We may well see some of our young people choosing other faiths or no faiths at all if their experience of church is incompatible with their understanding of God.

Let us now go back to the apostle Paul and look again at some texts that, in the past, have been much misrepresented in the debate on 'homogeneous versus heterogeneous' churches. Paul says:

> There is neither Jew nor Greek, there is neither slave nor free, there is neither male nor female; for you are all one in Christ Jesus.
>
> (Galatians 3:28)

> [You] have put on the new man who is renewed in knowledge according to the image of Him who created him, where there is neither Greek nor Jew, circumcised nor uncircumcised, barbarian, Scythian, slave nor free, but Christ is all and in all.
>
> (Colossians 3:10,11)

Enormous effort has gone into interpreting these verses as meaning that Paul is adopting an 'it doesn't really matter' attitude. This is then used to stifle debate on diversity and difference, and, in particular, it is often put forward to support the argument that the homogenous unit principles is erroneous. But the real heresy, it seems to me, is to ascribe to Paul views that he did not hold.

It is true that Paul is demanding the breaking down of barriers between Jews and Gentiles. However, he is not doing this from inside the camps of either Judaism or Jewish Christianity; rather, he is firmly on the outside, in the camp of the Gentile Christians. It is from this vantage point that he is both critiquing the practices of the 'insiders', and, rather like a team coach, boosting the confidence of the outsiders, telling the latter that they do belong, that the work of Christ has now made them equal to their tormentors: 'You have equal rights and equal access to God,' he was saying to them. 'You are not abandoned by him, nor has he made you second-class citizens by giving you less abilities, opportunities or gifts to exercise in his kingdom.' Paul is confirming their status as children of God, 'heirs of God and joint heirs with Christ' (Romans 8:17). Those who belong to God are joined together as one spiritual family, with Jesus as 'the first-born over all creation' (Colossians 1:15), and the rest of us, his brothers and sisters, having equal entitlement to access and to share in his inheritance, gifts, grace, love, acceptance, commitment and divine favour (v 12). I see Paul's words in Galatians as being primarily about the status of Christians before God. If this is the case, it easy to see that, although we are all equal in his sight, we can still maintain our uniqueness and be different from each other, both as individuals and as people groups, in our diverse human dispositions. Unity does not necessarily equal uniformity. The issue, then, for the church is about locating where each piece fits into the jigsaw.

Paul did not attempt to transform the socio-economic circumstances of the people with whom he worked. It is not surprising, therefore, that his advice to Onesimus, the escaped slave, was to return to his master, Philemon. Both Onesimus and Philemon were new converts: Philemon was Paul's 'beloved brother and fellow worker' in the gospel; Onesimus had become like a son to Paul during his imprisonment (Philemon 1,10). Although some may find this hard to understand, Paul was not interested in placing Christian slave owners at a disadvantage within the societies in which they lived: rather, he saw them as primarily benefiting from the work of slaves who were fellow Christians (1 Timothy 6:1,2), who had fully accepted the values of Jesus; who were committed and obedient to the law; and who understood that all human beings were created in the image of God and this image must be preserved at all cost. It was only on these terms that slavery became acceptable. This is not to say that Paul condoned every aspect of the condition of slavery: he included slave traders in his 'blacklist' as the very people that the law was intended to restrain (1 Timothy 1:9,10, NIV).

In my view, Paul chose carefully the battles he was prepared to fight in order to maintain the spiritual, social and economic cohesion of the communities he was serving. This does not mean that the ones he chose not to fight should forever remain unfought: on the contrary, we too must wrestle with the issues of our day. One of the great challenges that Christians face today is to ensure that the value and social standing afforded all human beings matches their spiritual status, whatever their sex, religion, ethnicity or geographical location. No doubt this will make us out of step with the spirit of globalisation that is traversing the world today. However, the church must take its stand. We may be one in Christ, yet we live in separate rooms. We should do everything possible to ensure that the day-to-day experience of those who do not live under the same roof as we do are reflected in their privileged status before the Lord.

Endnotes

1 Donald McGavran, *Understanding Church Growth*, third edition, Eerdmans, 1990, p69.
2 McGavran, p174.
3 McGavran, p177.
4 McGavran, p177.
5 Z Nia Reynolds, *When I came to England: An Oral History of Life in 1950s and 1960s Britain*, Macmillan, 2001, p54, 55.
6 Jack Hywel-Davies, *The Kensington Temple Story*, Monarch, 1998, p86.
7 Wynne Lewis, in Hywel-Davies, p104.
8 Lyle E Schaller, in McGavran, p165.
9 Lewis, in Hywel-Davies, p121.

5

What on earth is a Black Majority Church?

There are at least five identifiable segments that could be included under the term 'Black Majority Church', each with its own distinctiveness that reflects either its origins or allegiances:

- Churches emerging from the African Caribbean diaspora;
- Churches emerging from the African diaspora;
- BMCs within the historic denominations;
- BMCs within the White Pentecostal denominations;
- African and Caribbean Spiritual churches.

Churches emerging from the African Caribbean diaspora

These churches emerged as a result of migration after the Second World War, when many people from the British colonies in the Caribbean answered the call to help rebuild a ravaged Britain. One historic example was the arrival of the *Empire Windrush*, which moored at Tilbury docks on 21 June 1948, carrying on her 492 migrants. These pioneers became known as the 'Windrush generation'. They established churches which were first called 'West Indian churches', then 'Afro-Caribbean churches' and now 'African Caribbean churches'.

The earliest church on record to be established was the Calvary Church of God in Christ. The date of its commencement depends on who is credited with the honour of pioneering the work. The settled position is that the church was started in 1948 by Mother Mary Mclachlan, but it was not until 1952 that a bishop was appointed to the UK.

Other churches in this category include the New Testament Church of God, the Church of God of Prophecy, the New Testament Assembly, the Wesleyan Holiness Church, the Bethel First United Church of Jesus Christ, the Assemblies of the First Born, the African Methodist

Episcopal, the African Methodist Episcopal Zion churches and the Ruach Inspirational Church of God, to name a few. In addition, if we are to be faithful to the above categorisation, the Seventh-day Adventist churches would also fit comfortably within this category.

The distinctive features of the African Caribbean churches are wide and varied, and often reflect the traditions of their pioneers. While it is accepted that the majority of these churches are both Trinitarian and Pentecostal, there are a significant number which are not: for example, the Unitarian (commonly known as the 'Oneness' or 'Jesus only' churches), the Wesleyan Holiness, the African Methodist Episcopal, the African Methodist Episcopal Zion, and the Seventh-day Adventist churches, do not fit into either of those categories.

Churches emerging from the African diaspora

Churches emerging from the African diaspora can be traced back to the 1970s. Although there were congregations before that time, their development is largely attributable to students from that continent coming to study in Britain. In need of spiritual support, fellowship and pastoral care, many of them organised themselves into fellowships and initiated many of the early African churches. Reverend Dr Paul Jinadu, General Overseer of the New Covenant Church denomination, who was then the evangelist of the Four Square Church, became one of the early pastoral workers sent from Nigeria to support African students in the UK. Matthew Ashimolowo, now the senior pastor at Kingsway International Christian Centre, also came to Britain as one of the first pastors to support the growing number of students and student fellowships.

This student movement saw the birth of the Overseas Fellowship of Nigerian Christians, which provided a student support base; and the African Christian Fellowship, which had a much wider remit and several chaplaincies. Alongside these were the Christ Apostolic Church, one of the first denominations to be established, and the Redeemed Christian Church of God, one of the fastest growing denominations. A notable feature here is the large number of independent churches, notably House on the Rock, Glory House, New Wine Church, The Everlasting Arms Ministries and Christ Faith Tabernacle, among others.

In the 1980s, a surge of growth took place. Many 'twentysomethings' were returning, having been born in the UK while their parents were students. A further factor encouraging students to remain was the instability of many countries in Africa. Overseas churches began to plant churches to cater for their members residing in Britain – a trend that continues today. The majority of these churches are Pentecostal, having a heightened sense that God has called them to transform the nation and be a light shining in the darkness of unbelief. They continue to be the fastest growing churches in Britain today.

Black Majority Churches within the historic denominations

When talking about historic denominations, I am referring to the likes of the Church of England, Methodists, Baptists, United Reformed Church and Catholic Church. BMCs in this category are very varied and tend to reflect the historic traditions of their denominations.

Between the 1940s and the 1960s, many immigrants to Britain went to churches belonging to the same denomination as those they had attended in their home country. However, factors such as worship and preaching styles, community cohesion and racism caused many Black Christians to switch to the churches that were then emerging from the African and Caribbean diaspora. However, this did not deter many others, who felt called to stay and serve in the historic denominations or who genuinely believed that they had no reason to leave. It is important that we remember this, as it would simply not be true to say that all Black people were treated appallingly when they came to Britain. As a matter of fact, I have met a number of people who have no complaints whatsoever. Their testimonies are that 'God is altogether wonderful' and has brought them 'a mighty long way', spiritually and temporally.

Nevertheless, although there was a degree of acceptance, what transpired as a result of Black Christians remaining in the historic denominations has done some harm both to the Black community and to the church. One of the notable features of the migrants who remained was that a large proportion of them were well-educated or from the middle classes. This meant that much of the intellectual capital needed in the emerging Black Majority Churches was unavailable to them. As a result, a view developed that the churches emerging from the West Indian (Caribbean) diaspora were predominantly 'simple rural folk'. It also sowed the seeds of a class divide within the community, and belonging to the 'right group' became important. Theological spats were common; the notorious notions of 'live' and 'dead' churches were bandied about; and every effort was made by the 'living' (ie the Caribbean churches) not to associate with the 'dead' (the historic churches).

It is also clear that all was not, and indeed is still not, well for Black Christians in the historic denominations. Many have suffered, and continue to suffer, racism within these churches. Often this takes the form of exclusion from decision-making processes, little or no encouragement to enter pastoral ministry, poor pastoral care, and even 'White flight', because too many Black people were joining their church. While the churches themselves have given a public response to the issue – almost all the historic denominations have employed racial justice officers – most of these officers are frustrated with the unwillingness of the structures to change. One of their main challenges lies in dealing with their liberal colleagues, whose open-mindedness has made it possible for issues to be raised, but who do not always notice that they themselves need to change. Unfortunately, bias and prejudice leaves few uncontaminated.

Nevertheless, the BMCs are the fastest growing in all of the historic denominations, and Black Christians are becoming a permanent feature of their landscape. There is room for more, especially from the African continent where migration is still occurring. Moreover, some Black Majority independent churches are now forming alliances with leaders in the historic churches for pastoral oversight, or 'covering'. It will be interesting to see how far this goes.

Black Majority Churches in White Pentecostal denominations

The main churches in this category are the Assemblies of God, Elim Pentecostal and Apostolic Church.[1] The number of BMCs in these White Majority denominations has accelerated since the 1980s: Kensington Temple has established over eighty of them as part of its London City Church network; equally, the rise of the Elim Camberwell network of churches, the Emmanuel Christian Centre in East London, the Birmingham Christian Centre (the last two are both Assemblies of God churches), and the Apostolic churches mirror this trend. However, although these BMCs come under the 'White Pentecostal' umbrella, there are no major differences between them and other Pentecostal BMCs. Apart from the London region of the Elim Pentecostal Church, and Kensington Temple in particular, it appears that no proactive effort was made in the past to target minority communities. BMCs therefore emerged organically owing to their geographical location and to other factors such as transfer growth and because independent churches were joining the denominations. A criticism of these denominations is that their structures have been slow to identify Black or other minority ethnic leaders and to include them at the highest levels of their decision-making processes. Issues of racism, inequality, poverty and social action are never very high, if they are present at all, on the national or corporate plan, and therefore remain outside the churches' collective conscience. It is left to local churches to set the agenda on these matters.

On the other hand, BMCs in these denominations resemble those in any of the other categories. Their social action and community involvement tend to reflect the needs of their community or their members: this is vital, as it makes it easy for new converts to join them. It is certainly the case that fewer and fewer Black Christians are paying attention to the label of the churches they attend. The criteria that ACEA receives from individuals looking for a church tends to be that they must be Pentecostal, in a particular locality, of a particular size, progressive, dynamic and a BMC.

African and Caribbean Spiritual churches

Many of the other BMCs would argue that this category is a misnomer. First of all, and quite rightly so, they would point to the fact that all of the previous classifications are 'spiritual' churches, since they focus on worship and foreground the importance of a relationship with God who is Spirit. Second, it could be argued that to call these groups 'churches', in the orthodox sense of the word, is misleading, as their faith and practice would preclude them from such a classification. However, the reality is that these churches are already regarded as legitimate churches by Britain's main ecumenical organisations – Churches Together in Britain and Ireland, and Churches Together in England. The World Council of Churches also accepts them as legitimate. These objections, if not rejection, by the other BMCs are largely because they have either lived alongside, were themselves members, or have members who were part of these groups in their country of origin. The belief is that there is a degree of syncretism as well as of practice, depending on the group, which is inconsistent with biblical orthodoxy.

The practices of these churches vary significantly, and if we fail to recognise this then we are doing these churches and ourselves a disservice. Some of them see their founders or primates as 'Jesus Christ Incarnate': for example, the Brotherhood of the Cross and Star, whose founder is Olumba, Olumba Olu; the initials 'OOO' are seen as divine. Although

Olu now refutes this, members of the church still believe this to be the case. 'Jesus Christ Church on Earth by his special envoy Simon Kabangwist' (commonly called Kabangwist) churches view their founder in a similar light. Other churches in this category are syncretistic, allowing the practices of 'African traditional religion' to be grafted onto Christianity.

By and large, the other main criticism of these churches concerns their use of visions, dreams and prophecies which, it is argued, are not in line with biblical understandings of the disciplines, but seem more like divination. The fact that a leader can tell you what you ate for dinner or exactly where you have been is not to be viewed as discernment or working to the edification of individuals, but rather as controlling them. Another distinctive feature of these churches is that they do not have a written theology. In Virginia Becher's analysis of these churches, she argues that 'the validity of many African churches is not found in their propositions of beliefs, but in their effectiveness for daily life. This is particular so in the older Spiritual Churches'.[2]

Spiritual churches emerged in Britain during the early 1960s, and are sometimes referred to as 'African indigenous churches' or 'African initiated churches', mainly because they have their origins in west Africa, mainly Nigeria and Ghana. The Caribbean churches from this group also claim their roots in Africa, and believe that their tradition of worship was handed down from their ancestors during slavery. However, 'African initiated churches' is a very broad term as it used to refer to all the churches started *by* Africans *for* Africans. Essentially, these were 'protest' churches which rejected missionary churches and practices.[3]

Other examples of Spiritual churches include the Aladura church, the Cherubim and Seraphim, the Born Again Christ Healing Church, the Celestial Church of Christ, the Spiritual Baptist Church, the Mount Zion Spiritual Church, and the Evangelical Spiritual Church, to name but a few.

In conclusion

In this chapter, I have tried to identify what BMCs are and to demonstrate that a wide spectrum of churches fit into this category. More significantly, I want to emphasise that if we are to engage with these groups effectively, we need to acknowledge their distinctive characteristics and their uniqueness, and to revise our notions of a homogeneous community, so that the contributions of all the parts in the whole can be properly affirmed.

There is a challenge in recognising this diversity, but Black Christians within these churches should be able to identify the things they have in common, to respect each other and to contend for the faith in a way that enhances dignity, promotes equity and provides opportunity for solidarity. This kind of solidarity might be extended to emphasise their collective strength and provide a counterpoint to many of the negative perceptions of BMCs that exist in British society. Simply being identified with these groups might present us with opportunities to rethink how we give each other pastoral support. Each group might act as independent arbiters in disputes, and offer specialist counselling and support, without undermining each other's integrity. To be a BMC is not about making a journey to the margins of life, but, rather, is all about participating in enhancing and extending the kingdom of God.

Endnotes

1 'Apostolic' here refers to the Trinitarian churches.
2 Virginia Becher, *Black Christians: Black Church Traditions in Britain*, Centre for Black and White Christian Partnership & Westhill RE Centre, 1995, p17.
3 Olugbenga Segun, 'Robed in White: Syncretistic, Sects or Just Another Denomination?', *Focus* Magazine, African and Caribbean Evangelical Alliance, August–October 1999, p10, 11.

6

Black Christian heritage in Britain before 1948

The legacy of Black Christians to the church over the ages has been wide-ranging and impressive. Contrary to popular opinion, for centuries Black missionaries were integral to the evangelisation both of Africa and of the UK. Their resolute faith in the midst of adversity is outstanding, and should be an encouragement to us all. What is evident from their stories is that the majority were selfless in their commitment to Christ and to transforming the societies in which they lived out their faith. It is this ministry of our forebears which sets the context for Black Majority Churches today.

Although I studied theology at one of Britain's premier theological institutions, I feel a sense of deprivation that throughout my studies I was not enlightened as to the contribution made by the individuals I have alluded to in this chapter. Many of the issues they faced are no different from those that constantly crossed my desk in my office as General Director of ACEA. Notably absent are the stories of women. I have not deliberately omitted them; they simply did not surface during my search. This is regrettable, and an omission that needs urgent redressing. The other issue is that those who wrote the histories of these people were not interested in their Christian contribution, often viewing it as incidental to their lives. This has made it difficult to know the real debt that we owe to Christians who served the Lord in years gone by.

As with any such survey, there is too much information available to include it all in one chapter. I hope, however, that I have offered a start sufficient to inspire students to undertake a more comprehensive piece of work. Those wanting to do so could do no better than to begin searching the websites listed in the 'Endnotes' at the end of this chapter. I have drawn on a wealth of material and find it encouraging to know that so much work is being done to ensure that Black heritage is not forgotten.

Black Christians in Britain before the *Windrush*

As I said before, Black Christians have long played a key role in British church life and society. In the same way that Black people travelled widely in biblical times, it should not be unthinkable that they have been part of British society for centuries. Jos Williams, principal and founder of Clearview College in Coventry, has even argued that it was the invasion of Anglo-Saxons which saw the demise of Black people during the fifth and sixth century.[1] The current thinking among scholars seems to be that Black Africans can be traced in Britain as far back as between AD 193–211, when around 500 North African solders were stationed at the Roman military garrison at the fort of Aballava (modern day Burgh-by-Sands) on Hadrian's wall in Cumbria.[2] However, there is no evidence to suggest these soldiers' religious beliefs.

As early as 1565, St Mary the Virgin, Aldermanbury, in London, logged the baptism and burial of Black people, so they were converting to the faith at the time. Its earliest record is of the baptism of 'John the Blackamoor' on 6 May 1565. Ironically, it also lists its earliest burial – 'John a Blackamoor' on 23 May 1566.[3] There was evidently a sizeable Black population and a growing one. By 1596 their numbers had become large enough for Queen Elizabeth I, to issue a decree that they be deported – for the reason of 'tendering the good and welfare of her own natural subjects'. It was felt that these 'negroes' (or 'blackamoors' as they were known) were taking advantage of the 'troubles' between the Queen and the King of Spain; and they were receiving relief, 'to the great annoyance of her own liege people that which co[vet] the relief which those people consume, as also for that most of them are infidels having no understanding of Christ or his Gospel'.[4] If, as the queen declared, the majority of Black people were indeed 'infidels', then it is reasonable to assume that at least a minority of them were Christians.

In the seventeenth and eighteenth centuries, the slave trade was at its height. One of the justifications for slavery advanced by Europeans for the enslavement of Africans was their 'heathen state'. However, it was not unusual for slaves to take on Christian names or to convert to the Christian faith in the belief that they would then become free men and women. This state of affairs, however, was very unpopular with slave owners, who were often wealthy men of power, and there was pressure to clarify the law on this issue. On 14 January 1729, the Attorney General Sir Philip Yorke and Solicitor General Charles Talbot ruled that 'baptism doth not bestow freedom on [a slave], nor make any alteration to his temporal condition in these kingdoms. We are also of the opinion, that the master may legally compel him to return again to the plantations'.[5]

By 1764 an article in the *Gentleman's Magazine* cites that there were 20,000 Black people living in London, which then had an overall population of 676,250. The article complained that this was too many:[6]

> The main objection is that they cease to consider themselves as slaves in this free country. Nor will they put up with an inequality of treatment, nor more willingly perform laborious tasks or offices of servitude than our own people, and if put to do it, are generally sullen, spiteful, treacherous and revengeful. It is therefore highly impolitic to introduce them as servants here, where that rigour and fervency is impracticable which is absolutely necessary to make them useful.

The following year (1765) the same magazine reported the ordination of a Black minister:[7]

> At an ordination of priests and deacons at the chapel royal at St James's by the Hon. and Rev. Dr Keppel, Bishop of Exeter, a black was ordained, whose devout behaviour attracted the notice of the whole congregation.

By 1817, it was not unusual for Black preachers to be the star attraction at open air crusades. *La Chronique de Jersey*, 4 October 1817, carried the following advertisement:[8]

> By permission of the Police, John Jea, the black African Preacher, will preach to-morrow, on the Grand Parade, at a quarter past nine, in the morning, and at four o'clock in the afternoon, if GOD spares him in health and strength, and the weather permits.

The Black Christian presence within the British church was not a passive one. As we will discover, Black Christians were actively occupied not only as evangelists and missionaries, but also as important agents seeking to bring about transformation within the church and society. Moreover, they would often serve as missionary ambassadors to their countries of origin. They would succeed where others failed because they were not treated with the same level of suspicion as their White counterparts, and they had a better understanding of local conditions and customs as well as of local dialects.

A few good men of faith

Notwithstanding the struggles and hardships they faced, there have been many outstanding Black Christian leaders and preachers. We now go on to explore the contributions of just a few of these 'men of courage' (1 Corinthians 16:13, NIV).

Scipio Africanus

We know very little about Scipio Africanus (named after the Roman general who invaded Africa in 204 BC). *The Methodist Archives Biographical Index* records that Africanus was 'a correspondent of William Seward . . . a friend of George Whitefield' in 1739, when Africanus was living in London:[9]

> The name Scipio Africanus and other internal evidence from the letters show beyond reasonable doubt that he was a black man. The tone and content of the letters suggest that he was either a slave of the Seward family, or more likely, a free servant. Seward refers several times to Africanus attending meetings of the early evangelical societies in the capital, although it is not clear if he could be regarded as a convert. There are unfortunately no extant letters from Africanus to Seward.

Africanus' connection with the evangelical movement is of symbolic significance, even though his involvement may only have been peripheral. At the very least, it represents early documented evidence that Black people were involved in the beginnings of what was to become Methodism. Seward's first surviving letter to Africanus was sent in February 1739, prior to John Wesley's first ventures into open-air preaching. 'It is a great pity that nothing further is known about this man outside of the William Seward correspondence from that year.'[10]

Olaudah Equiano

Olaudah Equiano is one of the best known and most popular Black Christians. He was born in around 1745 'in an area called "Eboe" in Guinea', and was the son of a chief or elder of his village. When Equiano was about the age of ten, he and his sister were kidnapped while out playing and were taken from the Benin Coast (Nigeria) to Barbados. Equiano was sold to a naval officer named Michael Pascal, who renamed him Gustavus Vassa after the first Swedish king who, in the sixteenth century, had led a rebellion for independence from Denmark.[11] As Pascal's servant, Equiano became a seaman and travelled extensively. Eventually, he came to London and lived in Blackheath with the Guerin family who taught him to read.[12]

In 1759 Equiano was baptised at St. Margaret's Church, Westminster.[13] He bought his own freedom for £40 in 1766, but it was around 1773 that he had a radical conversion. In his autobiography, *The Interesting Narrative of the Life of Olaudah Equiano, or Gustavus Vassa, the African*, he gives an account of his experiences while on a voyage to Spain, when he saw 'the bright beams of heavenly light' and was 'born again'.[14] This proved an important turning point in his life, and he went on to be a notable abolitionist, working closely with Granville Sharp, travelling nation-wide and speaking in Europe against the evils of slavery.

In 1777 Equiano is alleged to have appointed himself missionary to Central America, thought to be Nicaragua, with the hope of taking Christianity to the native people of the region. He is regarded as one of the first civil servants when he was appointed Commissary in charge of stores which catered for destitute Black people who were being resettled (repatriated) to Sierra Leone. He was sacked after complaining of corruption and claiming that the project would fail to achieve its objectives.

Equiano died in 1797. He was married to an Englishwoman, Susanna Cullen from Ely, Cambridgeshire, and had two children.

Ignatius Sancho

Ignatius Sancho was another prominent Christian and Equiano's close friend. He was born on a slave ship and spent his first two years in Grenada before being brought to England as a servant.[15] He was baptised as a Catholic between 1729 and 1730, by the Bishop of Cartegena (Columbia). However, Sancho became 'a staunch Anglican who toyed with Methodism'.[16] He was not encouraged to read by his mistress whom, he believed, 'judged that ignorance was the best security for obedience'.[17] However, the Duke and Duchess of Montague taught him to read and, when the Duchess died, she left him a legacy of £70 and an annuity of £30.

In a letter written in 1778, to Jack Wingrave, son of a friend, John Wingrave, a London bookbinder and bookseller, Sancho sets out some of his most trenchant criticisms of slavery, in particular of Christian involvement in it, which he saw as going against the spirit of the gospel:[18]

Look what the Lord has done!

See the effects of right-doing, my worthy friend – continue in the tract of rectitude – and despise poor paltry Europeans – titled – Nabobs. – Read your Bible – as day follows night, God's blessings follow virtue – honour – and riches bring up the rear – and the end is peace. – Courage, my boy – I have done preaching. . . .

In some one of your letters which I do not recollect – you speak (with honest indignation) of the treachery and chicanery of the natives – My good friend, you should remember from whom they learnt those vices: – the first Christian visitors found them a simple, harmless people – but the cursed avidity for wealth urged these first visitors (and all the succeeding ones) to such acts of deception – and even wanton cruelty – that the poor ignorant Natives soon learnt to turn the knavish – and diabolical arts which they too soon imbibed – upon their teachers.

I am sorry to observe that the practice of your country (which as a resident I love – and for its freedom – and for the many blessings I enjoy in it – shall ever have my warmest wishes – prayers – and blessings); I say it is with reluctance, that I must observe your country's conduct has been uniformly wicked in the East – West Indies – and even on the coast of Guinea. – The grand object of English navigators – indeed of all Christian navigators – is money – money – money – for which I do not pretend to blame them – Commerce was meant by the goodness of the Deity to diffuse the various goods of the earth into every part – to unite mankind in the blessed chains of brotherly love – society – and mutual dependence: the enlightened Christian should diffuse the riches of the Gospel of peace – with the commodities of his respective land – Commerce attended with strict honesty – and with Religion for its companion – would be a blessing to every shore it touched at. – In Africa, the poor wretched natives – blessed with the most fertile and luxuriant soil – are rendered so much the more miserable for what Providence meant as a blessing: the Christians' abominable traffic for slaves – and the horrid cruelty and treachery of the petty Kings – encouraged by their Christian customers – who carry them strong liquors – to enflame their national madness – and powder – and bad fire-arms – to furnish them with the hellish means of killing and kidnapping. – But enough – it is a subject that sours my blood – and I am sure will not please the friendly bent of your social affections. – I mentioned these only to guard my friend against being too hasty in condemning the knavery of a people who bad as they may be – possibly – were made worse by their Christian visitors.

Sancho married a Caribbean woman, with whom he had six children. He died on the 14 December 1780.

Quobna Ottobah Cugoano

Another Christian of note is Quobna Ottobah Cugoano. Cugoano is believed to have been born in Ghana during the 1750s. In his autobiography, *Narrative of the Enslavement of Ottobah Cugoano, a Native of Africa*, he gives a candid account of his past:[19]

> I was born in the city of Agimaque, on the coast of Fantyn; my father was a companion to the chief in that part of the country of Fantee, and when the old king died I was left in his house with his family; soon after I was sent for by his nephew, Ambro Accasa, who succeeded the old king in the chiefdom of that part of Fantee . . .

Cugoano goes on to explain the circumstances behind his enslavement. Once while on a visit to his uncle, a friend of his dared him to go into the woods and catch birds: 'because you belong to the great men, you are afraid to venture your carcase, or else of the *bounsam*, which is the devil'.[20] Cugoano was so incensed by this insinuation that he agreed to go and catch birds, an event that led to his being captured and sold into slavery. He worked in Grenada before coming to England.

Cugoano was baptised in 1773 as John Stuart. He argued passionately that 'an end to the wickedness of slavery and merchandising of men, and to prevent murder, extirpation and dissolution, is what every righteous nation ought to seek after; and to endeavour to diffuse knowledge and instruction to all the heathen nations wherever they can, is the grand duty of all Christian men.' He continues:[21]

> Were the iniquitous laws in support of it, and the whole of that oppression and injustice abolished, and the righteous laws of Christianity, equity, justice and humanity established in the room thereof, multitudes of nations would flock to the standard of truth, and instead of revolting away, they would count it their greatest happiness to be under the protection and jurisdiction of a righteous government. . . .

> We would wish to have the grandeur and fame of the British empire to extend far and wide; and the glory and honor of God to be promoted by it, and the interest of Christianity set forth among all the nations wherever its

influence and power can extend; but not to be supported by the insidious pirates, depredators, murderers and slave-holders. And as it might diffuse knowledge and instruction to others, that it might receive a tribute of reward from all its territories, forts and garrisons, without being oppressive to any. But contrary to this the wickedness of many of the White People who keep slaves, and contrary to all the laws and duties of Christianity which the Scriptures teach, they have in general endeavoured to keep the Black People in total ignorance as much as they can, which must be a great dishonour to any Christian government, and injurious to the safety and happiness of rulers.

Thomas Birch Freeman

Thomas Freeman was born in Twyford, Hampshire, in 1809, the son of an English mother and a freed African slave. He was a Methodist preacher and became head gardener on a Suffolk estate; however, he was sacked from this job owing to his Methodist activism. As a result, in 1837, he became a missionary to the Gold Coast on behalf of the Wesleyan Methodist Missionary Society with whom he worked for more than fifty years. In the library catalogue for the School of Oriental and African Studies, his colourful CV reads as follows:[22]

... sailed to the Gold Coast, West Africa, 1837-1838; missionary on the Cape Coast (where an indigenous Methodist church had been tenuously supported by a succession of English missionaries), 1838-1857; visited Kusami, the Ashanti capital; married, for the second time, Lucinda Cowan (d 1841) at Bedminster, Somerset, 1840; visited England to appeal for funds and recruits, 1841; the publication of his journals made him a celebrity; his pioneering work in founding many mission stations and chapels in the area underpinned later Methodist success in Ghana, western Nigeria, and Benin; married for the third time, 1854; financial controversy and other difficulties caused him to retire from missionary work, 1857; civil commandant of Accra, 1857-1860; remained in the Gold Coast, farming, writing, and preaching; returned as a missionary, to Anamabu, West Africa, 1873-1879; Accra, 1879-1886; retired and settled at Accra, 1886; died, 1890.

Freeman was involved in missionary work in Africa for half a century; he had a major impact on Ghana and on his Methodist colleagues in Britain. Two biographies about him were published in 1929 and 1950, both entitled *Son of an African*.[23]

Joseph Jackson Fuller

Joseph Jackson Fuller was said to be a very popular preacher who toured British churches to raise support for his missionary work. Born as a slave in Jamaica in 1825, he became a Baptist missionary to the Cameroon in 1850. Jeffrey Green records: [24]

> . . . people across Britain heard JJ Fuller's sermons and descriptions of Africa, as well as the story of the event he witnessed at the emancipation of Jamaican slaves in 1838 – the burying of their shackles to the singing of Christian hymns.

Fuller is also credited with the success and the endurance of the Baptist Missionary Society's work in the Cameroon. He was better able than his White colleagues to win the confidence of the natives, who were very suspicious and were refusing to cooperate with the White missionaries. Fuller was also commended for his involvement in negotiating the transfer of the Society's property to the Swiss in the 1880s. The Cameroon mission subsequently became the springboard for Christian work in the Congo, where his son also became a missionary. [25]

Married to an Englishwoman, J J Fuller died in 1908. His biography is said to have been published in the 1930s.

Samuel Barber

Surprisingly, very little information seems to be available about Samuel Barber, who was the son of Francis Barber (who was acquainted with Equiano and Sancho). He became a Methodist minister and joined the very popular Primitive Methodist Movement or 'the Ranters'. From small beginnings, with 200 followers in 1808, the movement's membership increased to nearly 80,000 including 500 travelling evangelists and more than 1,200 chapels. Membership continued to grow, and by 1875, had reached 165,410. Unlike the Wesleyan Methodists, the Primitive Methodists encouraged women evangelists. They also provided many leaders of the trade union movement in the late nineteenth century. [26]

Peter Stanford

Reverend Peter Stanford is listed as 'Birmingham's first black minister'. [27] He certainly lived an intriguing life. He was born in the Southern states of America, where he was nameless for much of his childhood. At about the age of three, he lost his mother to slavery and was fostered by another Black woman. He passed a few more years of his young life in a state of desperate neglect, before being captured by Native Americans. He lived with them for a few years and learned survival skills, then was abandoned again. Fortunately, he was rescued and taken by the Quakers to a Black children's shelter in Boston. He was later adopted by a Mr Stanford, who gave him his name; he then lived an itinerant life, taking any jobs he could find.

Stanford's Christian ministry began in 1872, when he met the Reverend Henry Highland Garnet, the pastor at Shiloah Presbyterian Church. Reverend Garnet assisted him in his education and in securing a job as a yard boy at Suffield College. This job enabled him to join the college as a student and to advance his education. He completed his college course in June 1881, and through the kindness of the Reverend Henry Ward Beecher and W E Dodge, was given work as a missionary to the Black community in Hartford, Connecticut: 'his lack of finances forced him to work in the foundry in the day and preach at night, taking services on Sundays'.

In 1883, Stanford travelled to England on 14 February, journeying to London on the same night of his arrival in Liverpool. After some time he left London and travelled to Leeds, Barnsley, and Keighley in Yorkshire; finally, in the latter part of 1885, he went to live in Bradford. Unfortunately, Bradford did not prove to be a welcoming environment, and he moved to Birmingham in June 1887, where he eventually settled. The turning point of his life in the Britain is probably his marriage, in August 1888, to a lady from West Bromwich, whom he claimed had an 'ardent zeal for Christ'. The following year he received the call to pastor Hope Street Baptist Church. The invitation read:[28]

Baptist Church, Hope Street,
Birmingham, May 8th, 1889

To the Rev. P.T. Stanford.

Revd. and Dear Sir,

At a meeting on Wednesday, May 8th, it was unanimously decided that we, the members and congregation attending the above place of worship, invite you to become our pastor. You know our condition will not allow us to offer you a large salary, but we offer you our prayers, willing hearts, and hands. Remember, dear Brother, this call is from God, and He has promised to supply all our needs. Trusting you will see your way to accept our offer.

We are, yours faithfully,
Signed on behalf of the Church

D. BRILEY
H. SMITH
T. BARBER
J. MADDOCKS
H. GREENHILL
HENRY RICHARDS
JAS. CLARK, Secretary

Despite the church's eagerness to benefit from his ministry, the reality proved very different. Later, Stanford commented in the column of an evening newspapers on 'his hard and wearing trials in his efforts to carry on the work. He was libelled, slandered, ostracised, suspected, and opposed but in spite of this he did have supportive Christian friends'. Amazingly, within this short time, the church 'grew with flourishing schools and organisations'.[29]

After leaving Hope Street Baptist, Stanford started an independent church called Wilberforce Memorial Church, out of admiration for the abolitionist. At the heart of his ministry was the cause of his own people, social justice and politics. He firmly believed that Black people were the best people to be missionaries to Africa, and set his mind on developing institutions that would train them to do so.

In 1889, Reverend Stanford published his autobiography, entitled *From Bondage to Liberty*, which gives a detailed account of his life in the USA and England.

Celestine Edwards

Celestine Edwards was born in Dominica in 1858. At the age of twelve, he became a sailor before moving to Edingburgh in Scotland. He then went to Sunderland and finally settled in London.[30] It was during his time in Scotland that he developed a social conscience and his faith. There he joined the Temperance Movement, which advocated abstinence from alcohol and later encouraged the virtues of being teetotal.

Edwards worked as a builder and pursued his passion for public speaking, for which he became renowned, especially in Victoria Park. He spoke about human rights (anti-racist), Christianity and the benefits of temperance. He also published 'penny pamphlets' on key issues of the Christian faith.[31] In 1891, he assisted Walter Hawkins, a slave from America who eventually became the Bishop of the Methodist Episcopal Church in Canada, to write Hawkins' autobiography. That same year Edwards gained a degree in theology. He was also an editor for several newspapers, including the Christian newspaper, *Lux*, from 1893–1895, and the Anti-Caste newspaper which was rebranded *Fraternity*, 'the Official Organ of the Society for the Recognition of the Brotherhood of Man', a mainly White organisation founded in 1893. The paper existed from July 1893 to February 1897. Edwards was probably the first Black man to edit a White-owned newspaper.[32]

With his growing reputation, Edwards' itinerant speaking engagements saw him travelling and speaking in America. On returning to England, he travelled to Bristol where, on 3 July 1893, he spoke against lynchings in the United States. The following week he spoke to 1,200 people in London on 'American Atrocities'. In August he was in Liverpool lecturing on 'Blacks and Whites in America'. Similar talks were given in Plymouth, Aberdeen, Newcastle, Edinburgh and Glasgow. Popular topics included 'The Negro Race and Social Darwinism' and 'Liquor Traffic to West Africa'.[33]

Despite his success as a speaker, Edwards had a strong desire to become a doctor. However, his hard work took a toll on his health. In 1958, during a period of enforced rest with his brother in Dominica, he died at the tender age of thirty-six.

Harold Moody

Harold Moody was born in Jamaica in 1882, and came to London in 1908 to pursue a career in medicine. He studied at Kings College Hospital, London. Much is said of his devout Christian faith which was nurtured by his family in Jamaica. He became a member of the London Missionary Society which had assisted him in securing accommodation in London, after landlords rejected him because he was Black. He later went on to become president of the Society.

Dr Moody married an English nurse, Olive Tranter, with whom he had six children.[34] Frustrated at the lack of opportunity to ply his trade in a hospital, he turned to general practice in Peckham, South London.

He wanted to ensure that the medical needs of Black people were met. On the 13 March 1931, in the central YMCA, Tottenham Court Road, 'The League of Coloured Peoples' was formed; Moody served as its president from its birth to its demise. Despite being heavily criticised by more militant pressure groups, the League never actually claimed to be a radical organisation. Its aims were clearly set out in its quarterly magazine, *The Keys*:[35]

1 To promote and protect the social, educational, economic and political interests of its members.
2 To interest members in the welfare of coloured peoples in all parts of the world.
3 To improve relations between the races.
4 To operate and affiliate with organisations sympathetic to coloured people.
5 To render such financial assistance to coloured people in distress as lies within our capacity.

Moody is credited with the success in removing the colour bar in the British Armed Forces. On 19 October 1939, the Colonial Office declared that 'British Subjects from the Colonies, and British Protected persons in this Country, including those who are not of European origin, are now eligible for emergency Commissions in his Majesty's forces'. To Moody, this approach seemed piecemeal, and he demanded 'that if this principle is accepted now, surely it must be acceptable all the time!' Two of Moody's children rose to the rank of major.[36]

Dr Moody was a practising Christian for all of his life. He was a deacon of the Camberwell Congregational Church, and preached in towns all over England.[37] As president of the Christian Endeavour, he supported not only children in the church but also those in the community by organising annual trips to Epsom Downs; he also treated them to a Christmas party every year.[38]

Daniel Ekarte

Daniel Ekarte was registered as 'George Daniel' on his seaman's Identity Service Certificate, which listed his date of birth as the 1 January 1904 in Calabar, Nigeria.[39] Marika Sherwood disputes this birth date, and suggests that the early 1890s may be more accurate.[40] As a child, Ekarte worked as an errand-boy for a Scottish missionary, Reverend Dr. Wilkie, and then for another missionary, Mary Slessor, who warned him not to come to England because the people there were not 'enthusiastic about heavenly things'.[41] After Slessor's death, and against her advice, Ekarte came to Liverpool in Britain in 1915.

Ekarte may have regretted not heeding Slessor's counsel, because he soon backslid, became a gambler and was involved in criminal activities. Added to that, he bought a gun and was determined to return to his native Nigeria and shoot all missionaries, Black and White, because he felt they had deceived him. He wanted to show the 'various chiefs my notebook in which I had written down all the insults I had received from the "Christian people" in the "holy country"'. But the Lord intervened:[42]

> One Sunday morning he was walking past 4 Hardy Street, where Africans used to meet to worship. He usually avoided this place, but on this day he heard a voice calling him and he went in. 'A great light came into my heart. I went in and knelt down to pray.' Soon afterwards Ekarte threw his gun and his note book in the Mersey and began a new life.

Soon after his radical recommitment in 1922, Ekarte started preaching in the open air as well as in private rooms. The police twice arrested him on the charge of obstruction. He refused to pay the fines and was eventually jailed. He was even referred to a mental institution for evaluation. However, ever determined, Ekarte continued his work and ministered to African seamen, the destitute and in hospitals.

During this period, there were two support organisations for Black people in Liverpool: the Coloured Men's Religious Institute, based at 4 Hardy Street; and the Methodist African and West Indian Missions Religious and Social Institute, based at 73 Parliament Street. However, neither of these seemed able to facilitate Ekarte's vision and aspirations. So, in 1931 he established the African Churches Mission at 122–124 Hill Street, Toxteth, Liverpool, possibly with a grant from the Scotland Foreign Missions and other sources as 'few of the congregation could afford more than a copper [for the collection] . . . The mission depends on donations and occasionally receives help from Africa'.[43] This helped to facilitate activities such as a Sunday school, which provided free or cheap breakfast to children who attended, handicraft for the women, a social club and Brownies. Amazingly, the church, led by Pastor Daniel (who was referred to as 'Nigger Dan'), held 'music and secondary school classes with 53 pupils. It also provided shelter for women and children fleeing abusive husbands. The church had 558 members and held daily services and all-night prayer meetings. In 1933 the mission served 13,336 free meals to both Black and White destitute in Liverpool. The Bishop of Liverpool was listed among its trustees. No wonder 'the Mission became the local centre for those in need'.[44]

Not all Pastor Ekarte's efforts were appreciated. There were racial tensions and complaints against intermarriage and dancing by Black people. In a letter printed on 12 March 1934 in the *Liverpool Daily Post*, Ekarte argued:[45]

Why do the complainants have a problem with Negroes coming to Britain when Englishmen go to Africa, driving Negroes into the backlands? Liverpool's Negroes neither held orgies nor do they figure disproportionately in the courts. Negroes are looking forward to see what place politically they will attain as Britishers – therefore we are expecting British Justice free of prejudice.

Despite his achievements, all was not well with Pastor Ekarte. At one point he allegedly had an affair with his housekeeper and refused to see the error of his ways. His attempt to build a children's home to support the war babies eventually failed. The mission was constantly struggling financially. Unable to get a mortgage due to racism, it was only because of an anonymous donation that he and his church were able to purchase their building and avoid eviction. A more serious setback occurred when the government offered grants to other churches and organisations, but bypassed the Mission. Consequently, membership decreased, and by the 1950s the church had become small. Pastor Ekate died on 12 July 1964, a few weeks after he was moved from the mission, which was then demolished.

Facing trials of many kinds

Not all Black Christians in Britain found their faith to be an asset or an agent for change. Some struggled with disillusionment; others were accused of heresy.

William Davidson, a Wesleyan Methodist, who was born in Jamaica in 1781, came to Glasgow at the age of 14 to study law. However, Davidson fell into a life of dissipation after being accused of seducing a young girl in his Sunday school class. He then totally lost faith in God after his friend, Richard Carlile, was jailed for blasphemy in 1819. Davidson was a political activist and, a year after Carlile's imprisonment, was found guilty of treason and hanged on 1 May 1820.

Then there was Arthur Wharton, who came to England from Ghana in 1882 to train as a Methodist missionary. However, Wharton was an outstanding athlete, and he eventually decided to abandon the idea of becoming a missionary to concentrate on a career as a sportsman. In July 1886, he ran the hundred yards at Stamford Bridge in ten seconds, setting a new world record. He became the first Black professional footballer, but after a life of uncertainty, he died, a penniless alcoholic, in 1930. His few surviving personal effects are his Bible and some pictures.[46]

Robert Wedderburn, born in Jamaica, was converted to Christianity by a Wesleyan minister. He became involved in the Unitarian movement, and a radical who advocated revolution rather than reform. He did not believe in controlling, centralised governments because of their corrupt values and endorsement of slavery. He is credited with reform of the freedom of the press. He referred to his Sunday Sermons as 'lectures every Sabbath day on Theology, Morality, Natural Philosophy and Politics by a self-taught West Indian'.[47] His staunch criticism and challenging of the orthodox position finally caused his incarceration in Doncaster Prison for three years, charged with blasphemy. In his rebuttal he says:[48]

Where, after all, is my crime? It consists merely in having spoken in the same plain and homely language which Christ and his disciples uniformly used. There seems to be a conspiracy against the poor, to keep them in ignorance and superstition; the rich may have as many copies as they like of sceptical writers; but if I find two most decided contradictions in the Bible, I must not in the language of the same book assert that one or the other is a lie.

As to my explanation of the doctrines of Christ, I must still maintain it to be particularly faithful. He was like myself, one of the lower order, and a genuine radical reformer. Being poor himself, he knew how to feel for the poor, and despised the rich for the hardness of their hearts. His principles were purely republican; he told his followers they were all brethren and equals, and inculcated a thorough contempt for all the titles, pomps, and dignities of this world.

On his release from prison, Wedderburn continued his campaign for freedom and was arrested again in 1831, at the age of 68. It is not known when he died, but it seems that this long-time member of the 'awkward squad' never gave up fighting against the injustice he saw around him, and his determination was fuelled by the light of the gospel.

It is my hope that this chapter has demonstrated the rich heritage of

Black Christians in the UK, and has successfully challenged the notion that Black Christians only came to prominence after modern migration to Britain with the arrival of Caribbean immigrants of 1948 onwards. What is clear is that they worked within the structures of the historic denominations for centuries. Any separation in later years could be seen as the turning of the tide – their way of going, like Jesus, 'outside the camp' (Hebrews 13:13) and away from corruption to shine a greater light on what God was about to do. The next chapter explores the spiritual and societal contributions of Black Majority Churches in subsequent years, and their role as the most cohesive representation of the Black community in Britain.

Endnotes

1 Jos Williams, in Selwyn E Arnold Snr, *From Scepticism to Hope: One Black-led Church's Response to Social Responsibility*, Grove Books, 1992, p13.

2 Richard Paul Benjamin and Alan M Greaves, 'The Archaeology of Black Britain: Approaches, Methods and Possible Solutions,' *The Black Presence in Britain*, 2003, Case study on North African soldiers at Aballava (Burgh-by-Sands); available at **www.blackpresence.co.uk/pages/historical/archaeology.htm**

3 Jeffrey Green, 'Black People in Britain: Before the Windrush', *The Black Presence in Britain*, 2003, Parish Records and News Clippings; available at **www.black presence.co.uk/pages/parish.htm** For further reading on the history of Black people in London, with a particular focus on slavery, see Seán Mac Mathúna, 'Slavery and London', *Flame*, Issue 1, Spring 1999; available at **www.fantom powa.net/Flame/slavery_in_london.html**

4 J L Hughes and J F Larkin (eds), Acts of the Privy Council, xxvi, 1596–1507, 16, 20 and 21, 'Licensing Caspar van Sanden to deport Negroes (1601)', *Tudor Royal Proclamations, 1588–1603*, Yale University Press, 1969, p221; in Nigel File and Chris Power, *Black Settlers in Britain 1555–1958*, Heinemann, 1995, p6. See also the National Archives, 'Early Times: Elizabeth I', *Black Presence: Asian and Black History in Britain*, transcript of Licence to Deport Black People, online exhibition, 2004; available at **www.nationalarchives.gov.uk/pathways/blackhistory/early_times/eliza beth.htm**

5 National Archives, 'Rights: Slave or Free?', *Black Presence*, The Yorke-Talbot Ruling; available at **www.nationalarchives.gov.uk/pathways/blackhistory/ rights/slave_free.htm**

6 *Gentleman's Magazine*, Vol. 34, 1764, p493; in File and Power, p1.

7 *Gentleman's Magazine*, March, 1765, p145; in National Archives, 'Work and Community: Relationships and Religion', *Black Presence*, transcript of Ordination of the First Black British Preacher; available at **www.nationalarchives. gov.uk/pathways/blackhistory/work_community/relationships.htm**

8 La Societe Jersiaise, 'Black History in Jersey' ('L'Histouaithe des Nièrs en Jèrri'), *The History Section*, 2004; available at **www.societe-jersiaise.org/history/niers.html**

9 See *The Methodist Archive of Biographical Index*, © John Rylands Library University of Manchester, 2004; available at **http://rylibweb.man.ac.uk/data1/dg/metho dist/bio/bioa.html**

10 *The Methodist Archives Biographical Index*, see above.

11 See Brycchan Carey, 'Olaudah Equiano: A Critical Biography', 2000-2003, *Brycchan Carey's Website*, © Brycchan Carey 1999-2004; available at **www.brycchancarey. com/equiano/biog.htm**

12 File and Power, p3.

13 File and Power, p3.

14 Carey, 'Olaudah Equiano'.

15 File and Power, p4.

16 See Carey, 'Ignatius Sancho's Friends and Family', 2002, *Brycchan Carey's Website*, © Brycchan Carey 1999-2004; available at **www.brycchancarey.com/sancho/ friends.htm**

17 File and Power, p4.

18 Carey, 'Sancho's Views on Empire and Slavery', 1999, *Brycchan Carey's Website*, © Brycchan Carey 1999-2004; available at **www.brycchancarey.com/sancho/ letter4.htm**

19 Ottobah Cugoano, 'Narrative of the Enslavement of Ottobah Cugoano, a Native of Africa; Published by Himself, in the Year 1787', *Documenting the American South*, 1999, © University of North Carolina at Chapel Hill; the electronic edition is transcribed from the Appendix to *The Negro's Memorial; or, Abolitionist's Catechism by an Abolitionist*, p120-127, Hatchard and Co. & J and A Arch, 1825; available at **http://docsouth.unc.edu/neh/cugoano/cugoano.html**

20 See Carey, 'Cugoano is Kidnapped and Sold into Slavery', 2003, *Brycchan Carey's Website*, © Brycchan Carey 1999-2004; available at **www.brycchancarey.com/ cugoano/extract1.htm**

21 Vincent Carretta (ed.), *Thoughts and Sentiments on the Evil of Slavery and Other Writings*, Penguin, 1999, p107-108; in Carey, 'Cugoano Calls For a Righteous Empire', 2003, *Brycchan Carey's Website*, © Brycchan Carey 1999-2004; available at **www.brycchancarey.com/cugoano/extract2.htm**

22 See School of Oriental and African Studies, 'Freeman, Thomas Birch', *Mundus: Gateway to Missionary Collections in the United Kingdom*, online library catalogue; available at **www.mundus.ac.uk/cats/4/991.htm**

23 Jeffrey Green, see above (note 3).

24 Jeffrey Green, see above (note 3).

25 Jeffrey Green, see above. See also School of Oriental and African Studies, 'Jamaican and Cameroon Missionary Papers', *Mundus: Gateway to Missionary Collections in the United Kingdom*, online library catalogue; available at **www.mundus.ac.uk/cats/ 10/1096.htm**

26 Spartacus Educational, 'Francis Barber', *Black People in Britain*, 2004; available at **www.spartacus.schoolnet.co.uk/SLAbarber.htm**

27 Birmingham City Council, 'The Reverend Peter Stanford - Birmingham's First Black Minister', *Black History*, 2004; available at **www.birmingham.gov.uk/peter-stanford.bcc**

28 Birmingham City Council, see above.

29 Birmingham City Council, see above.

30 Spartacus Educational, 'Celestine Edwards', *Black People in Britain*, 2004; available at **www.spartacus.schoolnet.co.uk/SLAedwardsC.htm**

31 Brickfields Project, 'Celestine Edwards, 1858-1894, Victoria Park', *People*, The Building Exploratory, 2004; available at **http://brickfields.org.uk/index.php/people**

32 Every Generation, 'Celestine Edwards c. 1858-1894', *Blue Plaque Scheme Nominations*, 2003; available at **www.everygeneration.co.uk/blueplaques/nomination2.htm**

33 Spartacus, 'Celestine Edwards'.

34 File and Power, p75.

35 Harold Moody in 'Black British Citizens', *The Black Presence in Britain*, 2003; available at **www.blackpresence.co.uk/pages/citizens/moody.htm**

36 Moody, see above.

37 File and Power, p75.

38 Moody, see above.

39 Marika Sherwood, *Pastor Daniel Ekarte and the African Churches Mission*, Savannah Press, 1994, p23.

40 Sherwood argues that Pastor Daniel may have given his birth date as the date he first joined the Free Church mission in Itu, which was run by Mary Slessor. See Sherwood, p24.

41 Sherwood, p24.

42 Sherwood, p25.

43 *Liverpool Daily Post*, 8 July 1931; in Sherwood, p 28-31.

44 Sherwood, p34.

45 Sherwood, p.40.

46 Spartacus Educational, 'Arthur Wharton', *Black People in Britain*, 2004; available at **www.spartacus.schoolnet.co.uk/SLAwhartonA.htm** See also FURD, 'Arthur Wharton – The First Black Footballer', *Football Unites, Racism Divides*, 2001; available at **www.furd.org/arthurwharton.asp**; and Arthur Wharton 'Black British Footballers', *The Black Presence in Britain*, 2003; available at **www.blackpresence.co.uk/pages/sport/wharton.htm**

47 100 Great Black Britons, 'Robert Wedderburn', © Every Generation, 2004; available at **www.100greatblackbritons.com/bios/robert_wedderman.html**

48 Spartacus Educational, 'Robert Wedderburn', *Black People in Britain*, 2004; available at **www.spartacus.schoolnet.co.uk/SLAwedderburn.htm**

Chapter 7

The development, role and contribution of the Black Majority Churches

In the previous chapter we saw that Black Christian faith has been thriving in Britain for over six centuries. We now turn our attention to the BMCs' development and contributions since 1948. When reflecting on this chapter, I found myself facing many challenges, the chief being what to include and what to exclude. Of course I wanted to go into greater detail about the great achievements of churches like the Kingsway International Christian Centre; and I wanted to explore more fully aspects of Black Majority Denominations, for example, the Redeemed Christian Church of God (RCCG), one of the fastest growing BMDs, with over 141 churches and 18,000 members in the UK since its inception in 1989.[1] Moreover, it would have been valuable to explore the history of the BMCs in greater detail, and to examine the issues around why some churches are thriving while others stagnate or are decreasing.

Looking through the pages of the *Black Majority Churches UK Directory*,[2] the task of deciding which churches to explore was certainly difficult! Another big challenge was how to give fair coverage to all the five segments of BMCs. I have therefore taken a pragmatic (even cowardly) approach and will explore the BMCs from the African and Caribbean diaspora in a general rather than specific way. Throughout the chapter I will be referring, where relevant and for statistical analysis, to the Churches' Profile Survey, which I constructed and to which churches have generously contributed for this book.[3] I had hoped to benefit from the published historical works of the COGIC, NTCOG, and COGOP, who all celebrated their jubilee anniversaries in 2003; but these have not yet been published. Otherwise, the history of many other churches and denominations is still oral, while some are very suspicious of researchers and make being secretive a virtue. It would be a mammoth task to reconcile the details in an analytical way. Nonetheless, I am sure that the journey chartered below will add to the reader's growing understanding of the BMCs.

The birth of a modern church movement

There is no doubt that the new wave of BMCs emerged soon after the mass migration of Caribbean people to the UK at the end of the Second World War. A pivotal landmark often used as a reference point was the arrival of some immigrants on board the *Empire Windrush* in 1948. While the majority of these were from Jamaica, they were drawn from several Caribbean countries including Trinidad, British Guiana (now Guyana) and Bermuda.[4] While some of the press campaigned for them to be turned back, it seems that the British government did indeed welcome them. The potential tensions and difficulties associated with the migrants' arrival were fully debated in Parliament and, despite the racial and cultural challenges they presented, the economic priorities of the government prevailed.[5] Others newspapers, like the *South London Press* on 25 June, reported that the Mayor of Lambeth and local Members of Parliament were on hand to welcome the immigrants who settled in Brixton. Among the arrivals were 'law students, dockers, potential chemists and scientists';[6] there were also ex-servicemen, police instructors, hairdressers, plumbers, electricians, typists, carpenters, musicians, artists and even a Guyanese judge.[7] Twenty-two per cent were white-collar workers.[8] Intriguingly, the average age of those arriving was 27.4 years, with the eldest being 63-year-old Margaret Campbell and the youngest 13-year-old Vincent Reid.[9]

From the names appearing on the ship's manifest, almost none are recognisable as playing a significant role in pioneering or taking on a major leadership role in the church. A notable exception is Samuel (Sam) King, who though not an ordained minister, was an active member of the Church of the First Born, a Pentecostal church in south London. He later went on to study part-time at Goldsmith College of Theology; then, as a member of the International Ministerial Council of Great Britain,[10] he was the Borough Dean in Southwark from 1984 to 1988. However, this is not to say that the immigrants on Windrush did not play a part in establishing churches or becoming active members in the historic denominations. On 8 September 1958, the *Daily Mirror* in a valiant attempt to overcome racial prejudice, ran an article entitled 'Introducing to you . . . The Boys From Jamaica'. The article answered the question, 'Are they heathens?' by saying, 'Three out of every five [i.e. 60 per cent of] Jamaicans are members of a Christian church or group. In Britain the churches they attend are packed.'[11] What is not clear is what percentage of *those in Britain* were Christians. It must have been somewhat alarming when only five years later, in 1963, Reverend Clifford Hill discovered that despite 69 per cent of the population in the Caribbean attending church, in London only 4 per cent were churchgoers.[12] In a conversation I had with Sam King, he explained that while 75 per cent of the new arrivals were Christians, the environment into which they had come was not a Christian but an imperialist one. The migrants' priority was survival – first find a home; then get your documentation; obtaining work was next, and church was fitted in at weekends. King also noted that, while many people did not attend church, they did not generally lose their faith.[13]

Migration continued unabated until 1962, when restrictions were imposed by the British government with the passing of the Commonwealth Immigrants Act. This Act brought about a complete reversal of the British Nationality Act of 1948 which had confirmed the rights of Commonwealth citizens, the colonies and the Republic of Ireland, to live unrestricted in Britain. The Commonwealth Immigrants Act was a racially motivated piece of legislation enacted to stave off criticism from White people that Black people were stealing their jobs, homes and social security, committing crime, even stealing their women, and, furthermore, they were heathens. It was a response no different from that of Queen Elizabeth I in 1598. The Act restricted the automatic right to enter, live and work in Britain only to those who had vouchers (like a visa), and stipulated that anyone acquiring a criminal conviction within five years of arriving in Britain would be deported. By 1965, the revised Act limited the number of vouchers to 8,500, most of which were to be offered to skilled professionals; of these, 1,000 were designated to immigrants from Malta.

People's reasons for choosing to come to Britain were varied. It must be remembered that although Britain was regarded as the 'Mother Country', travel to the USA was much easier and closer to the Caribbean, and there were established labour links between the USA and the Caribbean islands. There was seasonal agricultural work (pickers) and the building of the Panama Canal, to name a few. The primary 'push' factor, however, that brought Caribbean immigrants to England was economic hardship. Jamaica, for example, was still suffering from the effects of one of 'the worst hurricanes to have come out of heaven in 1944'; then the banana crops that had not recovered from hurricane damage were hit by 'Panama disease', and the coconut industry was ravaged by 'lethal yellowing disease'. The resulting economic hardship led to strikes and riots.[14] The ongoing poverty, 'un- and under-employment', 'the declining estates of Britain's sugar colonies' and the fact that there were no opportunities for young people and their children all contributed to the exodus to Britain.[15] Many soldiers who were demobbed after the war also wanted to return because, having travelled widely, seen the world through different lenses and acquired new skills, they were unwilling to settle for a life of impoverishment back home.

There were, however, also 'pull' factors. Initially, legislation like the British Nationality Act actively encouraged people in the colonies to come to Britain. The invitation to rebuild post-war Britain is legendary, with the slogan 'Your Mother Country Needs You!' Coupled with this was a change in American immigration law in the form of the McCarran–Walter Act, passed by the US congress in 1952, which 'restricted the number of British West Indians who could enter the USA from 65,000 to 800 per year'. Then there was the prospect of making a better life in Britain, with higher wages, better job prospects and wider educational prospects.[16] Later, it was missionary zeal and pastoral concern that brought many of the founders of BMCs.

In the case of the African diaspora, it was missionary zeal and prospects of a good education which started the influx of churches and leaders from Africa from the 1970s onwards. Then came growing economic migration, and the political fallout from the newly independent African nations that did not deliver the economic promise or benefits of self-rule. *Coups d'état* and political persecution brought leaders like Sam Larbie from Ghana; Larbie currently pastors the Camberwell Elim Pentecostal Church in south London, and provides apostolic oversight to the many satellite churches he has planted. Civil wars, like those in Eritrea, Ethiopia and Somalia also resulted in new forms of BMC.

Whatever their background, African or Caribbean, the majority of immigrants settled in Britain in the major industrial cities – London, Birmingham, Manchester and Bristol – where jobs were available or where they could be near family or friends.

Phases of development

The phases of development of BMCs in the UK have been described elsewhere by Joel Edwards, Roswith Gerloff and Bishop Joe Aldred. I have chosen here simply to outline, in Table 2 below, their individual perspectives on these phases as well as my own. You will notice that in my list there is some overlap between different phases and some even operate concurrently. Granted that there are overlaps, it is important that these phases are continually revised in order to update the historical records.

Table 2 Four perspectives on the periods of development in the Black Majority Churches

Stages	Roswith Gerloff[7]	Joel Edwards[18]	Joe Aldred[19]	Mark Sturge
1	The early mission	The inception of the Afro-Caribbean church (1950–1975)	Initiation	The scattered church (1948–1955)
2	Denominationalisation	The period of consolidation (1960–1975)	Rapid growth	The community church (1952–1960)
3	Proliferation	The period of initiation (1975–1985/8)	Consolidation	The denominational church (1955–1966)
4	Stabilisation	Period of dynamic transition (after 1988)	Fragmentation	The consolidating church (1965–1975
5	Interdenominational and intercultural partnership		Para-church organisation	The restless church (1975–1985)
6	Time to speak		Stagnation of old	The integrated church (1980–1985)
7			Emergence of new	The diverse church (1980–1993)
8				The revitalised apostolic church (1990–1996)
9				The recognised church (1997–2003)
10				The maturing church (2004 onwards)

The scattered church (1948–1955)

The immigrants brought with them their faith traditions – Anglican, Catholic, Baptist, Methodist, Presbyterian and United Reform Church. From the mid nineteenth century, 31 per cent of churchgoers in the Caribbean were Church of England, 29 per cent were Wesleyan Methodist, and 20 per cent were Baptist.[20] While many remained loyal to their church traditions, others concluded that it was not for them, as Sybil Phoenix explains:[21]

> To overcome I decided to be part of white society, the white church. I was not prepared to leave it. I've had squabbles with bishops, dug my heels in and said, 'You are going to recognise me, because I'm not going anywhere!' As I often say, 'It was the devil that kept me in the Methodist Church.' I was determined that they had no more right to be in it than me. Well, wasn't that the devil that made me so awful? . . . In those days I used to say I am only black on the outside and white on the inside. I know what I would say now, but that is what I once said. I was white, all my training was white; brainwashing does operate.

Not everyone was so resolute or so candid about their experiences. Many were not prepared to let the 'devil' have any persuasive influence on their lives, or to worship in a context that was no different to the hostile, prejudiced and disrespectful environments they experienced in their world of housing, on the streets or at work. Granted that there were churches who could be commended for their generosity and support for the migrants, it seems that their efforts were overshadowed by the prevailing culture and the actions of the majority.

We have already spoken in some detail about the reasons for the existence of this 'scattered church' among the immigrants; we get a sense of the upheavals faced by a community of vulnerable people who still found strength and new ways to worship God. A major characteristic of this phase is that the churches were without seasoned leaders. Nevertheless, they were determined not to 'defile [themselves] with the portion of the king's delicacies' (or, as this is the British context, the Queen's!) (Daniel 1:8). For many, estrangement from the church, home or even Christ was not a permanent condition. After all, they were only going to be in England for a very short time, five years at most; then they would return to their homeland, economically and educationally secure and ready to continue their faith walk.

The community church (1952–1960)

Racism and prejudice were not the only reasons for the emergence of the BMCs. Joel Edwards has argued that it would be disingenuous or even be doing these churches a disservice if they are presented as existing purely because of the shortcomings of White Christians, rejection and racism:[22]

> Black Churches were not brought into being solely as a result of racism. This would make them entirely a community by default. Whilst God is able to produce good fruits from our bad seeds this is not the whole story! Black Churches came into being to fulfil spiritual, social and cultural needs which would otherwise have gone unmet – and the African and Caribbean Church in the UK is an indication of God's ability to meet a people's need through their own ministry to themselves.

Even so, the tension between the demands for a culturally appropriate worshipping community and the rejection suffered by the migrants is very strong. If anything I believe they fed each other, as Oliver Lyseight, a founder member of the NTCOG and the denomination's first National Overseer, explains:[23]

> We ministered to thousands of people. However, with all the successes we were having, we still were not satisfied to be ministering only to the native population, while our own people were drifting away and backsliding as they poured into the country as strangers, unaccustomed to the ways of Britain. Some of them were despised and were made to feel unwelcome by some of the main-line churches. We saw their plight, and then decided to try and put the situation right. When we tried to start up the work – just to have fellow-ship and somewhere to worship – where our people from the Caribbean could attend freely and feel welcome, we suffered many adversities.

This interpersonal ministry often started as a prayer meeting in a bedsit or front room. Often referred to as 'the bedsitter church', their frequency, popularity and amplified intercessions often drew the attention and consternation of their neighbours and, consequently, the latter or the police would often interrupt. It became obvious that if the meetings were to continue to fulfil the needs of those attending, they would have to find alternative ways of congregating. The other motivation to move was the sheer success of these meetings: logistically, it was just not possible to continue unless other, larger premises were secured. The search was on to find suitable halls and churches where the brethren or 'saints' could gather. But there were very few social spaces where migrants could congregate, outside the dance halls. Few institutions or structures catered for their needs. The desire to establish a place for the Sabbath – for emotional, spiritual, psychological and cultural respite, as well as a place to call home – became a powerful driving force. Ironically, the historic churches assisted in this development by either providing spaces for worship or alerting Black visitors to their services to the fact that 'one of their churches was down the road'.

The migrants were also responding to a desperate need to rescue those who had either abandoned their faith or were no longer making it a priority in their lives or an essential part of their character. This sense of mission and rescue became a hallmark for the BMCs as they welcomed those still on their pilgrimage to the 'Promised Land'. It meant that when new friends, families or 'countrymen and country-women' arrived in Britain, there would be someone and somewhere to greet them – a church, actively functioning as a welcoming centre, sharing information and offering support, where the weak and discouraged could be strengthened by the testimonies of the victorious and 'the overcomers'. A people with a space to worship God in their own style, in their own time, without an identity crisis, provided the essential ingredients for the fledgling 'community church'. Driven by pastoral opportunities, the BMCs were energised by the missionary zeal of their members, who were eager to let others know that here was an alternative worshipping community.

The denominational church (1955–1966)

The community church could by no means be described as encompassing a single period or phase. In the initial stages, the driving force was the need to congregate for worship, fellowship, support and prayer, and cultural, theological and ecclesiastical differences took a back seat. The person able to provide the best exhortations, and thereby offer the best encouragement to lift the people's spirits, often took the lead. But there was another dynamic interaction taking place, as Joel Edwards explains:[24]

> Body ministry was lived out rather than verbalised. The priesthood of all
> believers was expressed rather than thought through. In this community,

the testimony of the illiterate man could be as liberating as the sermon from the preacher.

And, I might add, the 'special' song or solo did indeed set their spirits free.

Inevitably, it was not long before the sociology of groups kicked in. What started as a community of African Caribbeans soon became communities of various Caribbean islands; then came denominational tribes, and these were soon followed by theological tribes. The introduction of seasoned leaders who had been pastors of churches in their home countries brought added value in the form of pastoral care and organisation of structures, but may have had the undesired effect of exacerbating theological and denominational divisions. The motivation of the early pastors may have been simply to continue as seamless a Christian existence or experience as possible. From all accounts, both COGIC and NTCOG, the first two post-Windrush BMDs, joined their international denominations at the behest of those who felt they would be better supported if they did so; it may also have been regarded as an economically prudent move. But, if this was the case, it was surely a misplaced expectation. What they actually received was instant recognition and an identity within a wider and global body, but this did little to enhance their standing in the UK.

Beyond that, there was the leveraging effect of establishing churches which until now had very little or no roots in the UK. Numerical growth and the plethora of emerging churches provided much encouragement, leading to the conclusion that God was moving by his Spirit and doing a new thing. This effect was by no means accidental. As Overseer Lyseight recalls:[25]

> Most of us were very young and we launched out with fervour. We went about the work wholeheartedly, sacrificially and consecratedly. It was not easy, but we trusted the Lord and His presence was always with us.

The churches gained confidence as well an anthem: 'who knows whether you have come to the kingdom for such a time as this?' (Esther 4:14). This move of God continued to stimulate the BMCs growth and development as they evolved from pioneering into established churches. In just over a decade (by 1966) almost all, or at least the first wave, of the denominations from the African Caribbean diaspora were established. Quite probably, geography played a greater part in the diversity than any other factor: so, while CCOGIC led the way in London, NTCOG took root in Wolverhampton, Birmingham and the West Midlands. There is also general consensus that despite the varying nature of the denominations, their leadership initially worked well together to build the fledgling churches. It was only when fragmentation occurred within the churches themselves that those relationships became divisive.

In Table 3 below I have provided a chronological breakdown of some of the BMDs. This has been a challenging exercise. Often these churches had been in existence long before they were registered with any official body such as the Charity Commission. It was also difficult to determine at what point a church becomes a denomination – I have opted for the date of their first public meeting. I have resisted the temptation of letting them define themselves, because some churches consisting of single congregation consider themselves to be a denomination. I have also taken the view that using a minimum number of congregations as a parameter would not be appropriate either, since once thriving denominations have now diminished in membership and congregations. Equally, many churches with several branches do not consider themselves to be denominations. I have therefore created a table of the denominations as I understand them. Any exclusion is due to lack of available information rather than authorial oversight!

The consolidating church (1965–1975)

It is evident from Table 3 that each denomination approached these phases of development at different intervals. Conceivably, in the process of rapid growth they faced many new challenges. Dreams of returning home after five years of hard work and dedication had now all but evaporated. Young single people became grown men and women with families of their own. People were investing in houses as their need to make better domestic provision for their families grew urgent. They were also becoming better at dealing with British institutions. Improving relationships with their bank managers and lawyers affected how they went about purchasing church buildings, and helped to transform informal alliances or groups into institutions that could do business with the financial institutions and finally gain credibility from their parent organisation. As Overseer Lyseight comments:[26]

> We had no financial status in the early days and the Mother Church in the
> USA – although we asked for financial assistance – did not catch the vision,

Table 3   An outline of the denominational profiles of BMCs in the UK

Name	Start date	No. of churches to date	No. of members to date	Church background	International Headquarters
Pre-Windrush former White Majority Denominations					
Seventh-day Baptist Church	1650	2	50	Baptist	*None*
Seventh-day Adventist Church	1878	250	21,864	Adventist	Seventh-day Adventist, USA
Post-Windrush					
Calvary Church of God in Christ	1948	23	2,750	Pentecostal	Church of God in Christ International, USA, 1957 (date of affiliation)
Church of God of Prophesy	1953	86	6,000	Pentecostal	Church of God of Prophesy, USA
New Testament Church of God	1953	110	11,000	Pentecostal	Church of God, USA
Bethel United Church of Jesus Christ (Apostolic); formerly First United Church of Jesus Christ Apostolic	1955	42	6,000	Oneness Pentecostal	Rehoboth Church of God in Christ from 1957–1965; then First United Church of Jesus Christ Apostolic until 1993
United Pentecostal Church of God	1956	3	800	Pentecostal	*None*
Community Church of God	1957	4	350	Evangelical	Church of God, Anderson, Indiana, USA

Table 3 continued

Name	Start date	No. of churches to date	No. of members to date	Church background	International Headquarters
Bible Way Church of the Lord Jesus Christ Worldwide, UK	1958	27	2,000	Oneness Pentecostal	*None*
Church of the First Born	1958	3	150	Pentecostal	Church of the First Born, Kingston, Jamaica
Church of God Worldwide Missions	1959	9	1,200	Pentecostal	*None*
Miracle Church of God in Christ	1960	3	375	Pentecostal	None
Wesleyan Holiness Church	1960	15	400	Methodist	Wesleyan Holiness, USA; formerly part of Pilgrim Holiness Church
Assembly of the First Born	1961	18	650	Pentecostal	*None*
Church of God (Seventh Day)	1961	17	600	Adventist	Church of God (Seventh Day), USA
New Testament Assembly	1961	14	1,500	Pentecostal	*None*
Church of God World Fellowship	1961	7	1,200	Pentecostal	*None*
United Pentecostal Church	1963	42	2,450	Oneness Pentecostal	*None*
Shiloh Pentecostal Fellowship of Great Britain	1965	8	1,000	Pentecostal	*None*

Church	Year	No.	Size	Type	Headquarters
African Methodist Episcopal Church	1966	2	150	Methodist	USA Episcopal District 17
African Methodist Episcopal Zion Church	1970	13	600	Pentecostal	African Methodist Episcopal Zion Church, USA
Christ Apostolic Church Mount Bethel	1974	4	1,000	Pentecostal	Christ Apostolic Church Mount Bethel, Lagos, Nigeria
Church of Jesus Christ Apostolic	1975	8	500	Oneness Pentecostal	Church of Jesus Christ Apostolic Inc., USA
Christ Apostolic Church of Great Britain	1976	45	4,000	Pentecostal	Christ Apostolic Church, Ibadan, Nigeria
Deeper Christian Life Ministry	1985	18	1,800	Pentecostal	Deeper Christian Life, Nigeria
New Covenant Church	1986	18	1,500	Pentecostal	*None*
New Life Assembly	1987	5	800	Pentecostal	*None*
Redeemed Christian Church Of God	1989	141	18,000	Pentecostal	Redeemed Christian Church of God, Nigeria
Universal Church of the Kingdom of God	1995	20	4,500	Pentecostal	Universal Church of the Kingdom of God, Brazil

Note: It should be borne in mind that the size of membership of a church is not necessarily an accurate reflection of a denomination's true number of adherents.

so we missed out on many fine opportunities to expand the work. It was not until in 1959, when we formed the 'Revolving Fund' – that is where we had one Central Treasury – that we were able to make a start, if somewhat shaky at first. We were also able to prove to our bankers – Barclays – that we were trustworthy. It was some time in the 70s that we finally managed to command some grants and loans from the General Church in the USA to buy church properties.

With NTCOG members' salaries often a meagre £5 per week, it was no mean feat for the denomination to have purchased 35 buildings by 1978.[27]

By far the greatest challenge facing the BMCs was the new generation of young people who needed nurturing. This was indeed 'a clash of worlds'. Some children, those who were joining their parents after a period of separation while waiting to be brought over from the home country, often found the transition to British culture rather difficult. Racism in schools probably had a more devastating effect on families than it had in the wider society or in employment situations. It created what is often called 'an angry generation'. Children who until now had been normal were now deemed to have 'special educational needs' or be 'educationally subnormal', and were placed in schools with White children with various forms of disabilities. The demands of earning a living, supporting a family and keeping a roof over one's head, coupled with the need to serve God, did not always seem compatible with family life. Some of these children became angry with the church because they felt it was not only ignoring their plight but also blinding their parents from seeing their situation, believing what they were telling them, and taking appropriate action. They felt that their parents were giving 'their all' to church and very little to them. Those young people who did manage to adjust to the British environment were either very compliant or had strong support structures.

One way in which young people reacted against church was by 'voting with their feet' as soon as they were able. Some sought to balance their spirituality with justice as a mark of integrity; others turned to Rastafarianism as offering the most ideologically coherent option; and yet others sought to remove the shackles of church or the Caribbean (or predominantly Jamaican) worldview, and to create a more relevant Black British culture that formed an intersection between the British and Caribbean cultures. But, while some young people settled for straddling the two cultures, it was those who fought to make room at this intersection for permanent and fierce debate on the issues of racism, educational equality, and a more proactive and relevant church, who became the BMCs' Achilles heel. They insisted on their right to be treated equally, and for their culture to be valued, affirmed and respected. They saw participation in society as essential, but with mutual respect and on equal terms. They condemned the notion of some churches that 'education is not going to take you to heaven', and advocated that heaven needed to begin right here, right now. They refused to accept that they belonged anywhere else other than in Britain. Even if their parents were thinking of returning home one day, maybe in retirement, they would have to do so without them. Out of the fragmentation over policies, personalities, probity and the nature of the Black presence in Britain grew an urgent need for consolidation. The issues raised by the second generation brought about a greater sense of the need for permanence and the realisation that the BMCs were here to stay.

The restless church (1975–1985)

The hoped-for natural and organic growth that was to come out of the second and third generations of Caribbean young people in Britain did not materialise. Granted that significant numbers of young people still went to church, this in fact may have only represented one-third of those who might have been expected to attend. Additionally, the pioneers were running out of steam or, at least, felt they had achieved all they had wanted to. Evangelists were now 'pastors' – often a sign that they were no longer willing to take on the challenges of the road or cope with the uncertainty of ad hoc financial support which is part of itinerant ministry, or that they were becoming less effective in winning souls for Christ. Up till now, it had been the historic denominations – backslidden Britain – that they had presumed needed reviving; all that the BMCs needed was a 'fresh touch from the Lord' as part of their sanctification, submission and yielding to God's will. But now, for the first time, the need for a revival among the migrant church became a critical reality. With this admission of the need for revival came the recognition that merely 'fanning the flames' would not generate the size of fire needed to burn in the hearts of a new generation.

Nonetheless, these years of restlessness were proving some of the most fruitful in other ways. The BMCs were beginning to stand out as the hub of their communities. Some were even beginning to respond to the social needs of their community. They entered alliances with local authorities, joining committees or offering educational and work-related training under the Manpower training schemes in a bid to tackle the massive unemployment in the Black community. They began receiving Section 11 Funding, the forerunner to the Single Regeneration Budget. They ran youth clubs and sought to provide activities that they hoped would keep young people, especially boys, off the streets and out of trouble. It was a reversal of roles, with the community now coming to the church.

Yet there was a far deeper reason for restlessness. Despite their social involvement with their community, the BMCs themselves had begun to put up their own barriers of resistance. They were concerned to keep out 'the world's ways of doing things'. They saw their young people, many of whom were by this time graduating from further education institutions, as a threat or a plague that needed to be controlled. Insecurity in leadership was rife. The need for a new hermeneutic was growing ever more apparent. The preacher now had to reach his audience intellectually in order to get to their spirits – the younger generation were more intellectually able, and had greater ambitions and aspirations, than had their predecessors. Coherence in presentation and delivery became more important (not that this had been unimportant before). But, rather than celebrate and embrace this phase of development, many from the older generation made their young people feel marginalised, resulting in the withdrawal of their commitment and support, and robbing them of the inspiration they might have gained from older mentors and role models. More devastating was the effect that the vocation to ministry became less attractive.

During this restless church phase, the BMCs had to recognise they were not going to be the only ones to transform the world. They had to revise the notion that people would automatically become depraved and unsuccessful if they did not stay within their 'ark'. The restless church was becoming a declining church.

The integrated church (1980–1985)

There was an acceptance among the BMCs that they needed to form alliances in order to gain recognition and play out their role as equal partners in impacting both church and society. The integrated church phase was one that saw the establishing of several 'umbrella' and representative bodies. As early as 1968, the International Ministerial Council of Great Britain (IMCGB) was established by Archbishop David Douglas and Archbishop Malachi Ramsay, among others, to provide ministerial recognition and ordination for leaders, and representation of the BMCs. Yet, at the Council's inception and throughout its early years, there were many controversies or misunderstandings. Some leaders, especially those from the more established BMDs, were unsure of its motives. They felt that there was no need for BMCs to mimic the ecclesiastical hierarchy of archbishops and bishops within the Church of England. In their view, the IMCGB's founders were setting themselves up as the primates and representatives of the BMCs. Consequently, while the IMCGB worked successfully on behalf of the BMCs within the sphere of government and the ecumenical instruments like the British Council of Churches (later CTBI and CTE), it did not have the support of the wider leadership in the Black church community. Nonetheless, it was during this integrated phase of the churches' development that the IMCGB played a major role in supporting the African and independent churches that were being established in the UK.

The Afro West Indian United Council of Churches (AWUCOC) was established in 1977, with the aim of uniting the churches around faith, social, and political issues, and of making representations on their behalf. From its inception, the AWUCOC enjoyed widespread support among the BMCs' leadership and could be identified as the most authentic Black Christian voice in the UK. Overseer Lyseight (from NTCOG), the late Reverend Desmond Pemberton (from the Wesleyan Holiness Church), Bishop Malachi Ramsay, Reverend Dr Io Smith, Bishop Bernard and Bishop Powell (the latter three from the New Testament Assembly) and the late Dr Aston Gibson all played key roles in AWUCOC's development. The AWUCOC made a significant impact, working with the Department of Education on the issue of Black pupils' underachievement, and with the Departments of Health and Social Security on issues of children in the foster and care system, unemployment and mental health; they also worked with the Home Office, and represented the BMCs on CTBI among others. However, AWUCOC did face challenges. Bishop Eric Brown, National Overseer of the NTCOG, who served as its General Secretary, commented: 'Where AWUCOC failed was in its dependence on the heads of the church to push its agenda. So, when the time came to choose priorities they always choose their own organisations.'[28] This led to an inconsistency in delivery and meant that much of AWUCOC's potential was not realised. Despite several valiant attempts to breathe new life into the organisation, it has not actually been in operation for over a decade.

Also developing was the Council of African and Afro Caribbean Churches (CAACC), which was established by the Most Reverend Father Olu Abiola in 1979. The CAACC's main aim was to gain recognition and credibility from the historic churches, in particular the British Council of Churches (now CTBI), for the African and Caribbean Spiritual Churches (ACSCs). However, this integration had its limitations. According to Father Abiola, 'The African Independent Churches are shy and afraid to join the international bodies. They fear others might want to influence and change their beliefs and practices.'[29]

The African and Caribbean Evangelical Alliance (ACEA) emerged on 14 April 1984, to accelerate the reconciliation between Black and White Christians and to support the development of BMCs. ACEA's success has been largely due to its partnership with, and the support it has received from, the Evangelical Alliance. ACEA has developed, despite its many challenges, to become a respected national body representing over 1,300 churches and organisations in the UK. It has been a strong representative voice in the media, and has provided excellent support and resourcing of its members in the BMC community. ACEA has taken the lead in raising the profile of the need for provision in children's work and youthwork, and of Black children's underachievement in the educational system. It has also gained national recognition for its role in championing the hopes, values and aspirations of the BMCs. ACEA's inclusive agenda celebrates the participation of both African and Caribbean churches and organisations. More recently, there has been increased interest and participation from White Majority organisations in many of its activities.

Philip Mohabir, an ACEA pioneer, established Connections in 1988. Working with over forty churches, Connections sought to bridge the gap between the charismatic and Pentecostal movements, and to provide training, support and mentoring for leaders and small churches with the aim of developing their vision. There was also the creation of the Transatlantic and Pacific Alliance of Churches, led by Bishop Paul Hackman, and the establishing of regional bodies such as the West Yorkshire Council for Afro Caribbean Churches in Leeds, and the Council for Black-led churches in Birmingham.

The diverse church (1980–1993)

In the wider context of the BMCs' development, it may not actually be true to speak of this phase as that of a 'declining church' – for two reasons. First, numerical growth is only one indicator of the lifecycle of development; I suppose it is as wrong to say that someone stops growing when they have reached their natural height. However, leaving the philosophical argument behind, the second reason for not describing this phase of BMC development as declining is that a wave of new Christians was arriving in Britain from the African continent, predominantly from Nigeria and Ghana. For these two reasons, I have opted to view this phase as that of *the diverse church*. For the first time, a distinctive culture, spirituality and missionary zeal had arrived in Britain to rival that of the African Caribbean churches over the previous three decades.

During this era there was an explosion of gospel music, which began when The Heavenly Hopes group, led by Joseph Pitt, appeared on television on Hughie Green's *Opportunity Knocks*. Then came Kainos who, for two years, were seen as the radical group in the Black gospel music scene; this group also appeared on *Opportunity Knocks*. Kainos comprised Bazil Meade, Joel Edwards and Joseph Pitt who, between 1978 and 1980, crossed over into the White Christian festivals such as Greenbelt, with their fusion of jazz, soul, gospel and funk. Their album 'Changing' was recorded at ICC Studios in 1978. Following in Kainos's footsteps was a group from CCOGIC, The Harmoniser, which included Lavine Hudson. Hot on their heals came Paradise, consisting of the Edwards brothers – Junior, Philip and Kirk – from the United Pentecostal Church. There was also Bobby Clarke, Paul Johnson (from the Seventh-day Adventist Church), Dave Ayieola (Assemblies of God) and Devon Burke (the New Testament Assembly). In around 1982–1983, Paradise reached the top forty with a record called 'One Mind, Two Hearts'. This breakthrough encouraged groups such as Clarity, Innovation, Images, Trumpet of Zion, and The Latter Rain Outpouring Revival Choir (under the leadership of Bazil Meade). In 1982, the London Community Gospel Choir was launched, bridging the gap between secular music and the wider church; it was the first choir to be created solely for the purpose of being a concert choir.

The Inspirational Choir, led by John Francis, captured the nation's imagination by providing the backing track for the pop group *Madness*, and their record 'Wings of a Dove' made the top five in the record chart. The choir went on to clinch a record deal with Stiff Records and later Sony Records. They had top 30 hits with 'One Love' and 'Abide With Me'. By 1988 the Inspirational Choir had their own television show, *People Get Ready*. There was also the BBC1 weekly radio show, *Soul Train*, produced by Juliet Fletcher, which broadcast British and American artists live. Lavine Hudson was snapped up by a major record label in the best deal ever achieved by a Black female artist. In 1994, the London Adventist Chorale won 'Choir of the Year' award.

The presence of gospel music signalled to the British public that there were churches in their neighbourhood which sang and worshipped in a way unlike any they had encountered before. It generated a vibrant concert scene nationwide, and set the momentum for a generation of Black Christian musicians, groups and artists – like Noel Robinson, Gifted, Nicky Brown, the Wades, Nu Colours, Dizzy K, Muyiwa Olarewaju, Sinai, and Raymond and Co. – to minister throughout the country and around the world.

In addition, the social, political and economic context was right for the emergence of churches from the African diaspora. Conservative 'Thatcherism' was taking root, and Britain was regaining her pride as one of the leading economic forces in the world. The nation was in buoyant mood. Economic prosperity was accompanied by the rise of individualism and the mantra of 'there's no such thing as society'. There was, instead, the virtue of opportunity for all, privatisation and record low unemployment. This was the era of the yuppies (young urban/upwardly mobile professional and progressive individuals) and buppies (Black urban professional and progressive individuals). Under 25s were taking up serious management positions in society. They were the new entrepreneurs, especially in the explosion of information technology and the emergence of local and wider area networks (LANs and WANs) which preceded the Internet. In institutions like the NHS, the transport industry and the statutory bodies, experience was being shunted aside in favour of academic qualifications, vibrancy and fresh thinking. The 'battle against the unions' was won, and Britain entered into a new phase of progress. However, all these developments had their social consequences. We were introduced to the concept of a 'post-modern' society which both challenged and fragmented the historic institutions and their value systems. Church, marriage, and law and order, political ideologies and the classical arts were interrogated in a way that made it clear they had no right to take up positions of privilege or pre-eminence within society, or to dictate how individuals live their lives.

All this represented a threat to the Caribbean churches and placed a further wedge between the generations. On the other hand, it also brought other communities together, especially those who felt they had little or no place in this so-called 'progressive society'. Minority communities from the Asian continent, who until now had been losing their grip on both their culture and their young people, saw a resurgence in community spirit when it became evident that the majority of working class, poor and minority ethnic communities were being disenfranchised in the midst of the boom. The mentality of 'survival of the fittest', the lack of social cohesion and the level of family breakdown were countercultural to many minority communities; a society that was being socially and economically engineered to enrich the rich and disenfranchise the poor, became the biggest threat to their very existence. And into this fertile context came the churches from the African diaspora, an event that almost went unnoticed in its early stages until these churches exploded onto the scene in the middle of the 1980s.

A distinguishing feature of this influx of African churches is its impact on the entire spectrum of BMCs. Denominations like Christ Apostolic Church, the New Covenant Church and RCCOG came into being, as did vibrant churches such as Kingsway International Christian Centre, led by Pastor Matthew Ashimolowo, and Glory House (initially Green Pastures Ministries) under the leadership of Jonathan Oleyede, Dr Albert Odulele and Vincent Odulele. There was also New Wine Church, under the leadership of Pastor Tayo Adeyemi; Christ Gospel Church, led by Pastor Gabriel Ilori; and Christ Faith Tabernacle led by Apostle Alfred Williams, among others; and a number of congregations blossomed and grew in the Baptist Union, Assemblies of God, the Elim Pentecostal church and the historic churches. The growth of these African churches was rapid. Within the first five years of their existence, they were surpassing many smaller Caribbean denominations. For the first time, we encounter 'church bombing', where a congregation suddenly appears in an area, either on a Sunday or for a short period, and then disappears. This was because of the saturation of existing premises: for the first time buildings were just not suitable for the needs of rapidly growing congregations. A new type of church administration also took hold. Churches were beginning to rent offices in the high street or in office blocks, giving an early signal of their professional intent and desire to be successful along the lines of a corporate organisation. This phase also saw the early stages of establishing of bookshops and Bible colleges whose primary aim was to produce 'senders' (ie evangelists) and to develop much-needed home-grown leaders. While many of these colleges would not have met the criteria of accreditation from British institutions, the churches themselves did not see the need to pursue such accreditation. They wanted to be Spirit-initiated, Spirit-directed, Spirit-sustained and Spirit-commissioned. This is not to say that established institutions did not have the same aspirations; but, in a climate of relative barrenness, the existing provisions and practices were not presenting themselves as something to be desired.

The revitalised apostolic church (1990–1996)

The emergence of the diverse church offered Britain a revitalised apostolic church. At the heart of this phase was the emergence of the independent BMCs. These churches were not just from the African diaspora: integral to this move were congregations like Ruach Inspirational Church of God, Aka Ruach Ministries led by Bishop John Francis, Rhema Ministries led by Pastor Mark Goodridge, Victory Christian Centre (with a chequered history) led by Pastor Douglas Goodman, and Christian Life City led by Bishop Wayne Malcolm. One of the differences between the Caribbean Independent Churches and the African Independent Churches was that the Caribbean churches were led by young men and women who were expected to play key roles in the future development of the Caribbean denominations. In addition, large proportions of their membership were drawn from the already established Caribbean churches. Needless to say, their presence posed a treat to those established denominations while, at the same time, offering a degree of freshness and a place of renewal for young people and those disillusioned by lack of progress and development in their original churches.

It would seem that the revived church developed its apostolic ambitions because the BMCs did not see themselves as playing a significant role in the agenda of institutional or traditional churches; their passion was to win their generation for Christ, just as their parents took on theirs. Meanwhile the development of the churches from the African diaspora mirrored that of the Caribbean churches in their early years. The revived church had its own niche that appealed to an audience beyond regular churchgoers. The churches were committed to meeting people's needs, building their self-esteem and empathising with their trials and tribulations in a more strategic and forceful way. They looked to the USA for their new model of churchmanship, leadership styles and organisational methodologies. The rapid growth and, by all standards, success of these churches led to a plethora of new ones. Observers might have been forgiven for thinking that God was fed up with the denominations and passing the mantle on to the independent churches, calling men and women from a variety of backgrounds to take up the gospel challenge.

This phase also saw the emergence of what were by British standards 'megachurches', with congregations ranging between one thousand and seven thousand members. The issues of churchmanship and leadership faced by Black pastors of these churches were on a scale only dreamed of by their White counterparts. It was not just size that mattered but also the rate of the growth, which seemed to have no end in sight. Painful lessons were learnt; leaders and structures had to be developed rapidly. It soon became evident that this booming revitalised church needed 'leaders of leaders' and 'champions of champions'. Like all previous attempts to do away with obstructive and sluggish bureaucracies, the independent churches needed considerable support and assistance. Leaders who 'stood taller' than their peers and who were deemed to be successful provided help, guidance and mentoring for younger leaders. These mentors went on to become bishops, apostles and prophets according to their gifts and anointing. This pattern continues today and has cemented the solidarity among the churches.

The recognised church (1997–2003)

The year 2000 was a significant signpost for the citizens of the world. We were about to enter a new century and a new Millennium. Never before in our generation had both religious and non-religious people entertained the belief that something apocalyptic was about to happen. This sense was heightened by the uncertainty of what would happen to the various global institutions and infrastructures that undergird daily life. The 'Millennium Bug' was supposed to crash any computer, electronic-controlled device or piece of equipment that was not Y2K compliant. Companies seeking to ensure that this did not happen spent billions of pounds. Around the world people moved out of the major cities. Some hoarded food to last them at least two years: the Japanese and USA governments warned their citizens to stack up at least one week's supply of food and water. Others rented spaces in bunkers and removed all their finances from the banks. This sense of doom was compounded by a season of national disasters, with record loss of life and damage from earthquakes in Turkey, Thailand, USA and Japan, and massive floods in Mexico, Honduras and other Latin American countries. There were the horrors of war and ethnic cleansing in Kosova, and fighting in East Timor. No continent was spared. All this became a field day for end-time preachers, who were boldly stating that the world would end within a decade.

But something else was happening. Very early on Britain signalled its intention to lead the world in celebrating the Millennium and leaving a legacy for the next generation. Meanwhile, at ACEA, I recognised that, if the world was coming to Britain, I did not want them to see Black Christians merely as choirs on other people's stages. I was determined that if the wider church was going to celebrate the 2000th birthday of our Lord Jesus Christ, then the BMCs must play their part. Although I say 'I', there was little doubt in my mind that this was a prompting from the Lord to seize this opportunity to ensure that the BMCs took centre stage in this Millennium year. After all, they were the fast-growing and dynamic churches which people ought to encounter on their way to embracing Christ. So, in November 1997, I invited senior BMC leaders together to cast the vision for Black Christians' contribution to the millennial celebrations. I encouraged them to do things within their local and regional context but, most importantly, urged that we should not miss the opportunity to do something *together* to celebrate our unity and to validate our experience, faith and contribution to society and the wider church. Although many leaders had not yet thought through what their contribution might be, there was an overwhelming consensus that we should go for it.

Everyone went away and began to dream. I went away and began the task of canvassing the support of other key leaders. To help in this endeavour, I attempted to paint a picture of who the BMCs were as a body and to challenge leaders that, if we did not celebrate, who was going to recognise our contributions, achievements and value? A year later we came together again. I put before the gathering my ideas for a national convention that would be a unique event, one that would bring out the best of the BMCs in every area of our spiritual, social and economic experience. We were used to the idea of conventions, but this one would be different – this time we were going to show ourselves to the nation and to the world. I also said that I would not even begin the task of planning unless they pledged at least £25,000 to start up funds. A bishop took the lead by pledging £5,000, which did put some welcome pressure on the others. Some asked for additional time to consult with their Boards. However, one thing was certain: the churches had given their support for the event and, for the first time, they had decided to put their money where their mouth was. We were in this together.

We called our 'big celebration' *Faith in the Future*. By November 1999 we were ready to go public. We launched the event at St Mark's church hall in Kennington, south London, using the theme of 'The Black church must have their own schools' as a way to capture headlines and the public imagination. As we unveiled the logo and backdrop for the event in the presence of the gathered press, we conveyed a simple but powerful message: Black pupils continue to fail in the education system, with over 75 per cent achieving less than five grades A to C in their GCSEs. We argued that it would be a dereliction of duty on the churches' part if we did not seek for ways to address this problem; after all, every other faith community looked after the education of their children except the BMCs. We announced that, in April 2000, ACEA would be inviting Black educators and parents to a conference called *Making the Grade*. The aim was to garner their perspectives on the issues and to present them at the *Faith in the Future* Conference scheduled for July of that year.

This theme touched a raw nerve within the BMCs. While the congregations became excited, some leaders began to lose confidence. One bit of feedback we received was the fear that ACEA would become too dominant. Moreover, African and Caribbean church leaders held different perspectives on the issue of Black children's education failure. Some churches worried that *Faith in the Future* would eclipse their own millennial events; others were concerned about who would be profiled in the event. Finally, it seemed that the BMCs' most serious concern was the potential for backlash and marginalisation from White society if we are perceived to be inversely racist.

The situation improved when the Prime Minister, Tony Blair, confirmed that he would be attending *Faith in the Future*. This was a big coup for ACEA as, initially, the PM had declined our invitation; but, with further representation, this decision was reversed, and we were elated when we received a letter stating that the PM was available. For security reasons, we had to keep this acceptance secret until the day before the event. We also succeeded in getting the then leader of the opposition, William Hague, to agree that he too would address the conference. At last, it seemed to me, the BMCs were in the driving seat, exploring with the government and the opposition what their policies were on a number of issues affecting Black people and the church. We were being asked to attend meetings and join committees in a way that previously we could only dream about. For the first time I had a glimpse of what it really meant to be able to change and affect policies.

However, there was only one problem. ACEA did not receive the financial support that was pledged. We were convinced that the event would be oversubscribed and, from the outset, championed it as a leadership event, inviting delegations from each church. While, at ACEA, staff morale fell as the demands of the task became apparent, the churches themselves seemed to become oblivious and somehow failed to grasp the moment. By the time the big day arrived on 5 July 2000, we already knew we were in financial trouble. ACEA executive members and many of senior leaders had already determined that the event would not be cancelled: we had invested so much and, anyway, it was customary for members to leave things to the very last moment! We held our nerve.

Anyone walking into the Brighton Centre could not have helped but say 'Wow'! All our hard work and planning was evident to see. When delegates entered the main hall, they were in awe. We at ACEA had kept our word and had delivered an event to make the heart and spirit glad. Attendance on the opening night was, however, no more than 350 people. Then that night the Prime Minister's teenage son, Liam, was found in the streets drunk and in a stupor after celebrating the end of his GCSE exams. The press descended to Brighton in droves. Yet there was still some uncertainty as to whether the PM would turn up, given the recent chain of events. However, in the end he did, as did William Hague, and their presence sent a strong message as to the importance and value of the BMCs. That week we were in the headlines in all forms of media.

Faith in the Future proved a pivotal event. For the first time, many churches and denominations had to recognise each other. BMCs from the historic denominations stood side by side with those from the African and Caribbean diaspora. BMCs gained insight into what it takes to build unity. For the first time some churches dared to step outside their perimeter fences. There was equal representation between African and Caribbean, men and women speakers in a way not seen before. There was no evasion; strong debates were delivered. Our only regret was the numbers who attended – there were just over 1,500 adult delegates throughout the event. Nonetheless, the agenda, the opportunities and BMC aspirations were put firmly on the table. Many churches took it up and ran with it; other organisations captured the essence and momentum of our vision for Christianity in Britain in the twenty-first century, and embraced them. One thing was for certain, BMCs entered into the nation's consciousness.

In this recognised church phase, community development became normative. In 1998, the Black Christian Civic Forum was launched by R David Muir on Martin Luther King Day, to encourage Black Christians and BMCs to get more involved in the politics that affect them and in social and racial issues. Regrettably, this initiative has not captured the imagination of the BMCs, and the Forum has not achieved its aspirations. However, one of the boldest expressions of the recognised church is evident in by the plethora of ministries that now broadcast on radio and television.

The maturing church

This final stage – the maturing church – marks the state of BMCs today and what is yet to come in the future. The *Faith in the Future* conference had provided Black Christians with new lenses through which to see themselves, generating confidence, and offering benchmarks by which to shape BMC priorities, vision and aspirations for the future. It raised the issues of social engagement, of tackling the inequalities and injustices in society, working with children and young people, and valuing the contributions of body ministry. The churches' mission was refocused and reenergized, and they were challenged to participate in shaping the perception of Christianity in Britain, and to be ambassadors and champions of their local communities.

To take on this challenge, the church had to grow up and become strategic. A new way of relating came into being. Many churches treated each other differently, and the hand of friendships was extended. BMCs now had to 'walk the talk' and deliver what they boldly said they could. A recognised church is a scrutinised church. It is a new feeling for BMCs to be examined thoroughly to ensure that they are indeed what they professes to be. However, our response to the future, and how we build on our past and present achievements, will determine the fate of our faith in the future.

The role and contribution of the BMCs

We now turn to examine in more detail the impact of these phases of development on the churches. In doing this, we will look at their spiritual impact on the wider church and society, their social impact both in and on behalf of their communities, and their economic contribution. There should be no doubt that BMCs are one of God's gifts to the nation and the Black community.

Spiritual impact

The spiritual contribution of BMCs is as much a testament of who they are as what they believe and practise. Through their personal and shared life experiences, Black Christians are constantly grateful to God for bringing them out of the 'miry clay' onto a solid rock, and have a strong desire to praise him for the rest of their lives. This desire has had a life-transforming effect. BMCs have always rejected the form of 'grace-alone gospel' often present in some historic denominations, which suggests that 'it does not matter how you live your life, the grace and love of God is too powerful to let you suffer in the end'. Instead, they pose a direct challenge by embracing a faithful interpretation of Scripture that holds in tension the tragedy of the cross, where both the love and wrath (justice) of God were revealed. As disciples of Christ, they put the onus firmly on the saved to 'win the lost at any cost' and to set free those who are captives to Satan. They would want, therefore, to challenge the posture of Western Christianity that presides over falling church attendance, eroded personal, social and moral values, and a lack of conviction regarding the role of Christ, the Bible and the church. They would contend that, in a land of relative plenty, 'it is easier for a camel to go through the eye of a needle than for a rich man to enter the kingdom of God' (Matthew 19:24). BMCs are therefore quick to point out areas of deprivation in the human condition, and the need to separate one's earthly estate from that which Jesus is building in the kingdom of God.

Because they have emerged out of a survivalist context, spirituality of BMCs is expressed as a revivalist challenge. There is a battle raging between the kingdom of God and the forces of darkness, between the living church and liberal, lukewarm or dead Christianity. Failure to recognise this fundamental principle exposes the individual to the deception that everything they do is by their own free will rather than at the instigation of a greater power. Christians must take sides and show their allegiance: 'Choose for yourselves this day whom you will serve' (Joshua 24:15). That way the enemies and their tactics can be clearly identified.

This clear position and resolute approach to the gospel of Christ is the foundation to BMCs' relationship with God, which is enhanced through prayer, worship and the other spiritual disciplines. This relationship has generated obedience and boldness to the command to go into all the world and preach the gospel (Matthew 28:18,19). But, far from marginalizing the BMCs, such boldness has placed them at the heart of British church life, because of the fruits of growth they have produced. BMCs can now offer a template for the declining church. They have preserved the heritage of Christianity in the UK by purchasing defunct church premises that would have otherwise been used by communities from other faiths, or as development sites or, in some cases, pubs. Black Christians who are members of the historic denominations and of White Majority Pentecostal churches have added to the BMCs' credibility and given them a wider multicultural presence in the UK.

Community impact

The pivotal role that the BMCs play in their communities varies starkly. The overwhelming evidence is that they are the hubs for many communities, and they are the most cohesive representation of the Black community. They continue to provide essential services for community development, ranging from counselling and advice services to care and advocacy for older people. Some, like the New Testament Assembly Community Project in Tooting, south London, and Leytonstone, east London, have entered into contracts with local authorities to provide home-care services and residential care homes. And the Church of God of Prophecy has initiated the Nehemiah Housing Association in Birmingham.

Efforts are also being made to tackle gun crime and the drug culture by Ascension Trust in Brixton, south London; this initiative is being led by the Reverend Les Isaac who has also begun the Street Pastors initiative to provide pastoral support for young people in nightclubs and on the streets. Freedom's Ark is spearheading the Peace Alliance in Haringey under the leadership of Pastor Nimbs Obunge: using the slogan 'Not one more drop of blood', they have brought together the various communities and faiths in the borough to reclaim it from violent crime. All of these initiatives have had a significant effect on crime reduction and have been recognised by politicians and the Metropolitan Police Service.

In the 1980s, the Joint Council for Anglo-Caribbean Churches (JCACC) led the way in dealing with drug issues; JCACC's founder, Reverend Esme Beswick, went on to become a President of the Churches Together in England in 2000. The New Assembly of Churches has initiated the support of prisoners and their families; under the leadership of Reverend Carmel Jones, they provide training in information technology and computing (ITC) training for inmates so that they can achieve a City and Guilds qualification. At its headquarters in Luton, COGIC, under the name of 'The Dale Social Welfare Group', not only provides ITC training but also foundation courses in childcare, hairdressing and health-and-safety training for their local communities and organisations. They are also partners with the Luton Borough Council and the Primary Care Trust in delivering services generally for the local community. There is also the National 'Black Boys Can' Initiative based in Birmingham, which is recognised by government and local authorities, and provides a holistic mentoring and support structure for boys.

Many congregations like Handsworth NTCOG and the Victory 'I Care' Projects continue to provide nursery school provision, and others have made their premises available to do the same; there is also a plethora of supplementary schools – all the anecdotal evidence suggests that the BMCs are the largest providers of supplementary education. There have been some interesting attempts to follow the lead of Tabernacle Christian School, in west London, under the leadership of pastors Derek and Pauline Wilson. The BMCs are the largest providers of youth clubs and facilities for the Black community, with Glory House leading the way with a purpose-built youth sports centre. They are also involved in the XPECT school project, in partnership with Newham Council – a football academy reaching over 400 young people. Many churches, like the Bible Study Network, also provide ITC training for their communities, enabling them to gain access to employment. Others are committed to working with the victims of HIV/AIDS. Much is being done in the UK, and much more is being done abroad through missionary endeavours and child sponsorship programmes.

The contribution of the BMCs to their communities is indicative of who they are and what they have achieved. They are the a huge economic force within the Black community. Their membership is largely comprised of the middle classes in the Black community, comprising by far the larger percentage of professionals and graduates than elsewhere in the community. It is also extremely rewarding to know that the BMCs are the greenhouses for the continued success of Black people in society: for example, they provide musicians, artists, producers and trainers for much of the music industry in the UK. Celebrating these contributions, however, should not mean glossing over the reality that the BMCs have not taken up many of the opportunities available to them. Many are delivering their services at their own expense, and have not participated in local schemes like Neighbourhood Renewal, Local Strategic Partnerships, Sure Start (for very the young) or Connexions Partnerships (supporting young people aged 13 to 19 years). There is also the demand from those providing funds that the churches separate their community work from their church life and form separate charities. Some have conceded, but it remains an area of concern and of some resistance from the church with the result of marginalising their 'good works' – good works that are integral to the gospel of Christ and forming part of the Lord's 'measuring rods' when his Day comes (Revelation 11:1).

Endnotes

1 The Redeemed Christian Church of God have also started an additional 34 branches in the Republic of Ireland since its inception.
2 ACEA has published two editions of the *Black Majority Churches UK Directory*. The first, in 2000, was in partnership with the Centre for Black and White Christian Partnership in Birmingham, and the second, in September 2003, was in partnership with CTBI.
3 I undertook a survey of a representative sample of the BMCs to gain up-to-date information of their history, distinctiveness, contribution to the Christian faith in Britain, and the extent of their social responsibility and involvement in government priority initiatives.
4 R David Muir, *A Mighty Long Way*, ACEA, p2.
5 See Professor Stuart Hall, Introduction to *Many Winters On* (a reprint of *Forty Winters On*), ACEA, 1998, p4–5.
6 The *South London Press*, 25 June 1948, in *Many Winters On*, p5.
7 Muir, p3–4.
8 The *Daily Mirror*, 8 September 1958, in Nigel File and Chris Power, *Black Settlers in Britain 1555–1958*, Heinemann, 1995, p87.
9 The average age was calculated from the list supplied at the Appendix of Sam King's autobiography, *Climbing Up the Rough Side of the Mountain*, Minerva Press, London, 1998, p272–279.
10 Established in 1968, IMCGB is an international council dedicated to offering recognition to Black churches and ministers through a process of ordination and representation. Through its bishops, it also provides apostolic leadership and oversight for these churches.
11 File and Power, p87.
12 Joel Edwards, 'The British Afro-Caribbean Community', in Martyn Eden (ed.), *Britain on the Brink*, Crossway Books, 1993, p103.
13 Details were given as part of a telephone interview conducted on 3 August 2004.
14 King, p77, 82 and 87.
15 Hall, in *Many Winters On*, p4.
16 Muir, p2.
17 Roswith Gerloff, *A Plea for British Black Theologies: The Black Church Movement in Britain in its Transatlantic, Cultural and Theological Interaction*, Peter Lang, 1992, p55–61; in Muir, p6.
18 Edwards, 'The British Afro-Caribbean Community', p107–115.
19 Joe Aldred, 'The development of BMCs', presentation given by as part of the CTBI consultation with BMCs, 23 November 2002.
20 Edwards, 'The British Afro-Caribbean Community', p102.

21 Clarice Nelson, 'If the church was what it professed to be . . . an interview with Sybil Phoenix', in Paul Grant and Raj Patel (eds), *A Time to Act: Kairos 1992*, Black and Third World Theology Working Group and Evangelical Christians for Racial Justice, 1992, p21–22.

22 Edwards, 'The British Afro-Caribbean Community', p104.

23 Oliver A Lyseight, *Forward March: An Autobiography*, George S Garwood, 1995, p35, 36.

24 Edwards, 'The British Afro-Caribbean Community', p. 105.

25 Lyseight, p36.

26 Lyseight, p46–47. It is very difficult to ascertain the chronology of events from this piece of work, as it jumps backwards and forwards, randomly in places, often reflecting the primary conversational style rather than a historical chronology. However, the evidence suggests that, although the revolving fund was set up, there were never sufficient resources to purchase the buildings in the many areas that needed them, or to maximise the opportunities that became available.

27 Lyseight, p47.

28 Telephone conversation, September 2004.

29 Virginia Becher, *Black Christians: Black Church Traditions in Britain*, Centre for Black and White Christian Partnership & Westhill RE Centre, 1995, p33.

Chapter 8

Theologies and doctrines of the Black Majority Churches

Any conversation about theology can be treated as much with disdain as with affection. Often Black Majority Churches are regarded by their White colleagues as being 'not quite up to the job'. Theology, it seems, separates and determines the elite rather in the same way that money sets up barriers between rich and poor. There is, instead, an intellectual snobbery that ignores the 'fruits' of ministry in favour of the theological camp to which one belongs. The reverse could be said about BMCs from the African and Caribbean diaspora who, for too long, have ridiculed the historic denominations, sometimes with good cause, for neglecting the work of the Spirit in their ministry; yet instead of embracing both dimensions, they neglect the discipline of theological study. In fact the BMCs' usual approach to theology depends very much on the particular issue, its likely impact on the churches themselves or on society, and the perceptions of theologians held by those involved in the discussion. If theology can be defined as the study of God as he is revealed in Scripture or elsewhere in history, then, to some degree, most Christians are constantly engaged in theological discourse and reflection. In this chapter I have set myself two goals: first, to outline what BMCs believe and practise; second, to identify whether or not there are similarities and differences between these and the practices and beliefs of the historic denominations.

The way that BMCs express and practise their faith can give the impression that there are huge theological differences between them and the historic churches. However, on closer examination this does not seem to be the case. Few new theologies are emerging from the BMCs, and differences seem mostly to be about the application of key Christian doctrines and practices, and the priority these are given. The BMCs' distinctive qualities have not necessarily come about simply because their members are Black Christians, but seem mainly to arise out of the churches' historical origins, be they Pentecostal, Baptist, Methodism, Holiness or Anglican. Differences may also stem from leadership styles, the choice of leadership and organisational structures, leaders' theological training background, or whether they are simply a product of their time and environment. When married to factors such as cultural and sociological distinctiveness and the perspectives gained from experience that Black Christians have when approaching matters of faith, any differences become magnified. And there are other considerations. Most African and Caribbean churches established in the UK have adopted their theologies from churches or denominations to which they had previously belonged. There is also the eclectic mix of external influences such as the popular television preachers as well as other influential preachers of the day. All this tends to create a mosaic of theologies which, though mostly within the boundaries of orthodoxy, have not been thought through or revised before being adopted.

Where the current thinking is taking place is in the personal pursuit of individuals. Birmingham University has been the main hub for theological thought for Black Christians, chiefly due to the work of Dr Emmanuel Lartey, who is now Professor of Pastoral Theology and Care at Columbia Theological Seminary in Decatur, Georgia, USA. Dr Robert Beckford of Birmingham University and Dr Anthony Reddie of Queens Theological College are now developing this work. There is also the development of what is referred to as a 'womanist theology' which affirms women's roles without denigrating those of men. However, despite these contributions, there is still a gaping hole in the provision and accessibility of theologies that are relevant or acceptable to BMCs.

It would be impossible here to focus on every theological point worthy of discussion. Equally, I am resisting the temptation of being drawn into the debate over which doctrine is right and which is wrong. What I am seeking to do is reflect the theological positions as they are and to highlight those that demonstrate BMC distinctiveness. The theologies and doctrines of the historical denominations are well documented elsewhere. Instead, this chapter will focus on churches emerging from both the African and the Caribbean diasporas. For clarity, I will concentrate on three categories of doctrine:

- The work of Christ and the Holy Spirit
- Beliefs and practices
- Divisions in the church

At the risk of appearing dogmatic, I will affirm that I know of no dissenting voices within these churches concerning the reality of the virgin birth, the divinity of Christ, or his resurrection and ascension, so I will not be giving those issues any individual treatment here.

The work of Christ and the Holy Spirit

The atonement

The doctrine of the atonement forms the foundation on which almost all Black Christian theologies are built. This doctrine of liberation from sin has its roots in the Old Testament which tells how, in order to avert the punishment of God, abate his anger and escape its consequences, the people of Israel offered a ransom for their sins in the form of a blood sacrifice of animals (Leviticus ch 16). While the entire ceremony on the Day of Atonement is important for different reasons, the focus here is on the two goats offered up on behalf of the sin of people (16:8–10). The random act of casting lots means that the choice made has come about by 'chance' even though the process was ordained by God and at times controlled by him. One goat was selected for the Lord and one for the people, and atonement was achieved when the goat of the people was sent into the wilderness as a scapegoat for the people's sins, while the Lord's goat was sacrificed as a sin offering. This bloody act is seen as foreshadowing the cross, on which Jesus became the sacrificial Lamb (Matthew 20:28; 2 Corinthians 5:21), while the life of humankind was spared.

This deed shapes the BMCs' understanding of the doctrines of Christ (ie their Christology). The prevailing view among the churches is that this act provides unlimited atonement – that is, it was undertaken for and is available to all humankind, rather than limited to the elect or the predestined. Nevertheless, there is a strong belief in, and affirmation of, the doctrine of *predestination*; but this is regarded simply as a matter of 'delayed certainty' (ie knowledge after the fact), since predestination is ascribed to all those who are saved. Nowhere, however, is there any movement towards the concept of *universalism*, which treats everyone as saved and having to 'opt out' of the grace of God. Instead, the picture is painted of a slave whose freedom is bought but who chooses to stay and work for his or her master under the same or worse conditions.

For churches from the African and Caribbean diaspora, the atonement foregrounds the centrality and power of the cross, and identifies Jesus Christ as the sacrificial Lamb and Saviour of the world. As a ransom, Christ has redeemed humanity from the curse and consequences of sin;

thus the efficacy of the atonement is demonstrated in the gift of salvation. The atonement is the gateway to justification, sanctification and a holy life. The defeat of Satan and his demons through Christ's death, burial and resurrection has resulted in the triumph of good over evil and the subjugation of sin. More than that, the atonement places God as sovereign over all things, whether in the heavens, on the earth or under the earth.

In practice and in teaching, the BMCs often emphasise what the atonement is offering, in particular the prophetic words of Isaiah 53:4,5:

> Surely He has borne our griefs
> And carried our sorrows;
> Yet we esteemed Him stricken,
> Smitten by God and afflicted.
> But He was wounded for our transgressions,
> He was bruised for our iniquities;
> The chastisement for our peace was upon Him,
> And by His stripes we are healed.

The implication of this selfless act, and the churches' response to it, has given rise to other theological emphases which we now go on to explore.

Salvation

In the Old Testament, salvation means 'bring into a spacious environment (compare Psalm 18:36 with 66:12), but it carries from the beginning the metaphorical sense of freedom from limitation and the means to that; i.e. deliverance from factors which constrained and confine'.[1] And, for the BMCs, it is this metaphorical understanding of salvation that is most significant. They take it for granted that the most important reason for the existence of the church is to ensure that lost humanity is saved from their sins and its consequences. The belief is that all have sinned and are not fit for the presence of God or are undeserving of his grace (Romans 3:23). In addition, that everyone who sins and delights in sinning is a slave to sin and to the devil (John 8:34,42–47; 1 John 3:8). The only way to escape sin and judgement is to denounce sin through repentance (ie demonstrate a marked change of conviction and actions) and to accept the work done in the atonement through Christ (Romans 5:15). This call to repentance and acceptance is accomplished by the proclamation of the gospel through evangelism, preaching and teaching by all and every means. Communicating through radio and television is regarded as crucial to achieving this.

Salvation, it is firmly believed, is found only in Jesus Christ (Acts 4:12). Pluralism and any tacit acceptance that all faiths are equal or somehow lead to God are absolutely rejected. In fact, plurality is seen as a vice employed by the enemy to distract or hinder the Christian's goal of salvation in Christ. Yet salvation is viewed as a notion that contains two parts, which are that the Christian is both saved and is being saved. So, on the one hand, people who are perishing are rescued by a compassionate Saviour (Mark 16:16; Acts 2:21,47); on the other hand, the saved person continues to require salvation in order to live a faithful, fulfilling and fruitful life (Matthew 10:22; 1 Peter 4:17,18). It is at this point that a major divergence from Western Christianity often occurs. The majority of BMCs see the second aspect of salvation to include being spared from the trials and tribulations of daily life. This means freedom from guilt (Hebrews 10:22), fear (2 Timothy 1:7; Hebrews 2:15) and bondage (Galatians 5:1). Attention is also paid to the promise of blessing and not a curse, wealth and not poverty, success and not failure. Scriptures like 'No weapon formed against you shall prosper' (Isaiah 54:17), 'I have never seen the righteous forsaken or their children begging bread' (Psalm 37:25, NIV), 'The eyes of the Lord are on the righteous and his ears are attentive to their cry' (Psalm 34:15, NIV; 1 Peter 3:12), 'by his wounds you have been healed' (1 Peter 2:24, NIV), and 'The prayer of a righteous man is powerful and effective' (James 5:16, NIV) are all regarded as evidence that God looks after his children and responds positively to their circumstances.

The Holy Spirit and his work

The Holy Spirit, the third person of the Godhead, is central to the life of the believer and the church. BMCs believe that the Holy Spirit has always been active and is ever-present as God's divine power as described in both the Old and New Testaments. However, the Spirit's continuing presence in the church was manifest on the Day of Pentecost when, as the promised Comforter and Counsellor, he was sent to take the place of the resurrected Christ (John 14:16,25; 15:26; Acts 2:3); as such, the Holy Spirit is now God's presence on the earth. He convicts people of their sins. He dwells in those who acknowledge Jesus Christ, and is a seal of God's approval on their life (John 14:17; Romans 8:9; 1 Corinthians 3:16). The Spirit empowers the believer for service (Acts 1:8; 4:31) and is the

Giver of gifts to all who believe (Acts 10:45; 11:15). He is also the revealer and teacher of all truth (John 14:26; 1 John 2:27).

BMCs place significant emphasis on the activity of the Holy Spirit in the life of the believer. There is no point in having a god who is so transcendent that he becomes a mere spectator of human affairs, and people are left to freewheel in their own existence, trying to make the best of terrible situations. Instead, the BMCs' interest lies in an immanent God who intervenes in the affairs of humankind and reserves the right to do things his way, in his time and to whom he chooses. Equally, there is confidence that, as an Advocate, the Holy Spirit, will fight every battle to enforce the rights of God's children and the victory already won by Christ on the cross. The power of the Spirit is therefore brought into sharp focus. Pentecostal churches in particular emphasise the baptism of the Holy Spirit, which theologians call 'a second blessing'; it is also referred to as the second stage of salvation. However, both these perceptions are misleading and misrepresent the beliefs of almost all BMCs (except the Oneness churches, see below), who simply see baptism of the Spirit as a free gift available to all believers. If anything, it should be considered a continuous blessing, since it is not a one-off event, but rather the means by which individuals subject themselves to the control and direction of God's Spirit. Consequently, becoming more like Christ means taking on more of his personality, a process that is nurtured and developed by the Holy Spirit. Moreover, there is a recognition that 'the weapons of our warfare are not carnal' (2 Corinthians 10:4), and that the church's mission is greatly advanced or hindered depending on how God's people allow the Holy Spirit to function.

According the Holy Spirit his rightful role is also regarded as important. The churches do not view him as though he were an elderly parent ready for the retirement home because he is no longer capable of living independently. Worst is the assumption that there is no more useful contribution to be made to society. Instead, the Spirit is seen as eternal and life-giving, continually renewing the believer, and revealing the heart and mind of God to his people (1 Corinthians 2:10-16; 2 Corinthians 4:16-18). He is also the spirit of unity that binds the various parts of Christ's body together (Ephesians 4:11-16). Equally, he bears the same characteristics as Christ, being the same yesterday, today and forever (Exodus 40:35; Isaiah 63:11-15; Luke 1:35; 9:34), thus making him willing and available to establish the kingdom of God with signs and wonders in the same way that Christ has done: by restoring sight to the blind, healing the sick and infirm, casting out demons, comforting the broken-hearted and meeting the deepest needs of those searching for answers in their lives (Matthew 12:28; Acts 9:10-16; 10:3; Romans 15:19). BMC members therefore frequently admonish one another 'not to quench the Holy Spirit': in other words, whatever we do, say or think, let's not lock the Spirit into our world, put him in a box or exclude him from our lives and the life of the church; rather, let us let him loose to do great exploits.

Justification

Justification is one of the most liberating doctrines in Christianity. It is a concept drawn from the law to describe the act of allowing the one who is found guilty of a crime to be set free or pardoned. As a Christian doctrine, it signals the end of hostilities between the individual and God, and is itself part of the peace treaty. The BMCs believe that when an individual acknowledges his or her sin before God, instead of condemning, he declares that person righteous and exonerated of all past wrongs. It should not be surprising, then, that justification is used by the BMCs as a powerful evangelistic tool. The invitation of salvation to the unsaved, to those without a personal relationship with God, offers justification as an opportunity to make a clean break with the past and a chance to chart a new future with God as their helper. Confidence in the God who justifies (Romans 8:33) removes ongoing guilt, fear, a sense of unworthiness or lack of self-esteem that may arise from the individual's conscience or from the judgement of family, friends and peers. In offering hope and a new start, justification presents the believer with a new canvas on which to design his or her life, to become a new person who is acceptable and pleasing to God.

Significantly, the ability to receive justification is not determined by social or economic status, age, gender, ethnicity or nationality, nor can it be earned by works or tender. Rather, justification is a gift from God and can only be received through faith (Romans 3:27-31). Moreover, since justification is the means by which we are reckoned righteous (Romans 3:23-26; 4:4-8), it is no wonder that 'without faith it is impossible to please God' (Hebrews 11:6, NIV). This emphasis on 'by faith alone' creates one of the Christian distinctives, setting it apart from other faiths, cults and sects. The implication for Christians the world over is that justification has the same levelling effect as death: it is applied not on the basis of merit or deservedness but wherever and whenever we acknowledge that, like all of humanity, we have sinned

(Romans 3:9,10; 3:23). Justification is the gateway to all of God's blessings and rewards that come with being children of God and heirs to his kingdom.

Sanctification

The doctrine of sanctification forms part of the family of beliefs, alongside holiness and justification, which emphasise the uniqueness of the believer and his or her relationship with God. Sanctification involves *separation*, being set apart for exclusive use by God. For BMCs, sanctification should be in the context of Christ's work, rather than the Law. However, the consequences of defilement or of being made profane are mainly interpreted through Old Testament events and instances where God challenged those who were rebelling against him. Sanctification, therefore, could be either a work of God (1 Thessalonians 5:23; John 10:36; 17:17), of Christ (Hebrews 13:12) or of the Holy Spirit (1 Corinthians 6:11; 2 Thessalonians 2:13), or it could be an individual's response to God in the form of consecration (John 17:19). The main difference between sanctification and holiness is that, though both involve separation from sin, it is human beings who need to be sanctified in order to possess the holy character or characteristics of God. God is holy; the angels in heaven are holy; we are commanded to be holy if we are truly to reflect the character and nature of God.

Once again, the accepted position represents a duality: the people of God are both sanctified and are being sanctified: the former occurs when we encounter Jesus Christ and are cleansed from our sins as a result of his sacrificial death; the latter is the result of the ongoing actions of the believer who seeks to remain sanctified in a polluted and evil world. Together, these aspects represent the believer's endeavour to take on the character of Christ and to allow Christ's image to be formed and reflected in his or her life. Through sanctification, we die daily to sin, renew our minds and stand firm against thinking too highly of ourselves or boasting of our achievements. Thus, we resist all forms of temptation, evil works and deeds. Sanctification is the process that allows the Christian to be holy, as God is holy and to work towards the goal of perfecting the believer.

For the BMCs, sanctification is achieved through a prayerful life supported by fasting, and is enhanced through careful study, application and obedience to the Word of God. It is expressed through good moral and ethical conduct, and through living the servant life dedicated to effective discipleship, evangelism and being a faithful witness. The expectation is that a true believer should live a moral, sinless, guiltless and selfless life. For these reasons, many Black Christians take a dim view of those who profess to be Christians yet who seek to avoid the commitment and implications of a sanctified life. It is this view of sanctification that gives rise to the notion of 'nominal Christians' and questions as to whether someone is truly or 'sweetly' saved. Sanctification should be about dying to self and selfish motives, an attitude that, without doubt, reflects a powerful counterculture to the prevailing values in much of Western culture.

Beliefs and practices in the church

Water baptism

The BMCs, like the majority of Christians, regard water baptism as the public declaration to the world that a believer has made a commitment to follow Jesus Christ. The rite usually involves total immersion in a pool sited within the church, although African and Caribbean Spiritual churches prefer the 'flowing water' of a river or the sea. It is an act of obedience, performed after individuals have repented and professed their faith. It can only be carried out at the believer's request, and only when they are capable of understanding the decision and implication of their actions: this means that the mentally ill, people with learning disabilities and very young children are not usually baptised.

This raises the question of what function baptism serves. For the Jews who joined the early Christian church, baptism in the name of Jesus was seen as 'the deed of transfer,' an act whereby the 'baptisands' handed themselves over as 'the property of the one named'.[2] However, for BMCs, there is a clear position that 'baptism does not save you', and no legal or spiritual transactions take place at baptism. This is because, the argument goes, water in itself has no salvific effect. If someone is a sinner before they are immersed, they will only rise from the water a wet sinner. However, there is a general acknowledgement that baptism symbolises the death to one's old self and resurrection to new life in Christ. It is also accepted that, for some individuals, baptism is a pivotal point in their lives, an event that crystallises their infant faith and brings about transformation; but this change is ascribed to the work of the Holy Spirit (Matthew 3:16,17).

BMCs from the African and Caribbean diaspora do not believe in or practise infant baptism. Some will go to great lengths to emphasise that they dedicate infants to God but do not christen them; for others, it is simply an issue of semantics. The overarching reason for resisting infant baptism is that there are no concrete precedents in Scripture. There is also the belief that, since faith is the prerequisite for salvation, an infant is incapable of having that degree of faith: baptism can only be offered to those who consent and are aware of the implications and demands of their actions. This position, however, presents some challenges for BMCs, as it gives the impression that all children have to *opt in* to Christianity, a process that is not evident in any other religion. It also does not consider how we deal with the issue of household salvation (Acts 16:15,33; 18:8); neither does it deal with the full implication of Paul's perspectives on sanctification and holiness for the unbelieving spouse and children (1 Corinthians 7:14). The tenuous and arbitrary approach to determining the 'age of accountability', the point at which a child becomes personally responsible for his or her own destiny, offers little clarification on this issue.

A holy life

As we saw earlier in this chapter in the section on the Holy Spirit, living a life defined by holiness has always been fundamental to the BMCs. It is seen as essential to maintaining a healthy Christian life. The admonition in Hebrews 12:14 provides believers with a constant reminder: 'Make every effort to live in peace with all men and to be holy; without holiness no-one will see the Lord' (NIV). For many Black Christians, the outworking of a holy life is what distinguishes a Christian from a 'religious' or non-Christian person. It is what sets them apart from sin, the world and its vices, so that they can live a life of exclusive service for the Lord. It is the antidote to living in a corrupt, ungodly, perverted and unjust society. Holiness is the means by which one maintains purity and, by implication, piety. It is the arena in which God dwells and the environment in which he meets with his people. Holiness is part of God's character and essence. Being holy is humankind's reasonable response to the demands of a holy God (1 Peter 1:14–16).

Where the BMC distinctive lies is in the application, monitoring and expectations that I outlined in Chapter 2. The quest to be good ambassadors and witnesses of the faith has often caused confusion between biblical requirements and cultural exceptions. Despite my personal misgivings that some BMCs have harassed, abused and mishandled many people because of the high value placed on holiness, nevertheless I believe they are right to make it an essential doctrine. It is important for Christians to remember that, before God, all our righteousness can be like 'filthy rags' (Isaiah 64:6), and that Jesus himself on occasion refused to be called 'good' (Mark 10:18). In doing so, we also remember that we are all mere mortals seeking the grace and mercy of a holy God.

Worship

Besides personal piety, worship, praise and thanksgiving also play significant roles in the corporate life of the BMCs. Much has been made about the differences between these three outward expressions of faith: a popular summary of their relationship to each other:

- we worship God because of who he is;
- we praise him for his mighty deeds;
- we thank him for what he has done and what he promises to do for us and those we encounter, know and love.

The basis for worship is that 'God is Spirit, and those who worship him must worship in spirit and truth' (John 4:24). To worship God 'in spirit' means to worship him 'by the prompting of' or 'through the vehicle of' the Holy Spirit. The worshipper must therefore be in tune with, and have the same character, as the Object of worship. And the Holy Spirit, the God who is with us, is an integral part of worship so that it can be presented to God the Father.

Worship is not just the act (the *doing*) but a lifestyle (the *being*). It is not unusual for the speaker to proclaim from the pulpit to those in the pews that they did not attend church to worship as their worship is ongoing and an integral part of their lives. Alternatively, the worship leader might say, as a protest or chastisement to the congregation, 'I'm not going to prime or pump you to worship God – you should have started before you got here!' This continuum of worship can be seen in gospel concerts and entertainment events, where an artist will admonish the paying audience, 'I haven't come here to entertain you but to worship God.' Worship as a lifestyle reinforces the notion that believers are constantly in the presence of a holy God who deserves to be worshipped at all times and in every circumstance. Holiness codes and promises in Scripture aid and abet this worship lifestyle.

The preacher is at the heart of worship in BMCs. This is depicted by the amount of time allocated to preaching – between forty minutes and an hour[3] – which excludes additional time 'when the Spirit moves'. Other aspects of the service tend to serve as a warm-up for the preacher, during which there is a strong steering of worshippers towards the preached word. The onus is on the preacher to let the Holy Spirit 'fall' or to 'mash up the place', as on the day of Pentecost. This creates the worshipping preacher, who cannot rely merely on expository preaching or exegeting a text since he or she might then be considered dead, dry or to lack the anointing. Consequently, sermons are punctuated with 'call and response' interactions to ensure that the audience is 'feeling' the preacher: calls like 'Can I have a witness?', 'Is anyone there?', 'Hello?', 'Are you with me?' or 'Say praise the Lord somebody!' are responded to with shouts of 'Amen!', 'Hallelujah!', 'Preach it!' or 'Bless him, Lord!'

Although BMCs outside the historical denominations do not have a written liturgy, there are predictable worship patterns that regular attendees will identify. Joel Edwards highlights the following:[4]

- *Devotional service*, which includes songs, prayer and Scripture reading. This period is often used as the worshippers' 'settling down' time, and functions in the same way as the traditional church bell's call to worship.
- *Further singing and testimonies*. Testimonies are normally given during the evening service, although not exclusively, and may set the tone of the service by uplifting the congregation. Testimonies can also be sometimes used to test an individual's depth of spirituality. On occasion, they replace sermons, and visitors and members alike may be called upon to give theirs. Very often members choose to sing their testimony as a song to better express their sentiment.
- *Special prayer*, for the sick and those needing ministry.
- *An offering*. This is emphasised as an integral part of worship, with the clarion call 'God loves a cheerful giver'. The call may go out, 'It's offering time', followed by loud cheers, drum rolls and dancing. Increasingly, some churches spend up to five minutes examining a passage of Scripture to establish the basis and virtue of giving. In churches of the African diaspora, additional thanksgiving offerings are given to celebrate success in a job, birthdays, anniversaries or the birth of a child.
- *Special singing*, which can range from a soloist to the choir, and is often seen as the prelude to the preaching.

- *The sermon.* In some instances this was given by a member of the congregation or a visitor, without prior notice. This is becoming less frequent.
- *The altar call.* This is the test as to whether the preacher has made an impact. Non-Christians are challenged to repent of their sins, while Christians are asked to respond to the preached word. This is also a time for individuals to place whatever burdens they may still have 'at the foot of the cross'.

Additional aspects of worship include:

- *The Lord's Supper.* Some churches still re-enact the Last Supper, including the washing of each other's feet. However, communion services tend to be less frequent than in historical denominations.
- *Hand-clapping and dancing* is actively encouraged before the Lord as a sign of joy and thankfulness for good health and strength, and as a means of celebration. More recently, classical dance and use of flags have been borrowed from historic churches, to add variety or to form focal points.
- *The use of spiritual gifts,* and disciplines such as prayer, fasting and personal devotion, are actively encouraged. Not only are these seen as acts of worship but also means by which believers effectively worship.[5] In smaller congregations, members are actively encouraged to use the gift of prophesy and to pray 'as the Holy Spirit gives utterance'. It is less prevalent in larger congregations because of the less personal nature of the setting and the practical issue of verifying the credibility of the person bringing the message. Often the latter difficulty is overcome by the proviso that the message is mediated or communicated through designated individuals.

The Lord's Supper and the washing of the saints' feet

The Lord's Supper, or the communion acted out as a sacrament, is a doctrine affirmed by the wider church. From a theological standpoint, it should be pivotal since it deals with issues of holiness, personal renewal and the proclamation of the Lord's death (1 Corinthians 11:23–34). However, it is one of the most neglected areas in the worship and praxis of the BMCs. It is ironic that one of the most fundamental rites celebrating the death and suffering of Christ has become marginalised to the point of being peripheral to their church life.

One explanation for this omission is that, unlike the early church and many of the historic denominations, this sacrament is not the focal point of worship in the BMCs. As a result, it has (wrongly) been pushed to the edges in order to facilitate what are seen as more important issues. Some churches do practise the washing of the saints' feet, but this is often undertaken in light of the command to follow the example of Jesus in John 13:5–17 in demonstrating humility and servanthood. However, the primary two elements in this Scripture are often over-looked: first, the welcome and generosity of the host which, one can assume, had already been granted when the guests arrived. There was no guarantee that they would receive a fitting welcome: at any gathering some are more important, and therefore receive more privilege and cer-emony, than others. For Jesus, however, this acceptance of each other as equally welcome and equally valued was crucial if his disciples were to become one body. And second, it was essential that those present had the capacity to forgive each other of their trespasses before they could go on to fulfil the mission of the church. It is these two lessons that still provide the greatest challenges for leaders and the church.

The priesthood of all believers

Within the BMCs, there is a firm belief in the priesthood of all believ-ers. There is no need for a mediator, other than Jesus Christ, between the believer and God (1 Timothy 2:5); we are all equal before God, since we are all his children and joint heirs with Christ. However, there is much in the churches that undermines this belief. Some gifts of the Spirit – prophecy, healing and miracles – are seen as superior to the other gifts, and those who have them as being more honourable, deserving and noble. There is also the suspicion that this doctrine is used more as a means to induce servanthood and servitude to the leaders and the needs of the church, than to release disciples into the world to turn it in the right direction.

Prayer and fasting

Prayer is the lifeblood of the BMCs, dominating most church activities. Common admonitions include, 'Seven 'prayer-less' days makes one weak', and 'Everyone can do something: those without a ministry or a recognised gift can still pray'. Most BMCs will acknowledge that prayer is the tool that connects us to God. In addition, prayer can change individuals or the course of events and thus bring about the will of God. The prayerful lives displayed by Jesus, the apostles and the first Christians are sufficient to encourage and reinforce the need for prayer in the life of every believer. Prayer's effectiveness and the promises it undergirds are also motivations for us to pray. The injunctions that Jesus gave to his disciples as to how they should pray are the same as those he gives to believers today ('*when* you pray', not '*if* you pray'; see Matthew 6:5-15): for this reason, an individual's spirituality is also judged on the basis of his or her prayer life and devotion to God. Finally, prayer should be continuous (1 Thessalonians 5:17).

That said, prayer plays many roles in the life of both the believer and the church. Prayer:

- aids unity, oneness of heart and purpose (Acts 1:14; 2:1);
- is a channel for forgiveness, repentance, healing and solidarity towards each other and God (Nehemiah 1:6; James 5:13-18);
- forms the basis of spiritual warfare, to counter the plans and works of the devil (Matthew 17:18-21; 2 Corinthians 10:3-6)
- assists in laying us bare before God, allowing for sanctification, dying to selfish motives and ambitions, and placing God in his rightful place as sovereign Lord (2 Chronicles 7:14,15);
- is like a telephone to God, vital for developing a relationship with him and generating confidence that he is there for everyone in their time of need (Luke 18:1-8; 1 Thessalonians 5:17,18; James 5:13-15).

It is easy to see how prayer might become egocentric, but it would be wrong for this gift and discipline to be exercised solely for personal benefit or in the pursuit of a self-indulgence. Prayer may often be undertaken as a corporate activity or by an advocate who intercedes on behalf of others: in either case, only prayers that are carried out with the right motive and a clean heart are viewed as effective in gaining the desired response from God.

Fasting is used in the BMCs to facilitate concentrated or focused engagement with God. A fast might be initiated by the Holy Spirit (Matthew 4:1,2). It is a spiritual discipline (6:16-18) and may form part of a time of separation from the world and the busyness and routine of daily life. It can also function as a point of agreement and solidarity with other Christians where, for example, people agree to fast on a certain day for a particular situation. Either way, the expected outcome is for God to acknowledge the individual's dedication and sacrifice. Fasting promotes sanctification: by drowning out the influences of everyday life, by cleaning the heart and renewing the mind, the believer allows the voice and direction of God and his Spirit to speak clearly into his or her life. Fasting may be observed as either a partial or full fast: a partial fast may include abstinence from food or drink, or both, for a limited period of a day or for an extended period; a full fast requires total abstinence for a designated period. In practice, however, there is often not so clear a distinction between the two. Normally, those who require food at regular intervals (eg diabetics), or who have any adverse medical conditions, are not encouraged to fast.

The application of prayer and fasting, both in the local church and in the personal life of the believer, always points to two key areas: first, the ability to overcome Satan and discern his devices (2 Corinthians 2:11); second, to bring in the power of the Holy Spirit to fulfil the work of ministry, enforce the dominion of God 'against principalities, against powers, against the rulers of the darkness of this age, against spiritual hosts of wickedness in the heavenly places' (Ephesians 6:12). Prayer and fasting give the Christian the power to do the greater works which Jesus had predicted that his disciples would do (John 14:12). This power is mainly evoked through intercession; petition, prophetic utterances, thanksgiving, speaking in an unknown tongue, groaning and sighing. Depending on the circumstances, some prefer to walk up and down the aisles or around the perimeter of the building, to prostrate themselves at the altar, or simply to sit or stand. It is not unusual for churches to declare a month of prayer and fasting, especially at the beginning of the year, usually accompanied by weekly prayer meetings and monthly all-night prayer meetings. The RCCG hosts the largest prayer meeting in Europe: the Festival of Life takes place three or four times a year, with over 10,000 attendees.

Despite this, there is evidence that fasting and prayer is abused and misused in the BMCs. Because of their effectiveness, they can also be used as a means of manipulation and control. Sacrificial giving is sometimes asked for as a confirmation of faith: 'If you want God to do something extraordinary, you need to do something extraordinary'. At other times, prayer and fasting are treated as pharmaceutical prescriptions with which to coerce those seeking spiritual breakthrough in some aspect of their life: 'Your situation needs three days' prayer and fasting'. Moreover, prayers can be used negatively to invoke curses. There is no evidence in Scripture that Christians cursing Christians is God-inspired or God-condoned, nor is the effectiveness of this kind of cursing proven.

However, what this does reveal is the attitude and character of the curse's invoker, and the consequences of feelings of fear, victimisation and intimidation for the receiver.

Tithing

Tithing is the act of giving ten per cent of one's income or increase to God. It is a spiritual discipline, one that the Old Testament presents as being demanded by God with the consequence of blessing and cursing attached (Malachi 3:8–10). Therefore, the tithe is seen by BMCs as the portion of one's wealth that rightfully belongs to God and which should be used to maintain the institution of the church, support its workers and advance the kingdom of God.

There can be no doubt that tithing was commended by God in the Old Testament as a means of supporting the Levites, priests and those worshipping in God's temple, and of preserving national and local ceremonial rites (Numbers 18:23–29; Deuteronomy 14:22–29). The tithe later became a form of taxation to support widows, orphans, the poor, foreigners and strangers in need. It is this widening of the scope for biblical tithing that has caused so much contention over the centuries and which is still being contested today. The debate revolves around a number of issues.

First, is the tithe really necessary? Critics may well argue that there is no need for individuals to pay a tithe, since modern society has developed to the point of making provision for the vulnerable and needy through appropriate taxation and the welfare system. Furthermore, the context for the Israelites being asked to tithe was that they had at the time abandoned the worship of God, and what sacrifices of thanksgiving they did make were often insulting to him, incompatible with his decrees and done grudgingly (*see* Deuteronomy 9:4–14). (Ironically, those who are now demanding the tithe run no such risk, as they are presenting their praise wholeheartedly and sincerely!) Therefore, the tithe was instituted as a discipline and a means of reigniting the people's loyalty to him. This is not the case today, since the people of God are now no longer under the Law but under grace, and should not be constrained by the limitations of the Law. As a matter of fact, God does not own ten per cent of our income – all of it belongs to him. Our response as his people should be one that encourages a generous commitment to give. Finally, a more significant criticism levelled against the principle of tithing is that churches often do not use the tithe in the way that

Scripture stipulates; instead, much of it is used selfishly and with a very narrow focus.

The next question is whether one should tithe one's gross or net income. The prevailing view is that the tithe should be given from the individual's gross earnings (ie the total earned before tax is deducted) and not the net income (ie the total that you receive after taxation, the amount you actually take home or have paid into your bank account). Those who argue for the gross tithe contend that all of what you receive is your income and, if the government deserves to take its portion from the gross, God should have the same privilege. There is also a school of thought that says, 'If you want a gross blessing, tithe from your gross; and if you need a net blessing, tithe from your net.'

However, to my mind, neither of these positions are consistent with a biblical point of view. Gross giving seems often to be encouraged simply to generate the maximum amount of income for the church, rather than out of any desire to give God his true portion. As for the 'what you give is what you get' argument, it seems to me that a truer biblical perspective can be obtained from examining Old Testament practices like those relating to the harvest remnants left lying the fields. The Law of Moses forbade the Israelites from harvesting whatever was left on the ground or at the edges of the field, and from picking up the fallen fruit: instead, they were to give this surplus to the poor, the widow the orphans and the stranger (Leviticus 19:9,10). It would be quite reasonable, therefore, to draw a comparison between what fell to the ground or was left behind in the field and the taxes drawn from our earnings as, to an extent, they serve the same purpose. Moreover, there is no evidence that the Israelites counted their cattle in the field according to the number that were born; instead, they counted them on the basis of how many survived. Therefore, it would seem right that the tithe should come out of what you actually have within your remit to give, rather than out of what has been siphoned off before reaching your pay packet.

Another reason why net tithing would be the more acceptable method of tithing is that organisations which can prove they use gifts and donations exclusively for charitable purposes are entitled to receive a refund of the tax paid by the gift's donor. So, for a church to receive the gross of someone's taxable earning, all the individual has to do is pay the net amount and sign a 'Gift Aid' declaration; the charity then has the opportunity to reclaim the tax and maximise its income. Having highlighted the inconsistencies, however, we are left with another problem: what to do with those people who have continually overcommitted themselves by linking their gross tithe to a 'Gift Aid', thus giving over and above the demands of the church – and God, for that matter.

Another debatable issue is the question of where the tithe should be directed? No church I know would advocate that the tithe is for the kingdom of God in its widest sense: all the admonition is for it to be given to the local church, and to do otherwise is always presented as being disobedient to the word of God. Such admonitions, however, are simply matters of expediency. Their real motive is that the local church benefits if its income is increased; the converse is also true – the local church suffers if there is little or no income. The challenge for churches is to determine how biblical they really are. Scripture suggests that 90 per cent of the tithe was used by the givers in the presence of God – an example that, as far as I know, is never followed in practice today. Added to that, if a church does claim tax relief from the tithe, it would be illegal in the UK for the giver to receive direct benefit unless it can be clearly shown that this is part of the objectives or powers of the charity. An alternative would be to ensure that the beneficiaries receive services worth up to 90 per cent of contributions, with only 10 per cent spent on administration and staff salaries. Very challenging indeed!

Closely related to where the tithe should go is the issue of the 'tithe of a tithe', or what I call the *spiral tithe*. The spiral tithe starts with the question of where the leader's tithe should be directed. There is a growing trend for pastors to tithe to those who offer them 'pastoral covering',[6] thus mirroring the act of Abraham to Melchizedek (Genesis 14:18–20). It should be pointed out, however, that while this act may involve the giver in offering the tithe to someone greater than himself, it is in no way symbolic of the priest offering a tenth of the people's tithe to God – to assert this would have serious theological implications.

After the leader has tithed, the spiral of tithing continues as everyone who receives an income offers a tenth to someone else; and some churches may nominate a particular organisation or charity to receive a tithe of its income. While there is nothing wrong with the spiral tithe in principle, it is not a biblical requirement. It may serve as a means of blessing, or of covering the extra administrative burden when the costs are related to the support that is offered, or when those who are tithing feel that by doing so they are generating a spirit or culture of generosity within their church. However if spiral tithing is done out of a misguided belief that it serves some deeper biblical principle, or through coercion, then that is wrong.

In conclusion, tithing remains one of the fairest and most equitable ways in which the believer can make a contribution to building the kingdom of God. There are many issues relating to the way it is utilised and to the narrow parameters in which it is sometimes used within the BMCs. Integrity demands that tithing should be presented as an economical and freely given commitment to kingdom development rather than a 'biblical' demand that cannot be sustained when compared to the evidence presented in Scripture.

View of the Scriptures

Another distinguishing feature of BMCs is their very high view of the Bible. Their engagement with Scripture stems from the belief that the written word should be encountered in the same way that we encounter the incarnate Word, Jesus Christ (John 1:1-7,14). The belief is that an individual cannot be separated from the words they speak; ultimately, you are what you think, say and do (Proverbs 23:7; Luke 6:45). For Black Christians, the written Word takes on added importance because it possesses many of the same characteristics as the incarnate Word. If we are to respect and honour God, then we must also respect and honour his Word; and if we are to obey God, then we must also obey his Word. It is inevitably then that if Jesus is 'the way, the truth, and the life' (John 14:6), the written word would also be the way, the truth and offers us life (Psalm 119:50,105).

> All Scripture is given by inspiration of God, and is profitable for doctrine, for reproof, for correction, for instruction in righteousness, that the man of God may be complete, thoroughly equipped for every good work.
>
> (2 Timothy 3:16,17)

This exhortation creates a powerful stimulus and a mandate as to how we should engage with Scripture. If the Bible is to retain its cutting edge and effectiveness (Hebrews 4:12), there should be nothing added or nothing taken away. Such an approach to Scripture is undergirded by the conviction that if Scripture is 'God-breathed' (NIV) then it is inherent, in that it is true and can be relied on wholeheartedly. It is also infallible, which implies that it is without error. This is not to say that the versions of Scripture we have today are free of inaccuracies in translation. On the contrary, it is because of this recognition that some have given the Authorised Version of the Bible pole position.

Not much attention is given to the merits and debates as to how the Scriptures were actually inspired. Instead, a pragmatic approach has been adopted. If God is powerful enough to speak through a donkey (Numbers 22:28–30), then he also has the divine ability to ensure that human agencies represent accurately what he has to say. While the rightness of this statement may not be in doubt, its integrity certainly is. This is because it creates a self-generating hermeneutic (the way that we interpret Scripture) which treats every verse of Scripture with the same value. Equally, there is the danger of treating the Bible as representing or encompassing the history of the world, rather than the diverse book that it is, telling the redemptive story of God and fallen humanity. And, while it may capture some snapshots of history, the Bible in no way intends to be the historic annals of times past. That said, it is the role that Scripture plays in the life of the believer that is most significant. Often this is the basis by which one can appraise their spirituality. There is the expectation that God will speak to the individual through the word and that our lives must be transformed by it daily. Therefore, daily reading, meditation and study are actively encouraged (Psalm 1).

What then if Scripture does not match our experience? The uncompromising position is that we must 'let God [and his word] be true but every man a liar' (Romans 3:4). Often it is this position that has led Black Christians, and BMCs in particular, to be considered fundamentalist. My own position has always been that if, by 'fundamentalist', critics mean 'having a set of fundamental Christian beliefs and values, which are non-negotiable, whatever the political climate, shifts in culture or popular opinions', then I am happy to be a fundamentalist. But if they mean 'uninformed, irrational, brainwashed and undiscerning', I am most offended.

While most churches take a literal view of Scripture, they are by no means literalist in a theological sense. The nature of their cultures has created a heightened sense of symbolism and metaphor. There is no doubt that when Scripture speaks about 'break[ing] up your fallow ground' (Jeremiah 4:3), this is understood to mean 'preparing our hearts for a renewed fruitful and living encounter and relationship with God'; or, more accurately, 'getting ready for a revival and a spiritual move of God'. Books like Revelation and Daniel are interpreted with symbolism in mind. Equally, testimonies like 'he took me out of the miry clay and planted my feet on the rock to stay' have no other meaning than that God has brought an individual from a bad and dangerous situation and put him or her in a safe place, both spiritually and physically. Moreover, in songs like 'Meet me by the river some day' speak clearly about the hope of gaining eternal life. If anything, it could be argued that some preachers rely heavily on allegory, especially in stories like the Good Samaritan. But this is to be expected in the context of storytelling as a preaching style.

Generally then, Scripture is seen as God's revealed word to us which, if embraced, provides the bedrock for Christian discipleship and discipline.

Divisions within the church

We now go on to explore further the divisions that exists within the BMCs. This is not to say that the theologies, beliefs and practices we have already explored in this chapter have not been sources of tension. However, the issues we are now going on to explore have kept BMCs apart for decades and have created a climate of mistrust, hatred, disrespect and rejection.

Trinitarians and Unitarians

As we saw in earlier chapters, much of the theologies of the early African and Caribbean churches were brought to the UK from the Pentecostal traditions in the USA via the African and Caribbean. The two main Pentecostal traditions are the Trinitarian and Unitarian, or 'Oneness' (Jesus only), churches. Historically, both camps believed each other to be heretical, if not cultic, and without salvation. The key doctrine at the heart of their dispute relates to the nature or essence of the 'Godhead', in the case of Trinitarians, or of God in the case of the Unitarians.

Trinitarians affirms that there is one God existing in three persons – Father, Son and Holy Spirit. This doctrine provided a way to make sense of the encounters with God described in the Bible where the three persons were all manifest at the same time: for example, in Matthew 3:13–17, at Jesus' baptism, the Holy Spirit descends on the incarnate Son, while the Father gives his stamp of approval from heaven. However, this doctrine has led to the assertion that God is no longer monotheistic. Apologists for the doctrine of the Trinity have responded by using several metaphors to make their case, such as that of the egg which has three parts – the shell, the albumen and the yolk – but which is still essentially one integral whole as, by themselves, the individual parts are not an egg.

It is difficult to argue that Unitarian BMCs have their origins as far back as the Arian controversy in the early fourth century, which was considered to be heretical and was rejected by the Council of Nicaea in AD 325 and by the Council of Constantinople in AD 381.[7] An Alexandrian priest, Arius, had argued that there was once a time when God was not the Father and Jesus not the Son; instead divinity was bestowed on the man Jesus, who was never the same substance or essence as God.[8] However, Unitarianism as it appears in the BMCs cannot be regarded as similar to other forms of Unitarianism which rejected either the deity of Christ or took on a humanist face; rather, what we have is a Pentecostal church that has drawn its historicity from a developed form of conservative Unitarianism. Their central tenet is the belief in 'the *oneness* of God, who was the Father in creation, the Son in redemption, and today, He is the Holy Ghost in The Church (I Timothy 3:16)'.[9] Hence the name 'Oneness church'.

Another distinctive of the Oneness churches was the issue of conversion. An individual was only 'really' saved when he or she had received the baptism of the Holy Spirit. Water baptism, it is argued, follows the apostolic traditions which are distinct from that of John the Baptist, and is done in the name of Jesus only (Acts 2:38; 18:24 – 19:5).

Disagreement over these issues meant that for decades there was no dialogue between the Trinitarian and Unitarian camps. However, in recent years there have been massive steps towards developing links with each other, resulting in healthier engagement. This has been brokered mainly through the work of the Centre for Black and White Partnership in Birmingham, but there are other factors. The older leadership for whom those points of contention were fundamental are either retiring or dying. The level of intolerance and abuse that hailed from the pulpits is no longer acceptable. Equally, each denomination has given up its exclusive claims to being the only true church. Possibly one of the most significant reasons is the movement away from the Unitarian position by some of its brightest sons. The likes of Bishop Wayne Malcolm, of Christian Life City in east London, have made the transition; if not fully in the Trinitarian camp, they have certainly built their tent next to it. A rebranding process has also taken place in many churches: so, for example, when Bishop Leon White, of the Bible Way Church of the Lord Jesus Christ Apostolic, retired, his son Reverend Michael White took over the branch in Lewisham, south London, and renamed it 'The Tabernacle', thereby obliterating historical and visible distinctions. This process is by no means only a British phenomenon. In the USA, other prominent preachers have also abandoned the Oneness label in order to reach wider audiences: for example Bishop T D Jakes of the Potters House; and Bishop Noel Jones of the Greater Bethany Fellowship Church, who was the star in Sophia Phines' film *Hoover Street Revival*.

Sabbatarianism

The controversy surrounding Sabbatarianism is similar to that over Unitarianism. During the 1830s William Miller, a Baptist minister in New York, prophesied that Christ would return between 1843 and 1844. When this prediction did not occur, Miller revised his date to 22 October 1844. Once again, Miller's followers (Millerites) were disheartened and the 'Great Disappointment' that followed caused the church to split, with Miller accepting his error and leaving the movement.[10] The name 'Seventh-day Adventist Church' was finally adopted in 1860, and the church was incorporated in 1863 with around 3,500 members in 125 congregations.[11]

By far the area of greatest concern is the Adventists' view of Ellen G Harmon White, as the development and very existence of Adventism is incomprehensible apart from Mrs White and her large number of writings. During her lifetime, she is credited with writing over 46 books totalling some 25 million words, which touched virtually every area of Adventist belief and practice.[12] No Christian leader or theologian has exerted so great an influence on a denomination. The wider church felt that the Adventists were according White's publications a status superior to the Bible, and that her status as a 'messenger' implied much more than simply being a disseminator of God's truth. However, the official view of the Adventist church has now fallen in line with orthodox Christian thinking. While White is still regarded as a prophetess, Scripture is affirmed as the church's standard. However, members are said to be able to understand the Bible better after reading her work.[13]

There were additional causes of concern for orthodox Christians, to the point where Adventism was at one time classified as a cult. First, the Adventist doctrine of 'investigative judgement' seemed to indicate the existence of a two-stage redemption. Here the belief is that, in 1844, Christ entered the heavenly sanctuary – 'the true tabernacle which the Lord set up and not man' – to begin the second and final stage of his atonement ministry.[14] 'In this act he reviews the deeds of professing Christians to determine whose names should be included in the Book of Life.'[15] Some believe this doctrine was invented to save face after the

Great Disappointment, others that it undermines the completed work of Christ on the cross. There is also the view that it diminishes the reality of justification by grace alone, and encourages the notion of salvation through perfect obedience.[16]

Yet another contentious belief is that relating to the scapegoat in Leviticus 16:8; the Adventist view is that it represents Satan and not Christ. Since the cleansing of the sanctuary required two goats – the Lord's goat and the scapegoat – the interpretation is that Christ was the sacrificial Lamb and Satan will be the eschatological scapegoat. This will lead 'to the final end of the sin problem' – the banishment of sin and Satan. The full accountability for sin will be rolled back upon Satan, its originator and instigator. Satan, his followers and all the effects of sin will be banished from the universe by destruction.[17] Critics of this belief argue that Satan has no part to play in salvation. Adventists have responded by saying that their view is a symbolic one:[18]

> For most Seventh-day Adventists the identification of Azazel [the scape-goat] is an obscure side issue. Whatever the truth of the matter we certainly do not accept that Satan is in any sense involved in our salvation.

Equally fraught is the belief that Sunday worshippers 'will eventually receive the mark of the Beast' if they do not worship on the Sabbath. By implication, therefore, those who continue to worship on Sunday will be placed under the control of Satan and be disqualified from heaven:[19]

> . . . the Sabbath versus Sunday question will become a key issue in Christianity. When it does then Christians will have to make a choice as to which side they are on. It is this decision, choosing to obey God or not to obey Him that we think will eventually determine who has the 'mark of the beast'. We don't claim to have reached that time yet and we certainly would not say that any truly born again Christian who is currently worshipping on a Sunday has the 'mark of the beast' or is under Satan's influence. However, we would ask our fellow Christians to think about the question of the Sabbath.

Adventists, as with many of the other denominations mentioned in this book, have had periods in their history where exclusivity, obscure doctrines and theological and biblical errors have been their main preoccupation. However, there is evidence of change. The application of theological rigour has led to clarification of a number of divisive doctrines, leading many to identify large sections of the Adventist church as an important part of conservative evangelicalism.

Prosperity theology

Prosperity theology has turned out to be one of the most divisive theologies in the BMCs. It has its genesis in what is often referred to as the 'Word of Faith' movement. The term 'prosperity theology' was not one that was actually coined by the so-called 'prosperity teachers' but rather by its critics, who are usually middle-class, economically secure, and who would probably, by virtue of their churchmanship or theological allegiance, take a different position from their opposition on a wide range of issues. The objective consideration of this subject has not been helped by the dogmatic stance adopted by either its proponents or its critics. Frequently, prosperity theology has been portrayed as an abusive theology that uses Scripture out of context, making promises to vulnerable and gullible people, with the sole aim of profiting its proponents and prophets. It is not surprising, therefore, that it has drawn fire as the 'name it and claim it' or 'blab it and grab it' gospel – a rather unfortunate approach to a theological position that is in fact seeking to take certain, often neglected, aspects of Scripture seriously.[20]

Properly considered, 'prosperity theology', as its name suggests, is concerned with a fundamental human problem: what does a God – who owns all things, knows all things and controls all things – have to say to the poor, the disenfranchised, the downtrodden and the socially excluded, those who find themselves in a rut and feel that only a miracle, wherever it comes from, can make a difference? Is the 'divine exchange' at the cross, where Christ took our place, of no consequence to our lives apart from the salvation of the soul? Are we not marginalising and misrepresenting the Christian faith if we close off salvation from the cares of this life?

It would not be unreasonable to think of prosperity theology as being at the opposite end of the theological spectrum to liberation theology. While liberation theology starts from the point of the individual's experience and then explores what Scripture has to say about that experience, prosperity theology has its origin in Scripture and seeks to ensure that the individual's experiences matches what God has already declared it should be in his word. Both theologies seek the same basic objectives:

- to highlight, from Scripture, God's deep concern for the poor, the marginalised, the rejected, the suffering and the outsider;
- to renounce poverty as a quasi-blessing or a curse deserved by people from particular ethnic groups or geographical locations, or a specific tribe, caste or class;
- to dispel the myth that humanity's hope for the future rests only in our eschatological hope – when Jesus returns and we experience a new life in heaven. Instead, both theologies proclaim that we can and must experience God's fullness and blessings now, in this life, as well as in the future;
- to challenge people's negative perceptions of themselves, their circumstances and their future, and to offer hope in place of despair.

Where the two theologies part company is in their response to social, economic and political structures. Proponents of prosperity theology seem to be very favourable towards the idea that capitalist ideology, infrastructure and methodology can be used as vehicles for change. Unlike liberation theologians, they do not see identifying with the poor and disenfranchised to mean becoming one with them; rather, the emphasis is on transformation and transportation – that is, a change in circumstances and change in location, if that is what is needed. In other words, there are no 'Mother Teresas' here. Another area of difference is that prosperity theology focuses on the individual's ability to respond positively to his or her own plight. Not much is made of capitalism's discriminating structures, economic policies and political bias in favour of wealth. The desire is to share in economic prosperity in spite of how it is generated.

Some of this theology's key doctrines include the following:

- *Sowing and reaping:* The measure you sow is the measure you will reap (2 Corinthians 9:6; compare with 1 Corinthians 9:14). Giving with a willing heart is a prerequisite for blessing, as God loves a cheerful giver (2 Corinthians 9:7). This also includes the promise of a hundred-fold blessing (Matthew 19:29; Mark 10:30).
- *Covenant:* The believer is the seed of Abraham and therefore an inheritor with him of the promise. Although we have a better covenant in Christ, God did not cancel the old covenant; rather he made it available to the whole world through the death of Christ (Romans 4:11–12; Galatians 3:16–17,29).
- *Being the head and not the tail:* The believer is encouraged to see himself or herself as the leader of the pack, victorious and successful. This theme

is amplified in areas such as being overcomers rather than the overcome (2 Peter 2:19), and being 'more than conquerors' (Romans 8:37).

- *Blessing and cursing:* There is a blessing available to the righteous and a curse for those who reject God's way (Proverbs 10:6,22,29)
- *Divine wealth transfer:* The wealth of the wicked is being stored up for the righteous.

To live by these principles, believers need *the anointing of the Holy Spirit* (Acts 2), *the revelation of the Holy Spirit* (Ephesians 1:17), *the power of the Holy Spirit* (Acts 3:1-8), and *the divine favour and provision of the Lord* in their lives (Acts 2:44-47). God's favour is the basis for blessing, success in every area of life and the courage to pursue, against the odds, your purpose and destiny until you overcome and are victorious. God's blessing can extend from individuals (Psalm 1:1) to whole nations (Psalm 33:12).

In general, prosperity is seen as having an holistic dimension: for true prosperity to be achieved, the believer should exhibit faithfulness, obedience to God, dying to self, the renewing of the mind, holiness, righteousness and doing God's will. However, there is justification for some of the criticisms that have been meted out to aspects of prosperity teaching:

- Making every issue a spiritual battle between good and evil on the one hand generates an 'opposition mentality' and removes personal responsibility to the point where the believer becomes fatalistic - if something happens then it must have been God's will. This goes against the core teachings in prosperity theology.
- Prosperity theology can generate an irresponsible approach to ministry. Often leaders and their ministries are direct beneficiaries, and this raises huge issues around motives and conflict of interest. It also means that less care and attention is given to prudence, as the body of Christ is there to underwrite every adventure or misadventure.
- Despite the obvious blessings that believers receive from the constant challenge to change their mindset, there is often little generosity of spirit towards those who do not measure up to 'the measure of faith' so as to bring about transformation in their own circumstances.
- There is little critique within the movement itself when their adherents are either proven to be deceptive, exploitative, or lacking in integrity, or misappropriate resources.
- Finally, it is not enough to ignore biblical scholarship or hermeneutics because it suits the movement's purposes. Consistency must be maintained in the understanding and application of Scripture.

Fundamentally, prosperity theology has highlighted an area of Scripture that the church has neglected; unfortunately, in so doing, it has become reactionary and dogmatic. Even so, it has a significant sociological and physiological part to play in the life of the church. It generates what is often referred to as 'redemptive lift' which changes the socio-economic standing of an individual or family because they have made different life choices.

> Beloved, I pray that you may prosper in all things and be in health, just as your soul prospers.
>
> (3 John 2)

Endnotes

1 G Walters and Bruce Milne, 'Salvation', in *The Illustrated Bible Dictionary*, vol. 3, InterVarsity Press, 1998, p173.

2 J D G Dunn, 'Baptism', in *Illustrated Bible Dictionary*, vol. 1, p1371.

3 Joel Edwards, 'The Pulpit Response to Worship', in *Let's Praise Him Again: An African Caribbean Perspective on Worship*, Kingsway, 1992.

4 Edwards, 'Pentecostal Distinctives', in *Let's Praise Him Again*.

5 Mark Sturge, 'Black Churches' Worship UK', in Paul F Bradshaw (ed.), *The New SCM Dictionary of Liturgy and Worship*, SCM Press, 2002, p61–2.

6 'Pastoral covering' takes many forms. It could be a mentor, or an individual or group who offers prayer, spiritual and emotional support. It could also be a fraternity to which the individual is accountable, or with which he or she forms an alliance in order to enhance the credibility of their organisation, receive support and affirmation.

7 C G Singer, 'Unitarianism', in Walter A Elwell (ed.), *Evangelical Dictionary of Theology*, Paternoster, 1995, p1126.

8 Singer, p1126.

9 Statement of Faith, Church of our Lord Jesus Christ of the Apostolic Faith; available at **www.cooljc.org/Faith_Mission/faith.html**

10 M E Dieter, 'Adventism', in Elwell, p15.

11 *Encyclopedia of American Religion*, vol. 2, p681; in Dave Cave, 'Fundamental Beliefs of the Seventh-day Adventist Church', unpublished paper, 12 May 2001.

12 Cave, 'Fundamental Beliefs'.

13 For further information on the beliefs and practices of the Seventh-day Adventist Church, see their website at **www.adventistinfo.org.uk/about/fundamen.php**

14 No. 23 of the Fundamental Beliefs; see Ministerial Association of Seventh-day Adventists, *Seventh-day Adventists Believe: A Biblical Exposition of 27 Fundamental Doctrines*, General Conference of Seventh-day Adventists, p312; in Cave, 'Fundamental Beliefs'.

15 Dieter, p16.

16 Dieter, p16.

17 *Seventh-day Adventists Believe*, p318–319; in Cave, 'Fundamental Beliefs'.

18 Answer to Question No. 6 in 'Answers to Some Questions on Seventh-day Adventist Doctrine', *Fundamental Beliefs*; available at **www.adventistinfo.org.uk/about/fundamen.php**

19 Answer to Question No. 5, *Fundamental Beliefs*.

20 The Evangelical Alliance (UK) Commission on Unity and Truth among Evangelicals (ACUTE) carried out one of the most comprehensive studies done on prosperity theology. *Faith, Health and Prosperity: A report on 'Word of Faith' and 'Positive Confession' Theologies* was an attempt to bridge an increasing polarisation and impasse between British evangelicals, as evidenced by the explosive expulsion of Morris Cerullo's World Evangelism Outreach and the resignation of Kensington Temple from the EA. The establishment of the Pentecostal Churches in the United Kingdom (PCUK) closely followed these withdrawals. There were also major concerns over the future and direction of the British church. Clearly the opponents of prosperity theology were losing ground and influence to the fastest growing churches. ACUTE's intervention was timely. By bringing the various sides together to present their perspectives, it became evident that much more work was needed to inform the wider debate. My primary concern about the final report is that the passions, fallout and ill-feeling that preceded it skewed its conclusion. Last-minute changes, including stronger condemnatory language, became tools to appease opponents, which in turn diluted the overall evidence that there is an intrinsic and essential basis in Scripture for the proclamations of the Word of Faith movement. This is true, even though they sometimes overemphasise, exaggerate or use Scripture out of context.

Part 3
In search of unity

Chapter 9

Race, reconciliation and partnership

Calling it what it is

Christians and their representative organisations usually talk about unity and reconciliation in glowing terms. For many, it is a noble pursuit that we should all work towards whenever the opportunity arises. Others, it seems, only want to talk about unity when they are trying to persuade you to take up or participate in their pet initiative. However, frequently when Christians use terms like 'unity' and 'reconciliation', they are in fact seeking to avoid an unfortunate fact – namely, that churches are often divided, both within themselves and from each other. Time and again, instead of 'endeavoring to keep the unity of the Spirit in the bond of peace' (Ephesians 4:3), they lack coherence in their message, seek to devalue the efforts of others or, at best, merely accommodate one another in order to further their own agenda. In this way, they violate their ethos as the body of Christ. The unpleasantness, anxiety and conflicts that are stirred up whenever an attempt is made to address Christian disunity have led the churches to confine themselves to talking only about mutual aspirations and goals. Notions of unity and reconciliation seem utopian dreams to be abandoned because they appear unreal, impractical or impossible to attain.

The rest of society, on the other hand, talks continually about racism, homophobia, Islamophobia, sexism and xenophobia, regarding these as emotive issues in need of immediate redress. In fact, they are human rights. The least that every human being on this earth can expect is to be accepted and treated with dignity and respect. Yet the church, the one institution overtly charged with the responsibility of restoring God's image in humanity, has been lethargic and negligent when dealing with discrimination and prejudice within its ranks and within society. What is more, the BMCs have provided little or no leadership in this area. The level of pastoral care to deal with racism, both in society and in the church, is abysmal. It is a badly kept secret that, while many BMC leaders privately discuss racism and its impact on society, they feel too constrained to mention it in public; instead, they either adopt a neutral posture, ignore the issue as though it does not exist, or at best, say a few lines about God's justice in their prayers. Few have equipped their congregations with a biblical perspective on justice, and how to recognise and pursue it in their daily lives. Worse still, a faith that is often focused on righteousness does not even teach about ethics – an issue that is seen as the preserve of theological colleges.

The primary reasons I assume for such reluctance is 'What if'. What if I offend the one White member of my congregation? What if a White person walks into my church or prayer meeting and hears these issues being discussed? These worries are as much a sign of insecurity as insincerity: insecurity because, despite our proclamations, we value our reputation or others' perceptions of us far above the pursuit of righteousness; insincerity because we profess one thing in private and another in public. In addition, we are ignoring one of the most soul-destroying aspects of the lives of Black church members and communities. The BMCs' silence has prolonged the cancer of racism and prejudice in UK society.

The nature of racism in Britain

Very few people will readily accept that they are racist. Many point to the fact that they have friends or know people from other ethnic backgrounds, as evidence of their antiracist credentials. Yet, being racist or committing racist acts are not necessarily rational processes. In fact, a significant characteristic of racism is that it cannot be understood or defended rationally. Neither is racism the preserve of the White Majority population: minority communities can be racist against each other in equal measure, and may even be racist against White people. Some may argue that this type of 'reverse racism' is to be expected after a group has endured centuries of discrimination, injustice and prejudice. What is different, however, is that minority communities in Britain do not have the power or opportunity to make their racism a tool of oppression or one with such devastating and adverse effects on so many people. Having said so, the bombing of the Twin Towers in New York on 11 September 2001 has highlighted the evil that people are prepared to inflict on each other in order to make their case. So, we must conclude that wherever racism is found it is wrong and incompatible with the Christian faith and witness to the world. Racism is sin.

For me, racism is an inbred attitude based on assumptions, prejudices and stereotypes that are applied wholesale to an entire people group, which thereby disadvantages, excludes and negatively discriminates against them. Racism is an attitude rather than an act because it is intrinsic to a culture's traditions, social arrangements, policies, processes, education and faith, as well as to its development as a society. As a result, I take the view that unless and until someone has clearly denounced racism and has opted out of a racist culture, they remain, essentially, racist. Furthermore, I would describe Britain as 'a PART society': by this I mean that it is '**p**redatory', '**a**dversarial', '**r**acist' and '**t**erritorial'.

British culture is predatory in the way that it conducts business and enterprise, which are often seen as the wheels driving the economy, indeed the whole country. The aim always seems to be to marginalise, subsume or consume our competitors. Market forces are the new gods which we spend our whole lives trying to appease. The reality is that this is a greedy, selfish and dangerous ideology which is endemic in boardrooms of all shapes and sizes, up and down the land.

British society is adversarial in the way that it conducts a good deal of public life. The legal and education systems as well as the media are based on adversarial principles: discovering the truth is often not the main issue; rather, it is all about winning the argument and, more often than not, the one who is better at manipulating the circumstances seems to come out on top. Theological institutions are no different: more books are written with the aim of rebutting or refuting someone else's argument than of offering fresh thinking and a new perspective.

That Britain is racist is personified in the death of Stephen Lawrence, the young Black teenager who was murdered in 1993 by thugs in Eltham, south London. The circumstances of his killing, and the poorly conducted police investigation that followed, led to a public inquiry into the issue, overseen by Sir William Macpherson of Cluny. At the end of the Inquiry, Macpherson produced a report telling the nation that Britain as a society was *institutionally racist*, by which he meant:[1]

> The collective failure of an organisation to provide an appropriate and professional service to people because of their colour, culture, or ethnic origin. It can be seen or detected in processes, attitudes and behaviour which amount to discrimination through unwitting prejudice, ignorance, thoughtlessness and racist stereotyping which disadvantage minority ethnic people.

Macpherson defines racism in general terms as 'conduct, or words or practices which disadvantage or advantage people because of their colour, culture or ethnic origin. In its most subtle form it is as damaging as in its overt form'.[2] Since the Stephen Lawrence Inquiry, many British institutions have acknowledged the existence of institutional racism within their practices, but there is little or no consensus on how to rectify the problem.

British society is also very territorial in nature. There is the saying, 'An Englishman's home is his castle', and 'Nimby-ism' ('Not in my back yard') is a common factor when new communities or environmental issues are introduced to neighbourhoods, towns or cities. Yet most people in Britain are happy to enjoy the positive outcomes of globalisation, either as investors, tourists or the beneficiaries of cheaper prices in the supermarkets, and give little consideration to the effects on poorer developing nations. Trade tariffs, foreign subsidies and the flooding of cheap exports on to their local markets neutralise or cripple any economic advantages poor countries are likely to get from producing their own goods and services. It is in this context that minority communities live. They are the ones who subsidise the economies of the developing world, by offering financial and other forms of support to families, friends, communities and countries from which they came.

Yet how can racism ever be justified when half of all African Caribbean men born in Britain, and one-third of African Caribbean women, are in relationships with White partners?[3] If these couples can commit to affectionate love and allow themselves to be intimately vulnerable with each other, then living in harmony and respecting each other as communities should not remain unachievable. And in case you are tempted to think that interracial relationships must therefore be the solution then ask yourself the question, can we only to accept each other if we 'blend' each other out of existence?

God's shame: a biblical perspective on race

To develop a godly perspective on racism, I have chosen to focus on one event in Scripture. The Old Testament book of Numbers, there is, I feel, a clear indictment against racism (Numbers ch 12) when Moses, God's chosen leader and judge of Israel, was severely criticised because he had married an Ethiopian (Black) woman (v 1, NKJV). Painfully for Moses, the source of this attack was his siblings – his older brother, Aaron, and sister, Miriam. They contended that his marriage was evidence that he was not as close to God as he portrayed and, by implication, was the reason for his lack of judgement. They were therefore not prepared to follow his leadership.

God, however, viewed this rebellion as serious enough to summon the three of them to an emergency meeting (v 4). He severely rebuked Aaron and Miriam, and affirmed Moses' pre-eminent standing with him (vs 6–8). This alone more or less amounts to a vote of confidence on Moses' choice of bride, but the events that followed provide yet greater confirmation of God's endorsement of Moses' authority as a leader and decision-maker. God was ashamed of Miriam and Aaron, and, in his anger, did the equivalent of turning his back and walking away (v 9). Then, as punishment for her vindictive attitude, Miriam became 'leprous' – a condition that meant she must be excluded from her society (v 10).

In an instant, Miriam lost all her influence and authority along with her personal dignity. She had to remember again what it meant to be a 'nobody' and an outsider, just as she had been when she was a slave in Egypt (Numbers 12:11,12,15; Exodus 2:8). Moses is gracious enough to plead with God on behalf of his sister, but God's response implied that her offence was equivalent to that which would cause a father to spit in his daughter's face (Numbers 12:14): these words imply that God found Miriam's racist attitude totally abhorrent and thereby set a precedent within Israelite society that they should not take it upon themselves to discriminate and abuse the foreign peoples they encountered both in their wanderings in the desert and later when they had settled in the promised land. By sending such a strong message to the leadership of this fledgling nation, God ensured that Israel was given no leeway to discriminate or to reject the 'aliens and strangers' in their society (Exodus 22:21).[4]

The relationship between Black and White Christians

Any commentary on the state of the relationship between Black and White Christians can only be spoken of in general terms – mainly because there are often remarkable exceptions to the rule, for which credit must be given. So what follows is intended to provide an overall survey of the general 'state of play' rather than a detailed critique of the relations between Black and White Christians.

At the heart of many of the partnerships forged between Black and White Majority churches are organisations such as ACEA, the now defunct Centre for Black and White Christian Partnerships (in Birmingham) and the Evangelical Alliance (EA); there have also been invaluable contributions from the CCRJ, a CTBI Commission, and Contrast (in Nottingham), among others. Another avenue for unity and reconciliation is the existence of the Churches Together ecumenical groups, which are found in cities and boroughs throughout England under the guidance of Churches Together in England (CTE). There are also Local Evangelical Fellowships which bring evangelical churches together, as well as the borough deans' networks and numerous fraternities which seek to bring about unity between Black and White Christians as a sign of Christian witness to the world. Outside of these structures are initiatives such as Soul in the City which brings churches together to undertake social responsibility projects as a form of Christian witness.

However, the major challenge for ecumenical organisations is that they have yet to engage in a meaningful way with the larger BMCs and their denominations. This is not for want of trying. However, the criteria they have set up for churches wanting to join them have presented inherent difficulties for BMCs. First, churches must have a minimum membership of 2,000 people; and, secondly, as there is no theological assessment for participation, there can also be no theological basis for exclusion, even when a church falls outside accepted biblical orthodoxy. The ultra-liberal approach of the Quakers and other historic denominations to Scripture and issues relating to the African and Caribbean Spiritual Churches have not been addressed by CTBI and CTE. Yet it is possible to argue that forging a partnership does not require looking for agreement on every point, but rather to find those areas that will strengthen the union and to ensure that the perspectives of all are taken into account whenever dialogue takes place.

Despite the efforts of organisations like CTBI and CTE to tackle the problems of unity, injustice and racism, one of the consistent features is their inability to retain the unwavering commitment of the BMCs to this process. A key reason is the failure of CTBI to take an holistic approach to tackling these issues. During the 1980s and early 1990s, many White leaders felt that it was right to seek forgiveness – from Black Christians in general, and BMCs in particular – for past hurts and the historic rejection that was meted out to some of them. Unfortunately, more often than not, Black church leaders felt extremely uncomfortable by such actions, as they had already become reconciled to these issues within themselves. There was also the question as to why it was necessary to 'hold a conference' in order to demonstrate remorse. While the sincerity of these attempts at repentance are not in doubt, the expected outcomes in terms of relationships, acceptance and support are often missing. Equally, the Black Christians' response can really be no different than that of Christ: you are forgiven; 'go and sin no more' (John 8:11).

Another difficulty for Black leaders in dealing with racism and injustice is when it is personified. It is easy to speak about such sensitive issues in general terms, but when it comes to actually confronting an individual or group over their demeaning and disrespectful behaviour towards another people group, some simply prefer to walk away – too much painful emotion is involved. Recently, I was in a mixed audience of both Black and White leaders, some of whom were bishops and the leaders of denominations. However, when the host of this gathering, who was White, got up to speak, he was very disrespectful, calling all African leaders 'thieves' and accusing them of dishonesty. It was a breath of fresh air to see another leader get up and challenge his attitude. As one of the guest speakers myself, I added my rebuttal and affirmations; but I was left thinking – how could our people stoop so low! No way I am going to accept another invitation from that quarter without an unreserved apology and assurance that this will never happen again. Even more recently I was in another setting, in London, in which the matter of faith communities and their representation in the wider community was being discussed. Again, many prominent Christians, Black and White, were present when an archdeacon from the Church of England remarked, 'The trouble is that you Black churches can't get your act together.' The incensed debate that followed detracted from the fact that the meeting was about encouraging a cohesive witness from faith communities in their local areas. It is the endeavour to avoid such confrontations that has led many Black church leaders to avoid making themselves vulnerable through involvement in situations like these.

Many BMCs have also avoided getting involved in Racial Justice Sunday, which takes place on the second or third Sunday of September each year, and Black History Month, which has become a national celebration of the contributions and achievements of Black people in Britain. Instead, these events have become mainly the pursuit of the historic denominations. Then, as is often the case, when BMCs do decide to become involved in these events, they find that they have fallen so far behind that, to do justice to the process, they must rely on others for expertise and resources. Thus the cycle of dependency continues, and the churches forfeit the opportunity to take the lead on this critical issue.

The issue of racism has now become so explosive that those in positions of authority often find it extremely difficult to implement the necessary changes without offending either themselves or the wider White majority. It becomes a matter of 'Sed quis custodiet ipsos custodes?' – who will police the policeman and who will judge the judge? Whenever a key policy is about to be announced by government, it is preceded by a draconian measure to tackle crime, drugs or some other issue that has particular resonance with minority ethnic communities: the government seems always to have first to demonstrate that they are nasty and unsympathetic to minorities in order to do what is right and just for them.

More recently, we have seen a shift in the use of the 'R' word. 'Racism' as a term is no longer fashionable or palatable, and has been replaced with the 'D' word, 'diversity'. To my mind, all this amounts to is a repackaging of wrongdoing in order to rend it no longer offensive. But dealing honestly with the issue of racism need not be offensive. 'Speaking the truth in love' will only offend if the search for truth comes at the expense of seeking to love; but if the main motivation is love, then love should be able to constrain any anger, resentment, bitterness, ego trip and superiority complex that might come from knowing either that one is sinned against, or any guilt that one is the sinner.

How then should churches be responding? In Chapter 4, which explored issues around the homogeneous church, I argued that Jesus' parable of the wine and the wineskins demonstrates that it was impossible for a church to accommodate the freshness and new things that God is doing when it resists every opportunity to change and evolve. The mission of the church is to make disciples of every people group: Christians, like Jesus' disciples, are charged with the responsibility of going to the whole world and preaching the whole gospel (Matthew 28:18–20). It would be ironic, then, that we should be happy to go, to send our resources or even to support others in their going, and yet resent it when potential converts arrive on our doorstep. Church growth depends on the influx of new people who are sensitive to the things of God, as it is they who tend to rekindle the sparks of excitement in the daily walk with God of their 'older' brothers and sisters in Christ.

To be welcoming is imperative for mission for other reasons. It demonstrates Christ's love for his world, and provides opportunities for the church to be Christ-like and countercultural instead of 'going with the flow'. When, as Christians, we support the vulnerable, the fatherless and the victims of disastrous circumstances, we may, unwittingly, entertain

God's angels (Genesis 18:1–8; Hebrews 13:2). Such acts of kindness provide us with concrete opportunities to 'love our neighbours as ourselves' (Mark 12:31); they remove us from the ranks of the priest and the Levite, and make us more like the good Samaritan (Luke 10:30–37). In so doing, God's justice is established, and the barriers of suspicion, fear and resentment are broken down.

The second imperative is to reject tokenism. Often when organisations start to worry about 'unity' and 'building bridges', their first impulse is to get a Black or other minority ethnic person onto their committee or board. Although this is a noble aspiration, it is a fundamentally flawed approach and usually bears little fruit. There may be little or no examination of the reasons why the status quo existed as it did for so long. No one seems interested in unearthing the barriers to participation and engagement, or what the likely consequences will be if they ignore them. Consequently, the contribution of Black members on the committees and boards is diminished. A senior White church leader once told me that the reason Black Christians are often not invited to join committees is that 'they couldn't sit through meetings'. With attitudes like this around, any moves towards Black inclusion can only be regarded as at best superficial, and at worst insulting.

Of equal significance are the experiences of those who dare to expose themselves to these situations. Some are selected because they are pleasant and nice individuals who will not, or who feel unable to, challenge the status quo. Some are chosen because an existing member knows them, even though they are not representatives of any constituency and so are unable to influence, encourage or secure wider participation from their community. What is worse is the assumption that, once a Black person joins a committee, then he or she is an 'expert' on Black or minority ethnic affairs. This puts undue pressure on the individual and, at the same time, limits his or her competence to race and race-related issues. Rather than being given the opportunity to contribute their real professional expertise and, in so doing, add value to the organisation or group, they are instead marginalised to an issue that they may in fact have no interest in, or at least not feel competent to take the lead on. I have refused on numerous occasions to join committees which, on my first meeting with them, started with something like this: 'We are delighted to have Mark with us. He will be our ethnic minority representative'. Obviously, this is fine if their agenda is to explore some common goal; however, when it is just 'business as usual', it simply will not do.

A good way to understand the fundamental dilemma we face when we want to form real partnerships is to illustrate it by referring to an episode from *Tonight*, an American television show, hosted by Jay Leno. In this particular episode, Leno wanted to introduce the poorest person in the world to the richest person in the world. They found a grandfather in his seventies in Mexico and concluded that they would introduce him to Bill Gates, the founder and owner of Microsoft Corporation. Wearing his tee shirt clearly marked 'Poorest man in the world', the man was taken to Microsoft's headquarters in Silicon Valley. As expected, Bill Gates did not return the compliment by turning up; instead, a member of the public relations team offered the man a Coke and wished him all the best.

This episode left a lasting impression on my mind. What if Bill Gates had turned up? Supposing the poorest and the richest men in the world had decided to enter into a partnership to tackle the issue of poverty in the world. How would the poor man have ensured that his perspective and contribution were taken seriously? The reality is that all the coordination, administration, public relations, human resources, premises and finances would have to have been supplied by Microsoft. In so doing, it would be impossible to ever have an equitable approach to the delivery of the hoped-for outcomes. Not until the poor man has aides and resources of the same calibre of expertise as Microsoft would it be possible for him to have a genuinely equal and viable partnership with Bill Gates. Alternatively, Bill Gates would have to be the one to recognise the full implications of his powerful position, and make the effort to ensure that the poor man is treated equitably, or else disadvantage would undermine the entire process. BMCs should therefore be continually seeking to build their capacity in every area of church life so that they can enter any room with their White counterparts as equals.

Partnership between Black and White Christians

In thinking about how Black and White Christians can work together in partnership, one approach that I would reject is one that reduces Black participation to a mere 'blot' on a 'white canvas' – I call this the 'Dalmatian Effect or Co-opting model' (see Figure 1). In this model, the contribution of Black Christians is scattered, isolated and patchy, and led totally by the agenda of the White majority. The 'baggy' edges of the model suggest the lack of coherent framework or clear understanding of how the partnership should work. This model tends to happen when the goals and objectives of the lead organisation are fixed, and there is no intention of reviewing them in the light of discovering the needs or circumstances of their Black members. Instead, I would advocate a partnership that operates on the basis of covenant, rather like that of a marriage. What I call the 'Partnership or Inclusive model' acknowledges the difference and distinctiveness of each group (see Figure 2). Each can bring something valuable to the mix and has a valuable contribution to make. Individuals are encouraged to maximise their participation and involvement, and are supported in doing that. Everyone has the opportunity to grow and develop, and no one need betray or stifle his or her individuality, personality or priorities in order to belong. Neither is there a demand on participants to assimilate or conform to the status quo.

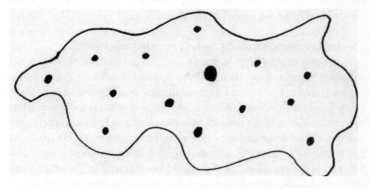

The Dalmatian Effect or Co-opting Model

The Partnership or Inclusive Model

ACEA has already learned many of these lessons in attempting to bring Black and White Majority churches together, and in seeking to engage with government departments, the Mayor of London and local councils. If anything, secular society is doing a better job than the church, not because it has higher and better values, but because it has made it mandatory that anyone receiving any form of support or grants must demonstrate fairness and openness. Possibly, these issues are discussed more openly in secular circles than in the church. People call it what it is and how they perceive it affects them.

A partnership model: the African and Caribbean Evangelical Alliance and the Evangelical Alliance

The relationship that exists between ACEA and EA offers one model for the pursuit of unity and partnership between Black and White Christians. Here are some key aspects of that partnership which, in my view, are essential for successful relationships.

Identifying common needs and aspirations together

ACEA began when Philip Mohabir and other leaders of the 'Black-led' churches, as they were then known, approached EA to express their concern about the lack of representation, recognition and support offered to Black churches. At that time, only one 'Black-led' church had become a member of EA since its inception in 1848.[5] The primary concern was that there was an emerging gulf between Black and White Christians. Black leaders were of the view that if something was not done at that time, then the church in the UK would be divided. On the other hand, EA wanted to develop relationships with these churches. Nothing could have been more profound than this insight and leadership. Identifying their common need provided both organisations with the basis for working towards shared goals and a set of strategic objectives. In April 1984, the West Indian Evangelical Alliance (WIEA) was formed.

Securing the involvement and blessing of key leaders

Among the key members at the beginning were Bishop Selwyn Arnold, National Overseer of the NTCOG; Bishop Melville Powell and Bishop Donald Bernard of the New Testament Assembly; Bishop Lovell Bent of the New Life Assembly; Bishop Eunice Mclean and Overseer Simpson of Light and Life Full Gospel Church; Bishop Oswald Williams of the COGOP; the Reverend Peter Burger and Philip Mohabir. They worked closely with the support and encouragement of the Reverend Clive Calver, the General Director of EA from 1984 to 1996. This level of involvement and participation offered a degree of ownership to the initiative, and represented a significant cohesive voice.

Clarifying the aspirations of both sides

The WIEA was established as a separate entity to EA, with Philip Mohabir appointed as its first Chairman. It later became a charitable organisation in its own right, with its own council and trustees. This ensured that the BMCs were entering into a partnership that facilitated their priorities, including promoting unity between BMCs and supporting their development. It was also about ensuring that the public perception of these churches was correct, and that the churches themselves could contribute effectively both to society and the wider church. From EA's perspective, it was important to build relationships with the new and emerging BMCs, as such a partnership meant strengthening what was an already powerful voice in mainstream evangelicalism. A helpful metaphor to understand the relationship between WIEA and EA is one I have used before, that of a marriage between two distinct groups of peoples who have covenanted their future together. This relationship exists through the fundamental belief that the best Christian witness is visible when Christians love, respect and value each other and the world around them.

Resourcing the work

EA was instrumental in supporting the work of WIEA (later ACEA) by paying the salaries of its General Director and a part-time secretary. It also provided office space and a car free of charge, and, in the early years, covered the WIEA's administrative costs. It is safe to say that, without these provisions, ACEA would not be around today. For its part, ACEA encouraged the BMCs to engage with the wider evangelical family and to identify with common concerns, including that they should become members of both alliances. There were opportunities to bring together disparate groups within the BMCs, and to encourage them to work together in areas of common concern. Moreover, ACEA became a pre-eminent voice for the BMCs, articulating their concerns and perspectives on key issues in the media and as part of their participation in the national forum, consultations and debates. As a result, the evangelical voice in the UK was enhanced.

Demonstrating the essence of partnership

In every sense, this partnership was an historic one, not only for the African Caribbean Christian community but also for the Christian community in Britain as a whole. It acted as a focal point for dialogue with Black Christians: prior to ACEA, the AWUCOC – the lead organisation for bringing together Black-led churches – was entering its death throes.

Even at this point, the 'Black-led' churches were an unrecognised entity, considered at best to be fundamentalist and at worst to be sects; they were certainly not considered evangelical. Nevertheless, although Mohabir was small in stature, he had the longest embrace you are likely to find in a Christian leader, and his passion for building bridges between Black and White Christians was infectious. These gifts allowed him to become an effective ambassador for Black Christians to both the historic denominations and the new church movements. In addition, members of ACEA's executive served on EA's council, and its General Secretary on EA's senior management team. In 1987, the Reverend Joel Edwards was appointed ACEA's first General Secretary (Philip Mohabir had used the title of 'Chairman'). Working strategically in a part-time capacity, Edwards introduced the work of the Alliance to the newly formed churches from the African diasporas. His gifting in promoting unity was recognised by EA which, in 1993, created a new post for him as their UK Director of Development. Eventually, in 1997, he was invited to serve as their General Director. It could be argued that if the only reason ACEA existed was to make room for a General Director to emerge from the ranks of the BMCs, then it has performed a noble task.

Undertaking regular reviews of the partnership

One of the weaknesses of the partnership between EA and ACEA was that it failed to carry out regular reviews of how the partnership was working – although there were reviews on staff performance and around the work itself. This came about mainly because there were no written agreements or 'Memoranda of Understanding'. It would not be fair or right to suggest that the partnership was founded only on 'a gentleman's agreement': there was a more fundamental issue. Although these were two separate organisations, for years their personnel and financial management operated as if they were one and the same. This lack of partnership parameters meant that no track was kept as to how the common objectives were being achieved, nor was attention given to what was needed to ensure that aspirations were on course. Instead, what transpired were unilateral adjustments from EA, seemingly to reflect changing times and circumstances, but in reality, evidence of an increasing lack of confidence in the partnership by some members of EA's senior staff and ACEA's Council.

Retaining independence

Integrity in any partnership demands that both sides are able to maintain their independence to some degree. This is essential if they are to remain objective and have the ability to critically appraise each other. Independence also gives confidence to members that the relationship is not reduced to one characterised by paternalism or the sense that 'Big Brother is watching you'. ACEA achieved this by developing its own programmes and operating on parallel tracks to EA. It sought to improve its management and governance on an ongoing basis, and was prepared to take the lead whenever the situation demanded. This approach did not forgo the need for any help and support, but it meant that ACEA's activities did not require sanction or approval from EA. That said, both parties were mindful of the need to maintain respect for each other within the partnership. On the very rare occasions where the two organisations disagreed over a principle, the disagreement was never so great as to become a matter for public debate. ACEA also ensured that it contextualised the delivery of services to the BMCs by using the appropriate communication strategies and remaining sensitive to their cultural and spiritual needs.

Maintaining a consistent message

Maintaining a consistent message does not preclude an organisation from expanding its vision. When the Reverend Ronald Nathan succeeded Joel Edwards in 1993, he encouraged the organisation to widen its brief to become representatives and advocates for the wider Black community. By utilising the press and media, ACEA was able to expand its work and constituency and to lead the way for BMCs to engage more fully in community action and social responsibility. My own aspiration as the organisation's General Director was to ensure that ACEA becomes an inheritance for the Black Christian community. This meant ensuring that the organisation's infrastructure was suitable for delivering services that matched the aspirations of its constituency, and that ACEA's message forms an essential part of its mission. Today the organisation's mission is 'to reflect Black Christian faith in Britain and to promote unity, reconciliation and understanding among all Christians in the UK'.

For EA, it was about taking the lead in public debates. Evangelicals were able to rally round the messages, 'Your voice for unity and truth', then 'Promoting unity, representing evangelical concern', and later, 'All uniting to change society'. This was a clarion call to become 'a movement for change' and to put 'values back into society'.

Facing up to new challenges

In the same way that children must learn their alphabet, every new member of staff, church and leader should be convinced about the need for partnership. Despite staff induction and training, it is my view that both ACEA and EA have failed over many years to convince new staff of the mutual value of their partnership and the need to maintain it. Possibly, the primary reason for this is that historic programmes and joint public activities – such as Accord (a national praise gathering of Black and White Christians attracting up to 4,000 delegates), and our Social Responsibility programme (promoting community development through an Active Community Unit) – ended and were not replaced, so people had to rely on rhetoric rather than a tangible experience. The same could be said for the churches: ACEA and EA have failed to educate them about the merits of two organisations working side by side, and the added value that each brings. The closest we have got in recent times was the GOAL (Governance, Openness, Accountability and Leadership) Conference, which looked at church governance and the way that church affairs were managed. Unity and partnership is hard work, and the pressing task of delivering services has left little time to clarify doubts and allay the fears of some church leaders.

One of the more ironic aspects of the partnership is that, despite their relative financial success and extensive human resource, the BMCs have not seen the need to finance ACEA beyond relatively small annual donations. My own view is that this has been the cause of significant tension, as EA supported ACEA financially to the tune of £40,000 per annum until 2003. Added to this were other support services such as personnel, press and media, payroll and the free use of premises. With the wide range of causes that people are being asked to support, many organisations suffer from falling contributions. ACEA's grant became a drain on EA's tight resources. A process of reviewing the partnership with the hope of clarifying anomalies, strengthening the commitment to each other and developing more tangible expressions of unity has brought a significant change in the relationship. An agreement is now in place and, in the process, ACEA is now EA's tenant. EA will be withdrawing its grant in the coming years, starting with a 48.5 per cent reduction in 2004.

Endnotes

1 Sir William Macpherson of Cluny, *The Stephen Lawrence Inquiry*, The Stationary Office, February 1999, paragraph 6.34.
2 *Stephen Lawrence Inquiry*, paragraph 6.4.
3 Policy Studies Institute Report, 1997; in Geraldine Bedell, 'Between Two Worlds', *The Observer* newspaper, 6 April 2003. She also identifies 1 in 20 (5%) of all pre-school children as mixed race.

4 Adapted from Mark Sturge, 'Why is the issue of racism such a taboo in our churches?', *Focus*, ACEA, 1999, August–October issue, p6, 7.
5 Ian Randell and David Hilborn, *One Body in Christ – the history and significance of the Evangelical Alliance*, Paternoster Press, 2001, p288.

Chapter 10

Unmet challenges

In any walk of life, such a large mass of people, with shared aspirations, common purpose and collective human and financial resources, would exercise considerable economic, social and political influence. In this regard, the BMCs could be regarded as a 'sleeping giant'.

Their economic clout would help them in demanding better treatment from financial institutions for their churches and communities. They could also do more to tackle the ongoing lack of employment prospects for many Black young people. It is not enough, and it is callous, simply to assert that those without jobs do not have them because they are unemployable. The BMCs' responsibility is to understand and respond to the implications of unemployment and extra low wages, which contribute so significantly to poverty, lack of ambition, mental illness, homelessness, drugs, crime, sexual promiscuity and all the other consequences of people trying to prove that they are 'somebody'. BMCs need to recognise the impact of over 64 per cent of Black pupils, both African and Caribbean, not succeeding at schools and leaving with less than five GCSEs at Grades A to C.[1] Their economic influence could be use to ensure that regeneration means more than work done by the rich, for the rich, in poor areas. Instead, it could ensure that housing really is affordable and not merely a 'mass income generator' that drives local people out of their communities and away from their support networks.

The BMCs considerable social influence could be used to raise the level of representation and advocacy for society's poor and vulnerable, including those attending our churches. They could defend the rights of new communities, refugees and asylum seekers. They could challenge the widespread assumption that economic migrants are somehow 'criminal', and declare that economic migration, although it may be unpalatable to some, is not in fact a sin; the daily pursuit of humanity the world over is to make tomorrow better than it was today. They could join in the work to ensure that the environments in which our children are brought up are safe and suitable for developing balanced and healthy adults. They could be challenging the use of taxpayers' monies to pursue policies conceived out of self-interest and those that will not benefit society in the long run. It is estimated that council taxes will have to rise by an average of £200 per annum to cover the cost of extending opening times for pub drinkers. Should the poor pay a 'drinking tax' to cover the consequences of irresponsible and badly behaved drunkards? But BMCs cannot respond to these issues without recognising their political implications.

Sadly, the majority of church leaders have not become reconciled to the fact that they are called to be transformers not only of people but also of the environment and the world in which they live. They have wrongly understood politics as being 'other worldly' and nothing to do with church. However, those same leaders would have no hesitation in confronting a painter or decorator who painted their church black instead of the buttermilk they requested. Why? Because the decorator has defaced their church premises, not followed their instructions and rendered the building unfit for use! What is certain is that they would demand that the decorator either correct the error or return the building to its original condition, and they would more than likely terminate the contract or refuse to pay until the job was done satisfactorily. Such practical concerns, then, are hardly beyond the consideration of faith.

Politicians, at best, are hired hands, tasked with the responsibility to administrate how society functions in both a local and a global context. It is therefore impossible and irresponsible for anyone, Christians or otherwise, to turn a blind eye when those whom they have employed to do a task do not comply with their brief or pursue a course that is detrimental to those affected by it. Politics is about the ideas, values and perspectives that people have on how national and international affairs should be run. But these ideas or values are not fixed: they are often governed by popular opinion, class and racial preferences or even personal conscience. If the church fails to engage with political issues, it has no right to complain when politicians violate or oppose Christian interests. It is worth considering this question: if the church succeeds in its mission of winning the world for Christ, who then will run the nations' affairs?

The call for ambassadors

BMCs have not given collective consideration to how they might exploit their enormous influence. There is a huge cry for credible ambassadors within the BMCs: where is the British version of Martin Luther King, Jesse Jackson or even Al Sharpton? How is it that the leaders of denomination have not managed to extend their influence beyond the portals of their organisations? This is not a plea for superstars or to inflate the heads of egotists: it is a plea for the Christian traditions to which Black Christians have committed themselves to find genuine expression in the public domain.

This call for ambassadors from among the BMCs provides a litmus test for identifying the degree of maturity that the churches have attained. And the testing ground is not confined to the public arena; it is also about how these ambassadors will relate and dialogue with the wider church. A critical contribution to this process must be the establishment of a Black Leaders' Forum that can bring senior church leaders together to examine issues of common concern, mutual trust, respect and understanding. This step requires solidarity among the denominations and the 'one voice' necessary to bring about key transformation. It goes without saying that such a forum would have to learn the lessons from similar attempts in the past, and to delegate its administration to an organisation with the capacity to ensure that the momentum is not lost. Failing to take up the challenge to be ambassadors leaves the BMCs open to the charge of toothlessness and inconsistency.

The call to realise the implications of being a diaspora

Belonging to a diaspora is closely akin to the role of the ambassador. Black Christians are often faced with the challenge of reconciling the need to make a living and leave their mark on their adopted nation while, at the same time, using their new-found opportunity and status to provide inspiration, encouragement, advocacy and support for their countries of origin. No doubt there are many activities taking place, but my observation is that these are not being done from any strategic national perspective. Instead, it is a matter of personality or a personal quest, where a church or individual is happy to build a school in the district or parish of their birth – this despite failing to engage with the education system at home or abroad. The priority, therefore, is to move away from the small-scale, even though that could enhance one's personal standing, and instead to concentrate on the large-scale which will transform the nation.

This realisation will affect the role that Black Christians play in seeking to resolve historic and national crises, including the way that the BMCs can put pressure or seek partnerships with institutions, the government or strategic politicians in order to put their priorities on the agenda. In doing so, Black Christians will be following in the footsteps of those from that earlier diaspora who were willing to make a difference at home and abroad: Moses, Nehemiah, Daniel and Esther. 'Who knows whether you have come to the kingdom for such a time as this?' (Esther 4:14).

The call for theological debate and dialogue

An area that has been much neglected by the BMCs is that of taking part in theological debate and dialogue, usually out of the belief that to do so would be divisive. Often church leaders would rather give up on a process, event or discussion rather than engage intensively in order to refine proposals. However, this is an unhelpful approach. The art of debate is critical wherever Christians are called upon to contend for their faith in the media and in the public arena.

The area of theological training also tends to be neglected, a deficit that is made worse by the BMCs' mistrust as to the value and effectiveness of theological institutions. Too often leaders have sought popularity by decrying the discipline of theological education. Meanwhile, the existence of a plethora of Bible schools and training taking place in BMCs gives churches the impression that they are preparing their leaders for ministry. However, at best many of these treasures prove to be no more than 'fools' gold'. The future of the church depends on good leadership backed up by excellent training, which in turn generates integrity in the handling of Scripture and the things of God. It is not enough to be educated in another field of expertise. While there is much merit to the kingdom in having people from all kinds of backgrounds in ministry, leaders must take seriously the vocation to which they are called.

I am not an advocate for disqualifying the untrained from ministry: what I am saying is that we should not make a virtue out of it, nor should we decry those who have obediently followed the call of God and have put themselves up for training. I am aware of the pitfalls and challenges that theological students face, but these challenges are often compounded because churches have not sufficiently supported and empathised with these students. I have no difficulty in suggesting that if the existing institutions cannot and will not produce the kind of leaders suitable for the BMCs, then either they should be challenged to do so and or we should consider setting up our own. However, there is no reason for wasting time, energy and resources on substandard training in circumstances that cannot be sustained or justified in the wider context; neither should students be encouraged to engage in costly study for certificates or qualifications that go unrecognised elsewhere, or be granted doctorates or degrees after one year of study. Such courses have no integrity and should not be thought of as such.

It must be the case that any congregation with over fifty members should consider seriously investing in the training of its current and future leaders. If we are asking young people to commit their lives to the ministry, such a course must be made attractive through promoting its excellence. No other profession would accommodate or give such great responsibility to untrained staff. Nowhere in Scripture is there a precedent for churches being exempt from the discipline of rigorous theological study.

While I recognise that the tide is turning, with more leaders taking up the challenge, I am aware that many individuals still have to pay their own way for the privilege of serving the church. The things that we invest in demonstrate the things that we value. If the BMCs continue to avoid theological engagement, then they will continually find themselves having to resort to a dogmatic approach to ministry. While this may bring them some benefits in the form of affirming unity and presenting a solid front, it is not always helpful in furthering their goal of spreading the gospel and bringing in the kingdom of God.

The call for a coherent policy on social justice

Where the BMCs lack political will, a sense of their own destiny and theological fervency, there is no doubt that this has had a knock-on effect upon their ministry. Their approach to critical issues is often fearful and cautious, which has led to the absence of a coherent theology, and hence a coherent policy, on social justice, thus stifling the churches' political engagement and aspirations. For encouragement, we can look to Scripture. The Bible is a book resonant with justice and the call to counteract inequality. It has much to say about corruption, the abuse of strangers and ignoring the poor (Proverbs 14:21,31; Isaiah 10:1,2; Ezekiel 22:12-16; Matthew 25:31-46; 1 John 3:17), and promises rewards for those who dispense justice (Proverbs 3:33; 21:3; Isaiah 58:6-12; Colossians 4:1). As Christians, we inevitably diminish our faith and damage our relationship with Christ if we neglect such an all-inclusive salvation.

The Hebrew word *Rephael* means 'God has cured'. It is the church's responsibility to give the people in our communities and throughout the nation the opportunity to experience *Jehovah Rephael* ('the Lord who cures') not only in their physical illnesses but also in the social and environmental structures in which they are living. As it is, however, many currently experience 'the sleeping giant' as a church that is *Rapheh* – slothful, slack, weak, idle, consumed or in its evening time. Uncomfortable though this may be, it is the perception of the majority, even of those sitting in the pews. It is not that BMCs are not actively involved in the institutions and the lives of the communities to which their members belong. The concern, however, is that community needs and the issues are increasing so fast that small, local and individual responses are not sufficient to bring about the transformation that is needed. A church that wants to be 'salt and light' to its communities must be ever present in every human situation and circumstance before it can be experienced as such. And not until the church has become a model for change, and undertakes what society calls 'best practice', can Christians authentically say that they are an example to the nation.

The call for an end to division

In calling it what it is, the BMCs need to identify the issues that are hindering them from being Christ to the nation – the lack of unity and of 'joined-up' mission, the undermining of trust and the evasion of mutual acceptance. It is the underlying causes of these divisions that I would like now to explore further.

An independent spirit

Anecdotal evidence suggests that more than 65 per cent of BMCs from the African and Caribbean diaspora are *independent* churches. When I talk about an 'independent spirit', I am not pointing a finger at independent churches; rather, the term refers to an attitude that can be found in both denominational and independent churches. Churches within denominations may struggle to preserve some degree of independence so as to gain much needed flexibility; meanwhile, other churches operate, or are established, independently so that they can have greater control over the vision and direction of their ministry and move into new areas of mission. This may be the result of a genuine call to work independently, or it may be the fallout of breakdown in relationships brought about by administrative differences, selfish ambitions or poor

shepherding. Whatever the cause, this freedom tends to nurture an attitude that reinforces the need to be separate or distinctive. These
churches will often legitimise their existence or justify their priorities by
highlighting the missed opportunities, 'sins of omission' or lack of credibility of other churches or organisations. Consequently, it becomes very
difficult to be at one with each other.

More subtle and sophisticated is the theological misconceptions that
can arise out of an overemphasis on personal calling and the privatisation of spiritual gifts. Such a combination puts leaders in a powerful
and dangerous position in which they are seen as 'set apart' by God for
the exercise of specific gifts. This lends a sense of exclusivity to the way
that they conduct their ministry and interact with others. It is no longer
surprising to hear the words, 'I cannot step outside the parameters of
my calling and anointing'. These leaders soon come to expect to be recognised exclusively in relation to their gift and to be accorded an appropriate status. Yet it was for the purpose of unity and the corporate
benefit to the whole community that the apostle Paul promoted the
wide use of spiritual gifts (1 Corinthians 12). He did not want those
using them to remain apart; instead he sought to ensure that everyone
within the body recognised their co-dependency and the need for
mutual acceptance. Is not the lesson that we are incomplete, less effective, restricted in movement, lacking in vision and insight, unable to
hear and to communicate effectively if there is not full cooperation and
participation with the whole body? Paul is clear about the reason for
these gifts being given: 'Now to each one the manifestation of the Spirit
is given for the *common good*' (1 Corinthians 12:7, NIV, my italics).

The competitive spirit

Another contributor to division is the existence of a competitive spirit
among the churches. This may range from the acquisition of premises,
where churches maliciously outbid and gazump each other, to having
the best line-up of preachers gracing one's pulpit. Churches may also
compete over the size of their premises or congregation. This may not
be a fixation that is all about being big, but churches who aspire to be
large are more likely to have this tendency, even if they do not realise it.
Sometimes, too, the earnest desire to be relevant means that activities
and ministries overlap or are reproduced. With the exception of the
RCCOG, the Seventh-day Adventist Church and the Universal Church
of the Kingdom of God, the area of rapid growth in the BMCs is among

the independent churches, and this growth is often presented as though it were a definitive sign of God's approval or that a church is best and right and therefore ought to be leader of the pack.

Relationships between African and Caribbean churches

One of the most sensitive points of division lies in the relationship between African and Caribbean church leaders, wherein lurks much mistrust, resentment, disrespect and misunderstanding. I have yet to find definitive reasons for the impasse that is preventing complete unity between the two communities. When I was interviewed for the role of General Director of ACEA, one of the objectives I presented to the panel was to 'speed up the reconciliation work between African and Caribbean churches'. Having remained faithful to this task, my observation, experience and reflection have allowed me to assess the situation in the following way.

There has been a huge assumption that the African and Caribbean communities really know each other. However, the truth of the matter is that until quite recently, over the last ten years, it is the British press which mediated much of their knowledge of each other. Because the two communities were assessing each other through the eyes of the media and from stories picked up through the grapevine, their relationship became characterised as one of 'stranger-danger' – the fear, suspicion and mistrust of those we do not know. Generally speaking, unless an individual had an Afrocentric or pan-African outlook, the two communities would not comfortably cross this invisible barrier. This has produced an environment ripe for stereotyping. No one likes to be typecast; instead, we all want to be treated as unique individuals. Stereotypes often lead to misrepresentation which, in turn, brings with it the danger of conferring excessive advantage or disadvantage on one or other group.

Both African and Caribbeans make a wide variety of assumptions about each other. Some common ones can be summarised as follows:

Things that Caribbeans think of Africans

- They are dishonest: they are liars and don't tell the truth. They are also likely to be fraudulent.
- Don't marry them: the men may already have a wife back home, and they are prone to violence. African women are subservient.
- They are too proud and think they are better than anyone else.

- They are power-drunk: everyone wants to be chief. This is why there are always wars and conflict in that continent.
- Whatever you do, their allegiance will always be to their tribe.
- Don't trust their leaders: they are all in it for the money and to line their own pockets. Just look at their economies and history.
- They are into voodoo, obeah and ancestral worship. They perform libations, offer sacrifices, use witch doctors and rituals to solve problems and for blessing and cursing.
- They lack etiquette; look at the way they eat and how they speak

Things that Africans think of Caribbeans

- They are slave babies and have a slave mentality. They are always blaming their plight on the past, always looking back and not to the future.
- They are very promiscuous and have too many babies out of wedlock.
- They have a chip on their shoulder. They are too proud and think they are better than us.
- They are muggers and thieves. They are always in the news, and give us a bad name.
- Every Caribbean is a Jamaican or a 'Jamo'. (A 'Jamo' is synonymous with being irresponsible or delinquent.)
- They are not interested in working and getting an education. They lack ambition. They prefer an easy life.
- They are into drugs.

Closer scrutiny will show that other communities secretly hold similar views about both Africans and Caribbeans. Our quest should be not only to disprove them but to discover their true source. More significantly, many of these traits ought not even to be named among God's people, and something has gone terribly wrong if any of them is proven to be true. Our Christian identity should have superseded whatever we once were. The apostle Paul is clear that those who lie, thieve, are sexually immoral or dishonest will not enter the kingdom of God (1 Corinthians 6:9,10), yet he acknowledges that the church is full of people who have left these characteristics behind (v 11). Paul offers good advice on how to deal with sinful attitudes that have not been redeemed by faith: 'Therefore, rebuke them sharply, that they may be sound in faith' (Titus 1:13). However, these stereotypical attitudes are not confined to the BMCs; they are found among Africans and Caribbeans throughout wider society. Moreover, it is possible to see that the divisions within the African and Caribbean relationship are deeply rooted in the historic events of slavery.

Some sections of the Caribbean community carry a huge resentment at the role that West Africans played in their enslavement. Some feel that the reason for their own inner restlessness is due to the fact that they were uprooted from their original culture, soul ties and bosom of nurturing, and pitched into a life of slavery, degradation and abuse. What is more, they feel that Africans, instead of empathising with their situation, in fact blame them for their current circumstances and are demanding that they pull themselves up by their own boot straps. Some Caribbeans are also angered that even today the practices of slavery and dislocation are widespread on the African continent; and many young people are forced into slavery for several reasons, including war, or because they have been duped by an increasing demand in Europe to support well-educated and professional families who wish to maintain their lifestyles and the culture of servitude. African silence on these issues is interpreted as turning a blind eye to the many injustices present today on the continent.

The African perspective, like that of many White Europeans today, has mainly been one of surprise that they should be subjected to such hostility, as this present generation were not themselves directly responsible for the enslavement and forced migration of Africans to the Americas and the Caribbean. Equally, many feel that there is no reason why this generation of Caribbeans should continually blame events in the past for their current plight: if they took a more proactive and positive approach, they would achieve success and progress socially and educationally. The cycle of anger and blame would be broken, and Caribbean children will grow up with a more positive attitude that they can achieve whatever they want to. Many Africans also feel that Caribbeans and their culture have dominated the debate around Black culture in Britain, and have become the yardstick by which all Black people are judged. Not enough emphasis is placed on the diversity of cultures that make up the mosaic of ethnicities to be found within the African and Caribbean communities. Despite the investment of Africans in educating themselves in Britain, somehow it is the African Caribbeans who have benefited from many of the top jobs, the higher profile and issues of representation in the wider society.

The first thing to do with such perceptions is to acknowledge that they exist. For too long there has been a failure in the communities to discuss them and apply the leadership necessary to resolve them. Instead, we have been disingenuous with each other, either pretending that there are no problems or not admitting it when attitudes and actions really hurt. In my own conversations with African pastors, they have confessed to feeling intimidated by reactions to their accents, by the fact that they do not have appropriate representation, and by the general lack of understanding of their culture and the issues that they face. This has led to a sense of dissociation and introspection. I would therefore like to propose a biblical example as a model for resolving what can reasonably be called the African and Caribbean Problem.

One thing to bear in mind, however, is that any model merely functions as an example from which we can draw parallels in order to inform our past, present and future realities. It does not, in my view, have to be all-encompassing and, since it is only a model, we must be willing to let it go when it has served its purpose and is no longer useful. Nonetheless, I hope the following exploration will stimulate further thinking and provide lenses through which we can view and understand what is happening within Black Christian faith in Britain today. I also concede that this model is not confined to Black Christians but has implications for the wider Black community.

Joseph and his brothers: a model for Black Christian faith in Britain

Whenever the plight of Black people is talked about, it is always from the perspective of liberation, and it is always the Exodus story, dealing with the liberation of the Israelites from oppression, that forms the basis of the discussion. However, I am convinced that Exodus cements Black people into the role of victim and demands that they adopt an antagonistic response towards their oppressors. Little room is left for reconciliation and affirmation; instead, separation from and dethronement of the oppressor is proclaimed as the only way forward. While Black people can indeed learn valuable lessons from Exodus, the story may in fact be unhelpful inasmuch as it seems to be saying that they are helpless and unable to change their condition without the intervention of a great leader like Moses and the miraculous work of God himself. While it is true that we all always need God to transform our lives and circumstances, it seems to me to be rather foolhardy if we were to limit ourselves to looking for redemption through confrontation, or national, regional or tribal misfortunes, in order to inherit our place of rest and security. God is not one-dimensional: he does not have to recreate a situation. Yet it is the lessons we learn about him and it is his aspirations for us that can transform our lives. This, for me, is one of the important lessons we can learn from Joseph.

Joseph was the favourite son of his father, Jacob (Genesis 37:3). Before he was sold into slavery by his brothers, he was economically and spiritually sufficient and surrounded by plenty – much cattle, beautiful clothes, the love of his father as well as divine favour (Genesis 37:5-10). He himself was the product of divine intervention: his mother Rachel was at first barren until God 'opened her womb' (Genesis 30:22-24): thus Joseph is accorded the same special status as his great grandfather Abraham, grandfather Isaac, and father Jacob. In spite of his comfortable circumstances, however, Joseph came to experience jealousy, betrayal, the loss of his family and his country, and the harsh state of slavery. But 'the Lord was with Joseph, and he was a successful man' (Genesis 39:2), rising to prominence in the house of his owner Potiphar, one of Pharaoh's officers and captain of the guard. Even then he suffered injustice and imprisonment when Potiphar's wife falsely accused him of sexually assaulting her (Genesis 39:7-20).

Nevertheless, out of his darkest hour, Joseph rose to yet greater prominence, this time in the house of Pharaoh himself. He eventually becomes second only to the king and is charged with managing the affairs of all Egypt (Genesis 41:37-45). Genesis depicts Joseph as one who had the potential to succeed at whatever he chose to do. Deprivation and hardship was only introduced into his life after he was sold into slavery, yet he did not let this degrade him or persuade him to surrender his gifts, talents and integrity; neither did he let it prevent God from working through his spiritual gifts (Genesis 41:1-36).

Films such as *Roots* and *Amistad*, however distorted or inaccurate, have captured Black people's imagination and helped a wider audience get a glimpse of the origins of African Americans and, implicitly, of African Caribbeans. Like Joseph, it could be argued that Caribbeans of African decent were betrayed by their brothers and sold into slavery to White slave traders. In my view, it is fair to say that rival or colluding tribes played a critical role in the capture and enslavement of their countrymen – the present situation in Sudan offers a modern example. This is not to suggest, however, that all Africans were culpable of these events: slavery was limited to specific geographical areas such as Ghana and Nigeria, and it is the case that not everyone in those areas were involved. It is important to recognise that Joseph had one good brother, Reuben, who was very much concerned for his welfare and who attempted to subvert the plot to murder his young brother (Genesis 37:23-30). Reuben's alternative scheme would have allowed him to rescue Joseph at a later date; however, to his great disappointment, he was not in the vicinity when there was a change of plan and Joseph was not killed but sold into slavery. Initially Scripture tells us that Joseph was sold to the Ishmaelites, but later that he is sold to the Midianites (Genesis 37:25,28). The popular view is that the Ishmaelites and the Midianites were nomadic tribes who were at times indistinguishable from each other. However, the point I want to highlight here is that Joseph was sold to his family's archenemies: Africans were sold as slaves to those who turned out to be the primary assassins of the African civilisation.

We can draw parallels between Joseph's rise to prominence in Potiphar's house and the experiences of Black people in the Caribbean. Over time, the privileges of indentureship and national governance culminated in independence. Unfortunately, many of the new Caribbean nations found that their aspirations for a new identity, self-determination and desire to establish an alternative system of governance other than the exploitative ideology of colonialism were greeted with hostility. They were falsely accused, like Joseph, of subscribing to Communism so as to threaten the freedom of the democratic, capitalist West and as a result faced punitive measures, sanctions, invasions and interference in their domestic affairs from Europe, the United States and the rest of the Northern hemisphere. Those whose ideas and ideologies were not welcomed by the powerful tended to suffer the consequences in the form of racism, unequal opportunity and at times the sheer corruption of human nature.

Pharaoh's elevation of Joseph to prominence can be compared to the British government's summons to Caribbean men and women, in a time of national crisis, to help rebuild Britain after the ravages of the Second World War. They were called on to help mitigate 'the famine in Egypt' – the devastation of the Second World War and the dearth of key public and private sector workers. Through hard work, doggedness and with God's help, they had many notable successes in the midst of hardship. Equally, BMCs, who were once considered to be Christian sects, are now at the heart of Christianity in Britain, helping to counter spiritual famine in British society. Resources from Africa were also being draw on to advance Britain economically: minerals, raw materials and the wealth and efforts of African students coming to the UK to improve their educational prospects.

Like Joseph and his brothers, African and Caribbean Christians and communities met again in Britain. Unlike the emotional scenes and convoluted plots that Joseph orchestrated in order to reveal his identity (Genesis chs 43–45), it could be said that the Caribbean churches were guilty of ignoring their African brothers and busily taking care of their own interests – purchasing and renovating their church buildings, obsessing over holiness to the point that each denomination believed they were the only true church with a divine responsibility to 'maintain the old landmarks'. A plethora of distractions or agendas competed for their attention while the injustices faced by the wider community were discounted. Instead, their accomplishments were celebrated among themselves. The African migration into this context took place almost unnoticed.

However, the emerging African churches made their own mistakes. There was an arrogance that supported existing stereotypes about Caribbean people as well as the view that the Caribbean churches 'were not doing a good enough job', and it was they, the African churches, who knew best how to break through to win the souls of the British population. African Christians were full of zeal and, like the early Caribbean churches, were often without pastoral experience. No doubt there were those who felt a definite call to mission in the UK, and there were those who mainly wanted to support Christians who attended their denomination or congregation back home. Yet there were also those who established satellites in Europe, either to support a global vision or to give financial support to ministries back home. ACEA's choice of name came to reflect the arrival of these new churches from the African continent. First called the 'West Indian Evangelical Alliance', the organisation later realised the need to identify the distinctiveness of the two communities, and became the African *and* Caribbean Evangelical Alliance. Once again, Black Caribbeans were being redefined, this time as *African* Caribbeans.

The neglect in pursuing, with a passion, reconciliation among ourselves is a scandal, and one of the most serious charges that can be laid at the feet of the BMCs. The African and Caribbean churches seem to have arrived at an impasse. My concern is that even where there is public affirmation of each other, behind the scenes there still remains a degree of suspicion, tribal loyalties and competition. There are notable exceptions but, granted that Black Christians have made significant progress, it is far from satisfactory and nowhere near what is needed for the task of transforming and serving the younger generation. The job of reconciliation is not for the next generation. If it is their task, then it is because their elders have failed in their duty. We need to make sure that we do not lay aside our responsibility simply because it is inconvenient for us to travel the road of reconciliation together. The season of forgiveness and reconciliation must take place soon if BMCs are to take advantage of the opportunities to exercise leadership in their areas of expertise and to follow the example of Joseph and his brothers in a land dominated by spiritual famine and indifference. In London, the BMCs are now on course to become the largest Christian presence in the city. Black Christians are 'on call' to play a central role in the leadership of the wider church. Responsibility for managing the affairs of our communities and the nation will only be possible when we demonstrate our capacity to manage that responsibility well.

The historical events of slavery and the slave trade have resulted in the dislocation of the African family – an experience that can be likened to that of Joseph and his brothers. While many African Caribbean people may feel aggrieved by the role that their African brothers played in betraying their countryman, they need to recognise that the time for resentment is past. The African Caribbeans laid the foundations upon which the African community was able to build. Now both communities have the potential to rise to greatness. The level and pace at which Black Christians grasp these opportunities will depend on how earnestly they pursue reconciliation. Those who pursue historical truth and a more balanced perspective of the African continent and the needs of its people should be assured that they can find biblical support in the story of Joseph for seeking to mitigate the effects of human sinfulness. It is my plea that we lay aside the weight that has done so much to hinder the BMCs from accelerating the vision and plans of God.

Endnote

1 Figures from Sarah Cassidy, 'Rapid Fall in Number of Black Pupils Achieving Good Grades', Black Information Link, 21 February 2003; available at **www.blink.org.uk**

Chapter 11

A biblical approach to unity

No compromises, no negotiations

In this chapter I have set to explore a biblical approach to unity, using as a lens Paul's first letter to the Corinthian church. For many, 1 Corinthians is primarily about church order, church discipline and the exercise of the gifts of the Holy Spirit. It is also presented as a 'hand-book' for solving problems in the church and as a resource for affirming the worth and value of each member of the body of Christ. Although all of these approaches may be fine, Christians have often missed the true value of the epistle because they have been thinking about it primarily in terms of personal and corporate ministry. But if we concentrate only on details, and fail to apply Paul's words to the context of the wider church, then we are in danger of minimising their impact.

Often in life there comes a point in time when we must either 'draw a line in the sand' or 'stand our ground' to ensure that a principle, value or decision is upheld, thereby clearly indicating that we are not prepared to go any further – there is no more room for compromises, no more negotiations, it is a choice of 'take it or leave it'. So, for example, when buying a house, there is a price above which the purchaser is not prepared to go; or, looking at it from the seller's perspective, there is a price so low as to induce negative equity on the property. In either case, to compromise would be to risk one's very future and livelihood.

This is the atmosphere in which we need to understand the purpose and contents of 1 Corinthians. It may be helpful if you read through the epistle before embarking on this chapter. As you do so, I want you to hear Paul speak again from his context, to understand anew his fears for the young church at Corinth, and why his concerns over the severe consequences of disunity brought him to the point not only of no compromise or no negotiation but also of no surrender. In 1 Corinthians Paul sets out his manifesto for unity, laying the foundations and general principles to which the reasonable majority of Christians should be able to agree.

I have chosen not to look at 2 Corinthians here, although the issues that Paul discusses in the second epistle build upon the approach he has adopted in the first, as he seeks to shore up his defense of Christian unity. So, let us first explore the apostle's motivation for writing to the church at Corinth and the context of his argument.

Do or die: the context of 1 Corinthians

The context of 1 Corinthians must be understood in the light of events recorded in Acts 18, when the Corinthian church was just established and its primary goal, set out in 1 Corinthians 10:32, was 'Give no offense, either to the Jews or to the Greeks or to the church of God'. Why has Paul come to this position? One key to answering this question can be found in the very first verse of 1 Corinthians, which says, 'Paul, called to be an apostle of Jesus Christ through the will of God, and Sosthenes our brother . . . '. The question is, what role, if any, did Sosthenes play to deserve this special mention?

At the time of the founding of the Corinthian church, ethnic cleansing was taking place in Italy with the expulsion of all Jews from Rome by the Emperor Claudius (Acts 18:2). No doubt, at this time, the Jews were feeling vulnerable and self-conscious about their heritage and religion. They may well have viewed the new Christian religion as a threat to their identity, as both Jews and Greeks were being converted to Christ, sometimes whole households like those of Rabbi Crispus and his family (18:4,8). It is likely that Crispus' synagogue became a place dedicated to the worship of Jesus as the Messiah, which would have put him in conflict with his friends and unconverted Jews in the other synagogues. Meanwhile, the fact that many Corinthians were being converted and baptised (18:8,10) led to Paul's arrest on the charge of persuading men 'to worship God contrary to the law' (18:13).

More trouble brewed after the governor of the province, Gallio, dismissed the case, ruling that Paul had not committed any 'wrongdoing or wicked crimes' and that he, Gallio, was not qualified to make judgements on matters of Jewish law (18:14,15). It seemed that, as far as Gallio was concerned, the Corinthian church and its followers were an integral part of Judaism. The Greeks, who we can assume were supporters of Paul, then turned on the leader of the synagogue, Sosthenes, and meted out to him what he had intended for Paul to receive (18:17). Although the apostle's freedom should be seen as a fulfilment of God's promise (18:10), the action of the Greeks represents rough justice, probably intermixed with some anti-Semitism. Gallio, seemingly principled up until now, did nothing to stop the vigilantes, who took the law into their own hands. We can clearly assume that the relationship between Jews and Gentiles, already fractured when the Jews had at first opposed Paul (18:6), was now split wide open.

Clearly, the Christian church in Corinth had become a hostile place for those antagonistic towards the faith. This flagship church, despite all of its success in communicating the gospel, winning souls and experiencing remarkable growth, had taken a different approach to its relationship with the Jews from that of the church in Jerusalem, for example. Therefore, if the church in Corinth was to receive recognition and endorsement from the apostles in Jerusalem, it desperately needed to become a place of unity and not conflict. This clearly mattered greatly to Paul. The church in Corinth represented a huge breakthrough in his ministry, and while the Corinthians were not the firstfruits of his work, he seemed to regard the church there as one of his best achievements.

Reconciling the Corinthian church

If we assume that the Sosthenes mentioned in 1 Corinthians 1:1 is the same person as that in Acts 18:17, then it looks as though his conversion bore some similarities to that of the apostle Paul, where the persecutor of the faith and the faithful became their defender (Acts 9:1–25). It is also consistent with Paul to befriend people who shared his background, such as Aquila and Priscilla (Acts 18:3). Even so, reconciliation was needed to prevent the Corinthian church from behaving as though they were a law unto themselves. Above all, Jews who believed that Jesus was the Messiah needed to feel free to worship in the church as well as in the synagogue.

Paul's motivation for writing his letter might, therefore, be summarised in the following way:

- First, Paul wanted to promote social cohesion between Jews and Gentiles, and between the converted and non-converted. There were no benefits in allowing ongoing public disorder and violence between Jews and Gentiles to continue.
- Secondly, Paul wanted to ensure that Christianity remained essentially a part of the Jewish faith. In so doing, he sought to avoid causing offence and to make it easy for Jews who were sympathetic or converted to Christianity to continue their worship in the synagogues.

- Thirdly, the decisions made in Corinth had the capacity to under-mine and bring into question the church in Jerusalem. Paul was not prepared to enter another face-off with the apostles there, especially over issues that were not fundamental to the faith. He had already won concessions over circumcision and the recognition that Gentiles had indeed received the Holy Spirit (Acts 15). 'Take it easy, you're going too fast too far and you're out of control' seems to be his message to the Corinthians.

Who, then, was best placed to assist him in this work if not Sosthenes? It is unthinkable that this former head of the synagogue would have such a minor role as merely being Paul's scribe. After all, he was conver-sant with the distinctive features of the culture, customs and practices of Corinth. Even more, he understood the points of convergence, as well as divergence, between the Jews and the Greeks. He understood the knowledge base, motivation, future plans and strategies of those wishing to cripple the fledgling church. He understood the church's weaknesses and the vulnerabilities that could be exploited by its enemies. Therefore, if these breaches were to be filled, Paul's edicts needed to be communicated effectively and contextually. Whatever the case may be, the apostle was a mere stranger and visitor to the province. Therefore, 1 Corinthians was probably written in consultation with Sosthenes, with his guidance and endorsement.

Ten fundamental principles for promoting unity

Once you start to look at Paul's concerns in more detail, you will soon recognise that the primary reason for Christian disunity is unfaithful-ness to God and Scripture. In my view, it is impossible for any two indi-viduals or churches who are consistently seeking to be faithful to God and the Bible not to walk in unity. But the truth is that everyone is right in their own eyes, and our biological differences, social status, educa-tion, culture and personal experiences all shape our perspective of reality. If unity is to be more than a utopian dream, we need to agree some basic principles that should at least allow us to feel comfortable in each other's presence and identify ourselves as playing for the same team. There are ten fundamental principles to be found in 1 Corinthians which can provide the church with a starting point for learning to live in unity. It is important that we take time to ponder carefully the issues raised by these principles, and to use Paul's reflections on them as building blocks for unity. If we get the task of unity wrong, it will be like building a house without foundations: everything is likely to collapse or be undermined at the first storm (Matthew 7:24-27).

Principle 1: Do not condone or initiate rivalry

At the heart of the Corinthian church was the spirit of rivalry (1 Corinthians chs 1-4). Rivalry at Corinth was like an invasive cancer, offering fertile breeding ground for envy, strife and division (3:3). It reduced Christians to behaving like unregenerated people, 'worldly', 'mere men'. If it was not addressed, it would soon hinder the mission of the church in bringing the true message of the gospel to the rest of the population in Corinth. Hence Paul's plea from the outset: '. . . by the name of our Lord Jesus Christ, that you all speak the same thing, and that there be no divisions among you, but that you be perfectly joined together in the same mind and in the same judgment' (1:10).

The main contention was over allegiance: it was about 'Show me your company and I'll tell you who you are' or 'Birds of a feather flock together'. The competition was between followers of the top leaders of the day – Paul, Apollos and Cephas (Peter) (1:11,12). Each of these men brought something distinctive to their followers:

- With Paul came miracles (Acts 14:8-10; 16:16-18; 19:11,12), a personal knowledge of who Jesus was (9:3-6,20-22), a passion for the salvation of the Jews (17:1-4), a considerable wealth of learning and knowledge of Jewish law (26:24), practical skills and a willingness to undertake hard manual work (18:3), and a solid track record in establishing churches among the Gentiles (see 14:19-24).
- Apollos was also learned and had 'a thorough knowledge of the Scriptures' (Acts 18:24, NIV), along with formidable skills of oratory and eloquence (vs 25,28). However, he had not had a personal encounter with Jesus in the way that Peter and Paul did, and this imposed limits, requiring him to seek the assistance and mentoring of Paul's disciples, Aquila and Priscilla (v 26). Apollos also needed a letter of recommendation before he could embark on new missions (v 27).
- Peter brought a different kind of status. Not only was he one of the twelve disciples of Jesus; he was one of the favourite three. He stood out from the other two because of his apprenticeship with Jesus, having been with him almost from the beginning, and he had received Jesus' personal commissioning. Peter was a big player in the fledgling

church and had played a major role in convening the Council of Jerusalem (Acts 15), bringing his considerable influence to bear on the direction that the future church should take.

There was no suggestion that any of these three men encouraged these attitudes of pride and disunity. This marks a huge difference between them and some leaders in the church today who, sadly, are guilty of fuelling division by exalting differences to the point where they become virtues, or who demonstrate insecurity, untruthfulness or other characteristics that undermine unity within the body of Christ.

I suppose the supporters of the three men viewed their partisanship as simply a matter of demonstrating loyalty to the person who had made the most significant contribution to their lives or who was responsible for them coming to faith. However, their behaviour exceeded a matter of mere preference: it had become more than simply a fondness for the linguistic styles and delivery of these preachers. Each man was bold in the face of Jewish opposition and had the ability to win an argument. For the Corinthians, it was probably the matter of who among Apollos, Paul and Peter was the best leader, who made the best assaults on the Jewish faith and on the paganism that was widespread in the Roman world, had the most effective method for evangelism, the best exposition of Scripture, demonstrated most the power of the Spirit, or provided most evidence of intimacy with the living Christ. The key to the problem at Corinth was an attitude of proud elitism: 'We are right, you are wrong. You are disqualified from our circle because you can't meet all our criteria'. Such attitudes are certainly not unknown in BMCs today.

The rivalry was not confined to personalities, but extended to the way that the gifts of the Holy Spirit were exercised (1 Corinthians ch 12). Some gifts were despised and others neglected. In a culture that put high value on power, wisdom, intellect, achievement, wealth and its associated lifestyle, status meant everything. I suppose this is akin to those who take great offence if one neglects to put the title of 'Pastor' or 'Reverend' in front of their names, or to list their academic qualifications afterwards; or who worry over which has the greater status, the 'Reverend' or the 'Pastor'. Whatever the case might be, at Corinth, the more valued the gift, the more respected the recipients. In his epistle, Paul had to present a lengthy exposition before he was able to convince the Corinthians that they were all one body in Christ, and that each and every gift was essential for the correct functioning of that body

(12:12–30). Very likely many of us today can think of experiences where something as simple as a lack of proper administration spoilt a beautiful experience, where maybe poor customer service or rudeness by an usher has caused us to feel differently about a place or organisation. The point is that these various functions, which may seem quite ordinary, are not just trappings – they are not optional or cosmetic; rather, they are vital to the effective running of any organisation. Therefore, they must function correctly and at the appropriate times.

Principle 2: Do not be proud or arrogant

Pride, therefore, was a central characteristic of the Corinthian church. Paul accused them of being 'puffed up' or arrogant (1 Corinthians 4:18; 5:2; 8:1). Arrogant people think of themselves much more highly than they ought to, and of others much less than they deserve. There is nothing wrong with self-affirmation or having confidence in oneself, one's church or community – false humility can be as bad as false pride. However, here that pride was leading to divisiveness and causing discord among believers. They were pretending to be different from and superior to each other, behaving as though the blessings they had received and the gifts of God's grace were the result of their own abilities and efforts (4:7). This attitude provoked a degree of scepticism and sarcasm in Paul: 'You are already full! You are already rich! You have reigned as kings without us – and indeed I could wish you did reign, that we also might reign with you!' (4:8). But Paul refused to 'reign with them' because they were foolish to think that they had achieved those blessings and those gifts by themselves.

What the apostle found lacking in the Corinthian church was the comparable evidence of their commitment to God and to God's work in their lives. For Paul and the other apostles, the role of honour read as follows (4:9–13):

- We were last.
- We were condemned to death.
- We were made a spectacle to the world.
- We are fools for Christ's sake.
- We are weak.
- We are dishonoured.
- We are homeless, hungry, thirsty, poorly clothed and beaten.
- We are self-employed.

- We are persecuted.
- We are defamed.
- We are the filth of the world.

'If then' Paul argued, 'we are all on the same side, why haven't you experienced any of these? On the other hand, if you continue in your arrogance, it may not be long before you will indeed come face to face with these hardships!' 'For the kingdom of God is not in word but in power' (4:20).

What then is the antidote to such pride and arrogance? The solution is to see ourselves 'as servants of Christ and stewards of the mysteries of God' (4:1). This combination takes us into responsible service rather than sterile servitude, demanding that we take every opportunity to be ambassadors for Christ (9:19-27), our sovereign Lord and King: at times to convey his best wishes, condolences and peace; at others his disappointment, disapproval or downright rejection of a plan or process. A good ambassador thinks and acts like the Sovereign himself.

Principle 3: Do not be immoral

God's righteousness and holiness demand that those who identify with Christ live blameless lives. Paul is clear that immorality bars us from the kingdom of God. By way of guidance, he lists the categories of behaviour and people that are immoral (1 Corinthians chs 5,6).

First, there are those involved in all forms of sexual and sexually deceptive and exploitative sins – fornicators, adulterers, catamites (boys kept for homosexual purposes) and sodomites (6:9). As evidence that sins like these were present in the church, Paul pointed to the man who was having an affair with his father's wife (5:1) – an act strictly forbidden under Jewish law (Leviticus 18:6-8). Failure to keep this law left the church open to the charge that 'anything goes' and provided a focus of disunity. Paul's antidote to this and other sexual sins was the sinner's excommunication and disassociation from the church (1 Corinthians 5:7,11-13).

Immorality is not confined to sexual sins, but includes those that violate and cause harm and distress to others (1 Corinthians 5:10). Covetousness is put in this category – one of the Ten Commandments (Exodus 20:17), and a serious sin since greed is the seedbed for envy, jealousy and hatred, all of which demand some form of action or redress. Similarly, the behaviour of extortionists (1 Corinthians 6:8) – deliberately preying on the vulnerable, deceiving them and demanding money or stealing property, while offering quasi-protection or other benefits – paves the way for a breakdown in law and order; and the words of the revilers – the slanderers, racists, bigots and xenophobes, who use abusive language and have nothing good to say about anyone – stir up much strife and disharmony. Unfortunately, as in wider society and the church, all these types of people exist in the BMCs, and I have seen and heard enough to cause me considerable concern.

Drunkards are listed among the immoral, probably because of the selfishness involved in alcoholism, the self-exclusion and isolation from day-to-day life. Drunkenness seems to have been the stimulant of choice in Paul's day, but those hooked on drugs or other addictions generate the same outcomes. They are never in a position to make a valuable contribution to family or society, and their unreliability of character makes them difficult to trust with responsibilities. In addition, the likelihood of them making bad decisions and poor choices makes them a poor witness to the saving power and work of Christ.

Finally, Paul included idolatry in his list of immoral behaviour, mainly because it invoked syncretism, the worship of God alongside idols (10:14–22). This would induce a kind of 'double-mindedness', wanting the best from both worlds: if one god does not work, there is another to fall back on. But there may have been another reason for condemning idolatry. The desire to be popular with everyone, or to please families and friends, might lead some of these new believers at Corinth to feel that they must attend all ceremonies, whatever the religion. But such involvement would undermine their Christian witness and reduce Christ to being just one deity among many, thus compromising the integrity of the faith as a whole.

One thing is certain: Paul directed his criticism towards Christians in the church: he did not expect any better from unbelievers (5:9–12). His call for Christian distinctiveness reinforces the point that unity in the church is unlikely to happen when there are disagreements over these issues of morality, and that the consequences for failing to meet these standards are often serious.

Principle 4: Do not seek gratifying justice

'Dare any of you, having a matter against another, go to law before the unrighteous, and not before the saints?' (6:1). In Paul's view, going to court represented a break in trust in God and his agency – the church and its leadership (6:2-8). He saw that going to the courts would start a cycle of litigation among church members, and breaking that cycle would mean that someone must suffer loss. Litigation also demanded that Christians be adversarial with each other. Some level of character assassination was required for a case to be proven: it would have to be shown that the other person was immoral, unregenerate, walking in ungodliness, deceitful and a wrongdoer. Surely this would compromise both the faith and the faithful, provide ammunition to the church's opponents, and further drive a wedge between believers by requiring people to take the side of one party or the other (Deuteronomy 19:15; Matthew 18:15-17). No wonder lawsuits among Christians represented 'utter failure' on the part of the church (1 Corinthians 6:7).

There is a saying, 'Don't wash your dirty linen in public', which is often used as a cloak for ongoing injustice within communities and the church. God's promise to right wrongs seems either too remote or all-consuming – 'Vengeance is Mine, and recompense; their foot shall slip in due time; for the day of their calamity is at hand; and the things to come hasten upon them' (Deuteronomy 32:35; compare with Romans 12:17-21) – and our natural inclination is to demand that those who do wrong pay for their sins. However, being a Christian does not mean being gullible or a doormat. It may at times be quite reasonable to bring an end to abuse and exploitation by asking the law to mediate. It is the spiteful self-gratifying of justice for its own sake that we are considering here.

In Matthew 18:17, for example, Jesus seems to be suggesting that if the offender does not recognise the authority of the church, then he or she should be treated no different to the ungodly: in other words, those subject to God should be subject to the counsel of God (his Word) or his agents (the church); otherwise, let them be subject to the law of the land. The challenge for the BMCs today is not to present to the world a context that depicts the church as failing to meet even the standards of the secular courts. Our selfish motives and personal ambitions should be sacrificed for the benefit of God's kingdom. There are no badges or crowns for condoning bad behaviour within the church, and doing nothing is not an option: either the matter should be resolved internally through appropriate guidance and discipline; or, if the situation demands, then the church should either deal with the wrongdoer through the secular system as a 'worldly person', or 'deliver such a one to Satan' (1 Corinthians 5:5) through excommunication. This will speak clearly to society as to what the church stands for.

Principle 5: Do not cultivate unhealthy relationships

There is no doubt that Paul was giving his advice from a Jewish perspective but, of course, the context into which he was speaking was not so straightforward. The Corinthian church was a multicultural church, and its members did not all share the same values and opinions, or the same levels of guilt and shame. What was a big deal to the Jews was not necessarily of consequence to Gentiles. At least the church recognised that if they were to worship and live together in unity, and be a credible witness to the rest of society, there had to be some convergence of ideals and ideas.

For the Jewish Christians and proselytes, the rules were straightforward and the laws governing sexual probity were clear (Leviticus 18; Deuteronomy 22:13–30). A young woman whose virginity could not be proven was to be stoned to death at the discretion of her husband. A false accusation regarding a woman's virginity fetched a hefty fine (one hundred shekels of silver; about £20,000 in today's money). Adultery incurred the death penalty, as did the infidelity of an engaged person who had had an affair, and the rape of an engaged woman. However, anyone who had sex with an unattached virgin had to marry her, pay compensation to her father and could not divorce her as long as she lived. There was also a severe punishment for illegitimate children. The situation for the Gentile converts was, however, vastly different. Aphrodite was the goddess worshipped at Corinth, and she was the patroness of prostitutes.[1] It seems as though an integral part of the Graeco-Roman culture included having sexual relationships with temple prostitutes of both sexes. It may well be that, in such a culture, which had at least 120 feast days, Paul had to assert to the Gentile members of the church that their new faith saw their formal liberty as *porneia* (sexually immoral).

While we know from Scripture that these punishments were not always meted out, they were often invoked, either at the demand of the Lord or through the zealousness of the pious. Their main purpose was to promote righteousness and holiness, but the consequences for families and the wrongdoers were harsh. Paul's comments on marital fidelity, fornication, divorce, widowhood and relationships between believers and unbelievers were all designed to generate confidence for the Jews, set new parameters for the Gentiles and reassure those who feared that their children would be outside God's grace because of their unbelieving spouse (1 Corinthians ch 7). This way, the distinctiveness of the church from the rest of society would be preserved, as well as the relationships within it.

Inappropriate or unhealthy relationships have serious consequences for church and family alike (1 Corinthians chs 6,7). In particular, families affected by them are likely to be permanently scarred. Nothing generates more controversy, pain and distress, and fractured relationships, both in the church and a large part of society, than infidelity. Often, when a Christian couple separates or divorces, one partner feels obliged to leave the church. If that person moves on to another church, how does it affect the relationship between the two churches? Moreover, members of both congregations are placed in the difficult situation of how to manage their friendships and to avoid taking sides in the fear that their attempt at neutrality might be interpreted as betrayal. For the Christian, it is not merely nitpicking to pay attention to the kinds of relationships he or she forms, and to take care to maintain the good ones. Not only is it vital for the well-being of the individual and of society, it also plays an essential part in preserving the harmony within the church.

Principle 6: Do not be insensitive to others

Multiculturalism has its benefits as well as its challenges. In the early days of the church, when a Jew became a Christian, he or she was free to continue attending the synagogue and celebrating the various Jewish feast days and festivals. This meant that, apart from the obvious theological divergence, Jewish converts were able to keep most of their relationships, culture and practices intact. However, when it came to Gentiles, the rules seem to change. This may have been because of fears that some Gentile converts would slip back into paganism, and concerns about the kinds of pagan rituals that took place at significant events such as births, deaths, marriages and other community celebrations. Very likely this divergence led to feelings of disgruntlement: 'Why aren't we allowed to attend our weddings in our temples and enjoy ourselves, when you [Jews] are allowed to do so? If we do attend, why must we behave as though we are fasting? And why should we be forced to spend our money in Jewish shops and make them rich, while our own shops are struggling for business and our neighbourhood is getting poorer?'

These feelings of discontent may well have come to a head over the matter of offering food to idols (1 Corinthians ch 8). The weight of contention is evident in Paul's appeal at the outset: 'If anyone thinks that he knows anything, he knows nothing yet as he ought to know' (8:2) – in other words, everyone has to set aside their presuppositions and entrenched positions so that he can enlighten them and provoke the level of sensitivity necessary to bring about unity.

Paul went on to affirm that idols are nothing (8:4) so, technically, food offered to nothing should have no repercussions (8:5,6). However, on the other hand, those offering the food to idols are offering it to something, which is certainly not God, so it must be to demons (10:18-20). This may have been why some converted Gentiles found it offensive for others to continue their association with the old ways (8:7). However, the answer to this issue cannot rest solely on human feelings or be merely a matter of convenience. Also, more importantly, what is God's perspective? Since what we eat is not what defiles or sanctifies us (8:8), this is in fact more about conscience and conduct of the individual. Three possible approaches emerge, represented by three groups – the advocates for abstinence, the libertarians and the enlightened.

Conscience may have dictated the necessity for abstinence on the part of both Jewish and Gentile Christians – more than likely those advocating abstinence demanded that everyone abstained. The libertarians, on the other hand, probably felt that it was nobody's business what they did; they were not going to own up or boast about their actions or convictions, nor were they prepared to condemn anyone else. They loved their people, their culture and their community, without making a 'song and dance' about it. They simply enjoyed their lives as they saw fit. However, this group was at greatest risk of being tempted or lapsing back into their past life (8:10-13). Remarkably, none of the above two groups would have had anything to fear if the enlightened group had been absent. The enlightened ones adopted a bold and open-minded approach which put them in danger of becoming insensitive to others and thereby causing conflict, as well as weakening the resolve of fellow believers who were weaker (8:9). For Paul, this kind of obstinacy was tantamount to having a confrontation with God (10:22).

All these are major issues for the BMCs. For example, many former members, including former evangelists, of Cherubim and Seraphim and other African and Caribbean Spiritual churches, are adamant that these churches cannot be considered orthodox. Having examined the requirements of Scripture, they have taken the view that there is a huge chasm between those churches and other BMCs, although there have been attempts to present them as 'one and the same'. On the other hand, many African Christians who attend either White Majority Pentecostal or the historic churches feel that they must have two ceremonies for occasions such as births and marriages, in order to fulfil both their cultural customs and the provisions made by the church. So, for example, often little or no provision is made for naming ceremonies as part of the worship service, which is regrettable.

Being sensitive to others' feelings and failings is not necessarily about taking a backward step. And looking for unity in a pluralist society does not have to mean uniting our spirits with other religions, whether they be other, or even secular, faiths. It is a good rule to bear in mind that if participating in an event or activity will damage our unity within the body of Christ, it may be that we should care about the concerns of our brothers and sisters in Christ enough to reconsider our motives or even to give up the pursuit (10:12–24).

Principle 7: Do not abuse your authority

As an apostle to the Corinthian church, Paul denied himself the privilege of enjoying the 'good life' or of demanding financial support for his ministry (1 Corinthians 9:1–18). Although the law and the Lord made room for such provisions, his conviction was that, even if it killed him, he was not going to have any one saying that he was in the ministry for the money (9:15). Unlike the other apostles, he even refrained from marrying (9:5). He viewed his reward for his hard work as being able to 'present the gospel of Christ without charge' so that he would not abuse his authority in the gospel (9:18). In this way, Paul liberated himself to serve all (9:19–22). And he saw the benefits to himself of adopting this approach: 'Now this I do for the gospel's sake, that I may be partaker of it with you' (9:23); and again, 'I discipline my body and bring it into subjection, lest, when I have preached to others, I myself should become disqualified' (9:27).

There are benefits and privileges that come with leadership. Any abuse of these undermines trust and generates scepticism within the followers. Notions of fat cats, poor corporate governance and outright manipulation and abuse are now familiar features of the social landscape. Chief executives and directors are often seen as looking after their own interests at the expense of their workers, often without any sense of remorse; instead, everyone gives the impression that they are worth it.

The way that Christian leaders raise money, whether by television, direct mail or in meetings, for very worthy causes or for the advancement of the gospel, can also lend itself to the accusation of manipulation or exploitation. The gospel, with its demands, is already an offence to those outside the church: if we then go on to exercise our rights and ignore our responsibilities, we are likely to attract even more antagonism to the gospel, and unnecessarily so. Our goal should be to refrain from putting up barriers between the cross and those needing to receive it as we preach the gospel of Christ. There are many other ways in which leaders can abuse their authority. They can do so by engaging in sexual inappropriate relationships, or sexually abusing children and vulnerable adults. I have even heard someone complain that their pastor was actively encouraging his church to borrow money from 'loan sharks' in order to upkeep his lifestyle! There is a very thin line between accountability and abuse. Some churches ask members to tell them exactly how much they earn; others demand that they seek the leader's permission before making personal decisions. In no way can these be merely marks of discipleship; rather, they are controlling vices.

Principle 8: Do not ignore traditions or conventions

Tradition seems to have ranked very highly on the list of controversies at Corinth (1 Corinthians 11:1–23; 14:26–40). Paul praised the church for keeping the traditions that he had delivered to them (11:2). However, this was precisely the problem! Those traditions were mostly Jewish customs and not those of the Gentiles. In addition, they were practices that were acceptable to the churches in Jerusalem and Antioch and which, on the surface at least, were useful in presenting the church in Corinth as being no different from the others. However, given Corinth's multicultural membership, this was probably not proving workable. No doubt Paul felt that he had to step in to stop dissension brewing, and to determine once and for all which customs were acceptable and which were not.

First, he seems to have made it mandatory for men to have short hair and to keep their heads uncovered, and for women to have long hair and to keep their heads covered (11:2–16). A Bible commentator has suggested that this may have been because he wanted to counteract a pagan custom in which the priest of a cult, who was often drawn from the elite of society, would distinguish himself from other worshippers by praying and sacrificing with his head covered.[2] A church leader imitating this custom could be accused of drawing attention to himself and his status, rather than to Christ. However, even if this was the case, it was not un-Jewish for men to have long hair: Samson, Absalom (King David's son) and those who took the Nazirite vow all wore their hair long (Judges 13:5; 2 Samuel 14:25-26; Numbers 6:5) . Paul even ignored the fact that removing their long hair may have caused difficulties for the Gentiles, given that those who wore their hair short could have easily been mistaken for slaves.

This contradiction waxed worse when it came to women, as Paul once again upheld the Jewish custom. In addition, he found support from an edict of the Romans that a woman who committed adultery, thereby shaming her husband, had to have her head shorn.[3] However, the apostle was being consistent by placing Jewish customs and practices, which obligated a man 'to divorce a woman who appeared in the streets with head uncovered',[4] above those of Gentiles. And since the houses in which Christians met and worshipped were often next door or very near to the Jewish synagogue (Acts 18:7,8), this issue took on greater urgency because of its potential for causing offence.

To crown it all, Paul was not prepared to condone any dissenters: 'If anyone seems to be contentious, we have no such custom, nor do the churches of God' (1 Corinthians 11:16). In other words, the Jews don't do it; neither do the other churches that have been started. So, tough luck if you don't like it!

There was a further realignment with Jewish customs when the apostle imposed a ban on women speaking in the church. Here again, Paul appealed to the Jewish law for support (14:34). He also pointed to the authority on whose behalf he was speaking. Wherever his hearers thought they were on the spiritual or religious hierarchy, they had to acknowledge that what he, Paul, was saying was from the Lord – anyone who did not acknowledge this fact should not be recognised by the churches (14:37,38). Controversially, Paul was prepared to go as far as placing the traditions of Jewish law above Gentile traditions. In fact, on this crucial point he was not prepared to make any compromises.

The value of traditions poses a tremendous challenge to BMCs and churches from other minority communities. Our traditions have tended to evolve from the customs and practices of our culture. They help us to define who we are and emphasise our roots, giving us a sense of belonging. They give meaning to our life and are the lens by which we judge the world we live in. However, when it comes to faith, our traditions are usually scrutinised from the viewpoint of Western Christianity. For many decades, particular Scriptures were used to excommunicate, or bar from membership, those who did not confirm to the traditions, customs and practices of their congregations. The wearing of hats or trousers, and the lengths of skirts, was the theme of many a sermon, prayer meeting and fasting day. Association with other churches were determined by whether or not their members wore jewellery. A classic confusion arose around the legality of married couples wearing matrimonial rings in a culture which assumes that if you don't wear one you are single and available. What customs and traditions remain permissible for Christians continues to be a matter of considerable debate.

Principle 9: Do not misrepresent the gospel

Two other factors involved in the trouble and strife at Corinth revolved around the misrepresentation of the gospel. First, there was the misunderstanding of the significance and symbolism of the Lord's Supper (1 Corinthians 11:20-22), which in turn undermined the profound reality of Christ's resurrection (11:23-34; 15:1-19,50-58).

In both the Jewish and pagan traditions there were many feast days involving lots of fellowship, eating and drinking. However, for new Christians who chose not to become proselytes, there was nothing; instead, the Lord's Supper became their focal point for celebration. However, rather than being an occasion to remember the death of Jesus Christ, and the need for individual and collective purification, it became an occasion for discord, and an opportunity for those who had plenty to eat and drink to despise those who had little or nothing (11:22).

Not only was the death of Christ brought into disrepute but also his resurrection (15:12). Those who claimed that there was no resurrection undermined the work of Christ on the cross and removed any possibility of life after death for themselves (15:13-19). Paul was dismayed that some in the church did not have knowledge of the things of God; it was questionable if some even knew God at all (15:34). This uncertainty had the potential to undermine their entire faith and to take away their ability to affirm, defend and proclaim the faith that they professed to believe in.

Paul sums up the message of the gospel simply and concisely:

- Christ died for our sins (15:3).
- He was buried (15:4).
- He rose again on the third day and was seen by over five hundred witnesses and the apostles (15:4-6).

In presenting theology in this concise way, Paul was wanting to focus their attention on what Christ had already done for them and what he was going to do in the future: because Christ has risen, they too would experience resurrection; and therefore they had hope both in this life and for eternity (15:50–58).

Poor theology is at the heart of much church disunity. A lack of understanding of Scripture and of basic theology can greatly reduce Christian effectiveness. On the other hand, a little knowledge can also 'puff up', and lead those who have attained academic qualifications to despise those who haven't. Nevertheless, it important that all Christians know the fundamentals of their faith. There is little virtue in refuting arguments with words like 'the kingdom of God is not in word but in power' (4:20), but not to know the theology that lies behind them. Neither approach – wilful ignorance or too much knowledge – is faithful to the apostle's argument. We ought to be of one mind as to who the enemies of the gospel really are: that plethora of vices of the devil, including cynicism, heresy, humanism and other philosophies of man; and the culture of syncretism, pluralism and liberalism within. However, it is poor theology – 'hobby horse' teaching and the narrowness of focus – that does the most damage. It prevents Christians from becoming mature and instead creates unbalanced people who, in turn, become poor witnesses for the gospel.

Principle 10: Do not neglect the poor

Paul was always careful to identify with the oppressed, outcast, abused and persecuted. It is in this arena that he found most strength, perseverance and purpose. It is in this spirit that he sets out to establish links between the Corinthian church and the churches in other provinces, and ends his letter to the church with a brief reference to a collection of money to be sent to the apostles in Jerusalem (1 Corinthians 16:1–3). On the face of it, this may well have seemed a straightforward exercise, but again the problems associated with multiculturalism might well have been at work. The resources were to be handled by the dominant Jewish membership. There is no mention of a collection for the local Gentiles, nor of any provision for their widows and orphans – unless the central fund was intended to be redirected according to need. Additionally, 'the saints' (v 1) are probably those who are in need either out of necessity (the poor) or as a result of their commitment to the ongoing development of the church (those in the ministry).

Failure to meet the needs and obligations of church members reflects badly on the whole church. In effect, it silences God and makes him out to be uninterested in the affairs of his people. To all intents and purpose, the church should be the hands of God. Christians who place a dichotomy between the gospel and social action often bring the gospel into disrepute. This attitude is usually an excuse for inaction, a pitiful response when the truth is that either there are not the human and financial resources and skills to deal with the issue, or it is not a church's priority but it doesn't want to say so.

'The greatest of these is love'

In exploring these ten principles to promote unity, I am sure that you noticed my omission of the other gems to be found in 1 Corinthians. In fact, I have resisted the temptation to look at love: this is because, to my mind, it covers all of the above. I felt it important to keep this as a summary of all that has been said in the ten principles outlined above. Love for God, love for others and love for self are all necessary to ensure unity in ways that present the gospel as it was originally intended to be shown. Love is the glue for unity. No wonder the apostle admonishes us to pursue love, and to desire this best of spiritual gifts. Love stands out above faith and hope as the greatest of the virtues (13:8,13), one that underpins all the others and that will never become outdated. Very often when the church approaches the text of 1 Corinthians 13, it is in the context of wedding ceremonies or intimate relationships between couples. Yet the context of this chapter does not give us any indication that personal relationships was what Paul had in mind when he wrote the chapter.

If we look carefully, we see that 1 Corinthians 12 deals with fragmentation and separation within the body of Christ owing to misunderstanding of the importance of one gift over another. Then 1 Corinthians 14 challenges the use of gifts in the church either for private benefit or solely for members of the congregation. The chapter also deals with the confusion likely to be caused by the abuse or misuse of speaking in tongues that are unknown to those listening. Love, as Paul describes it in 1 Corinthians 13, is absolutely necessary to keep church unity. We need to take it seriously, and understand that somehow we must learn to appreciate other people's talents, skills and abilities. Ours may be unique and special but not superior. Love will constrain us from being selfish, self-centred and self-seeking, and will take us to a place where we can overlook one another's faults (not sins) and recognise that whatever spiritual gifts we have received come second to our love for each other.

Having re-examined the evidence, I can reach no other conclusion than that the number one reason for disunity is not disagreement over differences in culture, style and theology; rather, it is because we with-hold our unconditional love from each other. Too often we refuse to suffer long and to show kindness to one another; or we are so desperate to show that we are different and have it all together, we become arro-gant ('puffed up', v 4); or we behave rudely to each other, to the point of thinking that we don't need to return a phone call, our time is too important; or we dismiss everything another brother or sister is doing for the kingdom because we see them as having no value'; or our deter-mination to remain 'focused on our vision' leads us to seek only our own interests at the expense of others; or we become angry and frustrated people who are easily provoked and who, as a consequence, cannot help but feel 'ill will' (evil thoughts) towards those who offend us.

But Paul points us in a positive direction. If we rejoice in the truth – God's word, his justice and his righteousness – instead of sin and evil-doing; if we bear all things, believe all things, hope all things and endure all things (1 Corinthians 13:7), there would never be division in the church. There may be fewer congregations but probably more people in the pews. And, by our love, the world will come to know that we are indeed truly Christians (John 13:34,35).

You may also have noted that, throughout this chapter, it has been evident that, because unity with Jerusalem and the dominant Jewish congregations in the region was so important to him, Paul seems to have made demands on the Gentile church in Corinth to take on Jewish tra-ditions. To be honest, it seems to me that he often rode roughshod over the Gentile preferences and relegated their customs to a secondary posi-tion. This poses a huge challenge for the BMCs. Should we give way in areas of theology, church practice, our view on essential doctrines and the way that we worship and evangelise in order to conform to the models of 'Britishness' and British church life? Or should we operate with our convictions, distinctiveness and differences. After all, nearly two millennia have passed and society has learnt to be more tolerant, pluralistic and accepting of each other. Certainly it seems that, for the sake of unity, Paul gave the Gentiles less leeway than he could otherwise have done. This presents the church today with something of a chal-lenge. If the majority of us accept these ten general principles, then how far should we be prepared to go in order to maintain the unity of the church in the twenty-first century? Whatever our conclusions, our moti-vation and actions must be undergirded by love. We are all God's creation, and we are all on the same side. Like any successful team, we must work with and for each other, seeking to achieve the same goals, albeit applying our individual gifts and talents. This love is what qualifies us to be a part of the team in the first place.

Endnotes

1 E M Yamauchi, 'Prostitution' in *The Illustrated Bible Dictionary*, vol. 3, IVP, 1998, p1289.
2 Bruce Winter, '1 Corinthians' in *The New Bible Commentary, 21st Century Edition*, IVP, 1994, p1178.
3 Winter, p1178.
4 C C Kroeger, 'Head' in G F Hawthorne, R P Martin and D Reid (eds), *Dictionary of Paul and His Letters*, IVP, 1993, p376.

Part 4

Looking to the future

Chapter 12

The future of Black Majority Churches

This book first began to take shape fourteen years ago, at the point when God called me to serve the Black Majority Churches. This concluding chapter coincides with my decision to step down as General Director of ACEA after eight years in the post. The whole of my time there has given me a unique perspective on which to reflect, as well as the opportunity to forecast what the future of the BMCs may look like. I am well aware that, in attempting to chart the trajectory of these churches, this journey will be scrutinised thoroughly in the years to come. Nonetheless, I hope that the reflections offered in this chapter will provide a basis for future dialogue on how the BMCs embrace the future.

What does the future hold?

To carry out an effective analysis on the future of the BMCs, it would perhaps be helpful to adopt a three-dimensional approach.

First, we could look within the churches themselves, ask lots of questions and take note of what they think of themselves. Are they satisfied with the progress they have made? Do they feel that they have accomplished their mission? Is their vision compatible with the aspirations of their members? Do they have the credibility and the influence to promote and demand transformation within British society? Can they survive scrutiny and demonstrate integrity? Do they have the ability to influence and inspire future generations? The answers to these questions will demonstrate whether or not there is sufficient momentum within the churches to be self-motivating and enthusiastic for the cause of the gospel. They may also be challenging enough to banish any residual inertia from pulpits, pews and altars.

The second approach is to go outwards. In looking to the future, we ought perhaps to consider the context in which these churches operate. Here, the political and economic climate, issues around immigration and racism, the nature of morality and values, as well as ethics and the intellectual debate, will all have some bearing on the priority and relevance of these churches. The main concerns of the historic denominations, the theological debates of the day, and the way in which the BMCs relate to the wider church and to their critics, will all help to guide the future.

Finally, the third approach is to move upwards. Black Christians should be anticipating what God will do in the nation. If we accept the proposition that the emergence of the BMCs in the UK is the Lord's doing, then it is safe to say that our omnipresent, omnipotent God will determine what he will do with them in the future. Then again we can legitimately ask, will God cede his responsibility to the whole church, giving them the full responsibility of being his witnesses to society? Will he envelop the churches in spite of their character, strengths, weaknesses or credibility? Will this result in an awakening, or a shaking of both the church and society? Or will it simply be a matter of those who earnestly seek God finding him, and those who are not seeking him to freewheel into the devices and desires of their own hearts?

To make sense of these three approaches, I have opted to explore them in reverse order, starting with the move upwards and then outwards, before going inwards.

Moving upwards: what will God do in the future?

I hope that readers of this book will forgive me if I appear simplistic and suggest that the most straightforward route to discovering what God will do in the future is to ask him.

Like me, you may have had the privilege (or the misfortune) of hearing a plethora of sermons, or of reading deluge of books, all purporting to enlighten us as to what God is doing today, and what he will be doing in the future. And you may well have reached the conclusion that either no one really knows what will happen, or that God is and will be doing an awful lot. There is a huge distinction to be made between predicting the future and exercising spiritual gifts such as prophecy, words of wisdom, words of knowledge and discernment. Predicting the future can be a scientific or an intellectual exercise that allows for analysis that charts particular trends and patterns: this is how many businesses and organisations forecast their growth, profits or decline. It is the same process that enables meteorologists to predict the weather forecast well in advance, allowing people to plan their day, judge what to wear or decide whether to hold an event indoors or outdoors. Now, I have had no primary revelation from God on what the future holds for the BMCs. However, as a participant and observer of these churches, I have explored their development for nigh on nineteen years; I have seen them at their best and at their worst, through tragedies and in their effervescence. Throughout this experience, the one constant has been the work of God.

There is an adage that says, 'A chain is as strong as its weakest link.' Despite my argument that the BMCs are not a monolithic group, there is an underlining thread running through the tapestry of church life, so that the actions of one church, pastor or indeed any individual Christian can shape perceptions of the group as a whole. For example, I had a call recently from a BBC reporter who was investigating whether or not a particular denomination had an active policy to disinherit members' families from their legacies. As it turned out, a recently deceased member of that denomination had made the denomination a major benefactor in his will. His relatives were very displeased by his action and wanted to discredit the church publicly. After I had had a full discussion of the possible scenarios that could have taken place, and had explained that legacies are integral to Christian and non-Christian charitable giving, the reporter decided not to go any further with the investigation.

Unfortunately, if we are honest, we must admit that some of our prophets do place profits above probity. Many 'prophetic words' do not have their genesis in revelation or vision, but are essentially psychological or sociological constructs. This is not to say that they could not also be godly insights into the human condition, but often what is presented as revelation can be found in the latest leadership or personal development manual, or is a straightforward biblical response to a social problem.

Every generation must have an opportunity to embrace the power, wisdom, authority and saving grace of God. Equally, there are counter-forces at work which may tempt Christians to ignore God and take his statutes lightly. Yet God will work through his church to accomplish his purposes and plans. The BMCs may well be judged for any inconsistencies, false claims and unjust actions. Nevertheless, their eagerness to be spiritual, to demonstrate the power of the anointing and the gift of the Holy Spirit, and to place them at the centre of what God is saying and doing in his world should serve to prevent them from becoming apostates who are irreverent and misrepresent God. Certainly, as an emerging church, the BMCs have been guilty of inconsistencies which have generated some cynicism in the wider church. However, it is exactly this dearth of confidence that they should resist as they continue to exalt the virtues of God.

One reason why digital signals are superior to analogue ones is their ability to reduce the level of interference and noise attached to the pure signal; it is also easier to amplify a digital signal without inducing distortion. So even when a digital signal picks up unwanted interference and noise, or becomes distorted, it is easy to restore the original signal through a process of sampling or filtering. I believe that, to understand and see clearly what God will do in the BMCs, and the wider church, it will be necessary to do some spiritual sampling and filtering.

So what will God do with the BMCs in the future? I do not know. I do not have much confidence in many of the end-time predictions, and not all of the chatter and emotionally charged experiences have eternal value. However, I am confident that God will continue to act in my generation. As he does so, he may well continue to use those instruments likely to have the greatest impact for justice, peace and equality, and those that will advance the mission and dominance of his kingdom over the kingdom of darkness. To achieve this, he may use political systems, communities, charities, businesses or even those who have no faith in him: God has no exclusive contract with the church or Christians. Although they have always been his first choice, his grace will fall on the just and the unjust alike (Matthew 5:45).

It will be in this environment that the BMCs must define their role. The louder they allow God's voice to be heard, and the more visibly they display his character and work, the better they will be at fulfilling his agenda. God's ways are not our ways. All that we can do as God's ambassadors, servants, slaves, sons, daughters and workers with Christ, is to pursue, with urgency, faithfulness and sincerity, the tasks we have been assigned; and then to wait with eagerness and anticipation for new instructions and direction. He will not give the BMCs responsibilities beyond their capacity to bear. Rather, he will present them with opportunities to make a difference to the world according to their gifting and abilities.

Going outwards: in what context will BMCs be working?

In exploring the future of the BMCs, we must also consider the external context, or the environment, in which they operate. By far the most significant threats to the churches' future growth and development are the political, cultural and economic climate in the UK, which may conspire to hamper the churches' progress, and to limit their freedom and authenticity. There is no doubt that, following the invasion of Iraq in 2003, the BMCs have lost out to Islam, and Muslims have become the main spokespersons on issues of minority communities, justice and fairness in society. It is also the case that the imbalanced and preferential treatment that is meted out to other faiths by government, local authorities and other institutions is not taken sufficiently seriously by BMCs. Often they are seen merely as a derivative or put in the same category as the historic denominations, because they are all Christians. This has a significant impact on the development of government policy, and the churches' engagement with politics and society. Seen this way, if the historic denominations are sidelined, so will the BMCs.

As a consequence of this, the needs of Black people, especially from former English-speaking colonies, are often not catered for. The assumption is that, since they already speak English, all they need to do is to apply sufficient dedication and effort, and they will find their way. Furthermore, other minority communities often have institutions, programmes and provisions established to assist them, giving them a distinct advantage and a supportive environment in which to develop and grow. Notwithstanding, here is where the BMCs can come into their own. They are frequently called upon to establish such support mechanisms and environments, and these, though costly to themselves, provide a bedrock for loyalty, commitment and growth and set a key agenda which the BMCs must pursue.

The future of the BMCs will be shaped by the UK's immigration policy. For example, will the government place quotas on the number of overseas students coming into the country? There may be an outcry if there are not sufficient places for British or European students in the British education system – this despite the fact that overseas students subsidise the education system. What if a future right-wing government implemented far more stringent measures such as forced repatriation? Or there was a break-up of the Commonwealth? What if Britain pulled out of the European Union, and ditched all their laws and treaties? History has taught us that Western countries are quite happy to underwrite flawed economic and social policies in order to achieve political and commercial objectives. The point here is that anything which further impedes migration will adversely affect the BMCs.

Immigration, particularly of young families, stimulates the current growth in the BMCs alongside the fruits of evangelism and mission.

Unless there is a wave of revival throughout the country, then the churches will need immigration, internal growth and evangelism in order to continue delivering adherents to the faith. However, the statistics tells us that the size of Caribbean families is shrinking. Another stark reality is that Black people only make up 2 per cent of British society. This means that there is only a pool of 1.1 million Black people in Britain (1% Black Caribbean, 0.8% Black African, 0.2% Black Other).[1] If the average of church attendance within this community does not rise above the current 33 per cent, then the church is bound to plateau at around 370,000 members. This is the case even if we allowed for a 5 per cent Black population growth and coupled that with a percentage of the 660,000 who have identified themselves as 'mixed race'. Further, if we make allowances for our brothers and sisters who do not appear on the official census register, the BMCs may still struggle to reach or surpass 0.5 million members.

This statistical reality has led to at least two perspectives. Firstly, there are those who see the BMCs as White Majority Churches in transition. This means that over time, as the Black population diminishes or saturates, then the BMCs will be forced to concentrate on other people groups. Those with expansive visions sees their future wrapped up in their ability to engage with other ethnic communities, including the majority White population. The second possibility is one that sees the trends in society continuing as they are. This means that there will always be a need for the churches to meet the particular needs of their people. While they should continue to maintain an open-door policy for everyone, there is no reason to believe that warfare, natural disasters or other human catastrophes around the world will stop. If anything, these things will get worse as we approach the return of Christ. More significantly, a depraved world will always have a need for God and his church. There may well be those who take the view that even these static numbers should not diminish or reduce the current and potential impact of the BMCs. To use the Jewish faith as an example, although small in size they continue to have incredible leverage in every area of society. It is this similar leverage that the BMCs need to explore, develop and exploit.

The political climate of a country changes the cultural and economic direction of its society. In the current debate about sexuality and gender, the law may well choose to ignore the issue of conscience and to demand that all churches should marry gay, lesbian and transsexual couples, since to refuse would be to impinge on their human rights and to treat them differently. The consequence may be to revoke a church's licence to marry or to preside over marriage ceremonies. To go further, if the government of the day takes a more radical line and rescinds their charitable status, this is bound to have an adverse effect on the churches. My own view is that these and other issues will be on the table in less than twenty years.

The way in which the church develops may be determined by legislation. Churches may not necessarily be able to set their own initial priorities. For example, new restaurants have to demonstrate that they meet the health and safety requirements of the Food Standards Agency and the other regulatory bodies. Similarly, the church will have to meet the increasing requirements of child protection, criminal record checks, equal opportunities, trustees and governance training from the outset. Obviously these policies and principles set the culture and the values of an organisation. For some, these measures may seem unnecessary, but it is when things go wrong that these policies, or their absence, turn out to be pivotal for an organisation.

However, leading the charge for change in the BMCs may have less to do with society and more to do with the historic denominations. I say this because, as pompous as it may sound, the BMCs are (or should be) a lens by which the historic denominations measure their own standing in, and perspective on, society and their relationship with God. This uncomfortable position may demand readjustments from both sides, but it is clear that to choose either to conform or to withdraw is out of the question. What is more likely, however, is that positions held by the BMCs will be undermined. For example, if it is accepted by the historic denominations that a belief in God is not a prerequisite qualification for the priesthood, then it will become extremely difficult to argue for Christian distinctiveness. Not that it is easy to do so currently: I have actually witnessed Christians leaders – sitting round the table, looking at how government departments should consult with faith communities – argue that there is no real Christian distinctiveness and that we are no different than other faiths. Consequently, it is likely that those who place a high value on Scripture, such as the BMCs, will be left in a precarious position because there is no consensus on the fundamentals of the Christian faith.

One might argue that the reason that the government was able to accelerate legislation relating to the reclassification of drugs, civil partnerships and gender reassignment was because the church had given up its opposition to the debate. Turning a blind eye to the use of drugs in the London Borough of Lambeth, and the subsequent reclassification of cannabis, was endorsed by the Church of England's Social Responsibility Committee, which called for doctors to be given permission to dispense drugs to addicts. Equally, the sexuality legislation was given impetus because Archbishop Rowan Williams expressed his willingness to ordain gay bishops who were still living with their partners. The ceding of such biblical principles and values will make life difficult for the BMCs, and may jeopardise the future and further unity of the wider church.

There is yet another challenge that will be brought to bear on both the BMCs in historic denominations and those within White Majority Pentecostal denominations. Successful BMCs within their ranks may well suffer as a result of predatory leadership: their healthy growth and development may make them the first choice of White leaders looking for promotion, with the result that up-and-coming Black leaders in those congregations are denied opportunities for attaining senior leadership responsibilities. While there is nothing wrong with aspiring to lead a progressive church, it would be unwise to assume that Black leadership within these churches will flourish. Unless there is a strategic and deliberate attempt, by both leadership and parishioners, to ensure that those called to pastoral and other leadership positions in the church are equipped to fulfil these roles, there may well be a drought of young eligible leaders.

The other buoy to look out for in any sea change is the neutralising and neutering of congregations. There is a tendency in the BMCs to play down the importance of dealing with the issues such as drugs, mental health, underachievement, unemployment, youth crime, family breakdown, racism and the lack of meritocracy within its ranks and society. Some years ago, when the BBC filmed one of the BMCs largest churches, all the contributors on screen were White – there was no footage of any Black person in the congregation, when over 70 per cent of the attendees were Black. When Black members of the congregation wrote to the pastor to complain, he responded in the pulpit the following Sunday by stating that instead of wasting their money on stamps, they should have placed it in the offering. This scenario is no different to the one in which the Ford car manufacturers removed all the minority ethnic faces from their posters, and replaced them with White ones, for a major advertising campaign. That pastor had disrespected the Black members of the church and disempowered the whole congregation, preventing them from dealing with this issue in a positive and open manner. Equally, the church lost the moral right to give prophetic leadership and a discerning response to a serious social problem. It is not only the leadership that loses credibility, but the members themselves. They lose the respect of their family, friends, colleagues and community. They are seen as not caring or of being out of touch with the 'real' world and the 'real' issues. It is this kind of perception that is most likely to affect the future of the BMCs. And, by the way, this credibility hazard is prevalent in every segment of the BMCs.

Looking inwards: how should the BMCs see the future?

I am in celebratory mood because, despite the challenges ahead, the future of the BMCs is extremely healthy. While it may sometimes seem as though there are those who secretly hope that the BMCs are a passing fad which will, like all other institutions, go out of fashion and favour, there are also those who are applauding because the BMCs have brought life and hope to the ailing church in the Britain. Even so, the voices that matter most are those that come from within the churches themselves. The BMCs must lift up their own voices and articulate their own history, aspirations and convictions.

In this book I have sought to outline a framework that has evolved over nearly sixty years. However, the BMCs are now at a strategic junction, and it is safe to say that the pioneering phase of the church has come to an end. Despite the ongoing church planting, growth and development, we cannot realistically describe what is taking place today as 'pioneering'. The pioneers are now citizens – they have become part of the system, institutionalised - and new issues are now on the table. In some instances, the former pioneers have retired, returned to their place of birth or have gone to be with the Lord. This is not to the churches' disadvantage but, rather, is an integral part of their growth and development process. The BMCs' numerical growth has to be complemented with organisational and strategic community development, and at the heart of this maturation period is good governance, transforming discipleship, integrity, and relevance that will undergird their dynamic expression of faith in Jesus Christ.

How will their credibility and integrity stand up?

Between October 2002 and January 2003, the BMCs' innocence came to an abrupt end. The bubble burst when the Charity Commission placed

Receiver Managers in two of the largest churches in the UK – Victory Christian Centre, under the leadership of Pastor Douglas Goodman; and Kingsway International Christian Centre, under the leadership of Pastor Matthew Ashimolowo. These churches were to undergo severe scrutiny of both their credibility and their integrity. The things that these churches had in common were that they were both BMCs and they were independent: they could also be described as having strong and independent leadership styles and organisational cultures. But in every other way, the reasons for the Commission's intervention were very different. This did not stop the shock waves of anger and anxiety engulfing the pews and the pulpits, and it sparked a widespread review within the BMCs of how we administer our churches.

From the Charity Commission's point of view, the critical trigger was a deep concern about the governance of these two churches. Their fear was that these churches were not being administered in the best interest of the charities, and that there were sufficient concerns about personal benefits to trustees and leaders to prompt action. From the churches' point of view, the main concern was about government interference in spiritual matters. To them, the regulator had overstepped the mark by predetermining how religion must be organised. More significantly, there was a lack of understanding of the culture of this new brand of church, and there was a concerted effort to remove or weaken the controlling influence of the strong, visionary, individualistic leader and to replace it with leadership by committee. No longer would the senior pastor be the head and final arbiter, but rather a board of trustees. No one, other than the Charity Commission, the Receiver Managers and these churches, will ever know the full range of issues that emerged. However, having had the thankless task of being one of the mediators in the process, I did gain some insight into the minds and actions of all parties.

The circumstances involving the Victory Christian Centre (VCC) were well publicised in the media. The police were already investigating allegations of rape and sexual assaults against the senior pastor when the Charity Commission responded to claims of misappropriate use of funds. They believed what they discovered merited the urgent intensification of their investigation and, to protect the charity's assets, they installed a Receiver Manager. Legally, the receiver manager became the custodian of the assets and was, in effect, the boss of the church: the church could not write cheques or conduct any business without the authority of the Receiver Manager. This stripping away of authority and control was met with hostility from members of the congregation and those loyal to Pastor Goodman.

By December 2002, VCC was in deep crisis as the details of the allegations became public knowledge. It is alleged that offerings slumped by two-thirds, and the church's overall financial position worsened after the receiver manager arrived. Coupled with that, the five-year lease on the property, which members thought they owned, was due to expire in January 2003; and the church faced the possibility of unlimited liability if litigation followed the allegations under investigation by the police. An emergency meeting was held to look at the possibilities of saving the church from closure. It was agreed that there were three possible options, and these were placed to Pastor Goodman. He, however, did not follow through on the undertakings that he gave and, because he broke the agreement, the receiver manager concluded there were not sufficient resources to keep the charity as a going concern.

Within a couple of weeks, Pastor Goodman started a new church, which is not a registered charity, called 'From Victory to Victory' (V2V) – a name which many regard as demonstrating contempt for the charity system. The integrity of the new church, V2V, hit rock bottom on 6 May 2004 when Pastor Goodman was found guilty of two counts of indecent assaults, one count of attempted sexual assault and one count of perverting the course of justice. The following day he was sentenced to three and a half years in prison. This verdict came after a second trial, the jury in the first failing to reach a verdict on fourteen allegations. To make matters worse, at the trial's conclusion, the Charity Commission announced that they were going to pursue Pastor Goodman and his wife for misappropriating nearly £3 million from VCC. Clearly, the issue at stake is not that VCC was a BMC but that the church had a pastor who clearly lost his way and failed to find 'The Way'. It is also true that the absence of good governance within the church allowed a bad situation to germinate and fester.

When the Charity Commission announced that they were sending a Receiver Manager into Kingsway International Christian Centre (KICC), it was as if hell had a lit volcano. Although, the church was concerned about VCC, there was sufficient doubt to be cautious. KICC was a flagship for the BMCs, representing everything we wanted the church in the UK to be. The church was large, it affirmed the people who attended and it was a beacon for what a successful church should look like. The word among leaders was, 'If the Commission can take over KICC, it can take over any church!' It would be foolish to pretend that all was perfect, but what is? Rumours abounded that the Commission had a 'hit list' with its targets lined up, which they strenuously denied.

KICC maintained throughout that they were in dialogue with the Commission for a couple of years, they were given a clean bill of health, and it was merely an overzealous investigator on a final visit to the church who misrepresented a situation she had observed. The Commission, on the other hand, argued that there were enough significant concerns relating to church governance to warrant a receiver manager being placed in the church. Trustees had been receiving 'unauthorised' salaries and benefits, and the charity had outgrown its management and accountability structure. For me, the critical point came when I was informed by an extremely credible source that 'the corridors of the Commission were very busy and they were considering closing the church'. Following meetings with both parties, a few leaders and myself persuaded the Commission not to appoint a Chief Executive for the charity, as this role had to be preserved for Pastor Matthew. We insisted that an agreed exit strategy needed to be in place. On the question of closing down the church, this was denied, but the Commission was adamant that changes had to be made. I do believe that the Commission got the message that to close the church would have been suicidal. They did not change their minds regarding what needed to be done; what changed was the method of achieving their objectives. So they opted to pursue a more low-key, integrated approach.

My source turned out to be correct. KICC was in fact registered with the Commission as 'The Kings Ministries'. Then, in February 2004 a new company called 'Kingsway International Christian Centre' was registered with the Commission, with new trustees. The assets of the Kings Ministry were to be transferred to KICC during the second half of 2004, and, as is usually the case, the cost of the receiver manager had to be paid out of the charity's own resources. In a press release issued in January 2004, KICC leaders listed the negative impact that all this was having on the church: including a reduction in income by 25 per cent, damage to reputation among the Christian community in the UK and internationally, and a reduction in the anticipated growth rate. My sincere wish was for this matter to be resolved much earlier. It might have been more advisable, once the principle that things must change had been established, for the church leadership to have offered greater cooperation with the process, and to have accepted the assistance of those in a position to help.

Something must also be said about the Charity Commission. My view is that at the time of these events, the Commission was going through a period when the government seemed frustrated with their performance and to have the opinion that the Commission was failing to carry out the regulatory aspect of its work effectively. The government response was to make more resources available for this task, and there were moves to replace the Commission with a Charity Regulatory Authority. There was also a review of charities and the 'Not For Profit' sector overall, entitled *Private Action, Public Benefit*. Had it not been for the reaction of the wider BMCs, at least one other church would have had a receiver manager installed.

At the beginning of the process, the Commission did not understand the BMCs and their cultural nuances, (something they readily accept). It is also true that they were far from even-handed in the way that they exposed these churches, and they undermined KICC in particular. I say this because other organisations who had their assets frozen were not vilified in the press. Notwithstanding, it is difficult to dismiss all of the Commission's concerns. It was evident that no other accountability structures or representative body could have resolved these issues. I do believe that the Commission have done their utmost to learn from their mistakes – in fact, they have proven to be much more open for dialogue, and are responding more eagerly, than one might have expected. Full credit is due to them for the swift way that they have agreed to produce new governing documents for churches (produced in the spring of 2005); in addition, they have relaxed the guidelines to allow for some trustees, especially pastors, to be paid. Further, they plan to arrange an amnesty for churches whose pastor was a trustee and was receiving a salary. Yet, it is the claim of the Commission that still challenges me: 'in all their history their staff had never been abused and humiliated as they were by Christians'.

No issue has so unified the BMCs, in fear, rage and concern, as has this governance issue. The issues involved are too numerous to explore in this book: in particular, I still have seriously reservations as to whether the Commission's model for the trustees' relationship with the pastor is appropriate in every situation. However, there were and are huge lessons for everyone. This episode led many churches to consider deregulation by withdrawing from the Commission. One Christian receiver manager has challenged this position: 'Only those who are crooked or have something to hide would give up the benefits of being a charity'. In any case the Commission would be unlikely to sanction such a move, and withdrawing organisations would be unable to transfer their capital or assets into any new non-charitable venture.

There is no doubt that some good has already come out of this situation. Many churches have bought into 'PPP' – perception, precedent and prudence – and have put their houses in order.

- *Perception* matters because it is important that an organisation really is what it says it is, and a charity should be run for the benefit of its members (in this instance, the congregation) and not for private benefit.
- *Precedent* matters because a church is not beyond the law the land, and we are held accountable. If we are genuinely faithful to God, we should have no difficulty with the law: 'Render therefore to Caesar the things that are Caesar's, and to God the things that are God's' (Matthew 22:21).
- *Prudence* matters because the cost of negligence is too high. Doing the right thing will keep both the leader and the organisation safe, secure and with an enhanced reputation.

I believe that if we take these matters seriously, we will build better and stronger churches. In a curious way, the BMCs' response has been to realign with White Majority churches. It is safe to say that they will be better able to face the future having learnt some hard lessons. KICC is well placed to expand and grow into one of the largest churches in Europe, but may yet face further challenges if London wins the 2012 Olympic games, since it is located on the very site earmarked for the Olympic stadium and village.

I do not believe that the BMCs have much to fear as a result of these challenges. Yes, we have received a spanking, but the righteous do not despise correction or chastisement (Hebrews 12:11). The BMCs' history is too short to lose all credibility so soon because of circumstances such as these. There seems to be no need for yet more regulation: not only is there the Charity Commission, there are also Company House and other statutory regulators. However, above all there is also Scripture with all its demands, which ought to be the churches' first and final arbitrator.

The challenge of relevance

The challenge for relevance is another issue that should concern the BMCs. There is nothing worse than trying to sell items that are already past their 'use by' dates. If a shop makes a habit of it, they will eventually gain a reputation of providing poor quality products. In any society, it is the circumstances that people currently face, or their aspirations for the future, that take precedence. They may well use the past as a reference point or even be anchored there, but the bottom line is always a concern for today and tomorrow.

BMCs cannot assume that they have a winning formula and so do not need to change or reassess themselves and their programmes. During my time as General Director of ACEA, I was single-minded in ensuring that BMCs moved from the fringes of society to centre stage, both in church life and in the Black community. I chose not to judge them by their potential but by their achievements. By helping them to see what they have achieved and the leverage they already had, it became much easier to show them the possibilities. It was always a pleasure to see churches converted to the reality that they could make a difference in their communities, regionally and nationally.

For BMCs to remain fresh and relevant, they need constantly to examine their spiritual impact and whether or not they are meeting the needs and aspirations of their members. They also need to 'face the music' when assessing whether or not they have succeeded in inspiring a new generation. Moreover, an honest review of their social and political engagement, and of their ambassadorial calling, is pivotal to their future success.

Confidence in the future

Growing up in South America, I encountered two types of dogs – bad dogs and 'rice eaters'. Bad dogs put the fear of God into you. You did not enter a yard or leave the premises where there was a bad dog without protection or unless the owner had succeeded in subduing and restraining their brutes. So fierce were these terrors that signs on the gates and fences warned, 'Beware, Bad Dog!'. Bad dogs were useful to their owners because they provided security for the owner and their premises. On the other hand, 'rice eaters' were pet dogs. They could not be relied on even to bark if someone came into your yard. You really had to prod, provoke and intimidate a 'rice eater' before you got a reaction. The strange thing was that many bad dogs behaved like rice eaters once they were outside the security of their homes! It was therefore difficult to detect the true character of the dog.

There are also three types of churches – those who lack confidence, those who are confident, and those who are overconfident. Amazingly,

size or 'success' is not the determining factor: it is often situational, cultural, the way that a church understands its roles and responsibilities,
or its theology. It is not the case that any of these positions is more detrimental than the rest – once we are humble in the presence of God, and
understand that we are mere 'hot air' without him, then we are free to
be ourselves in order to achieve our goals. Having said that, our confidence determines who we engage with, how we engage, and who engages
us. And this is the crunch of the matter.

BMCs need to be bad dogs, not only in their own homes but also
wherever they go. They need not be intimidated by their limitations, but
they must be able to recognise those limitations and seek to correct and
strengthen their weaknesses. Confidence will be misplaced if it rests
only in ourselves. Yet we know Who it is we believe in, and it is that confidence which should catapult us into areas we have avoided or that have
avoided us, which should convince us that there are no no-go areas for
the church. It is because of their genuine faith that the BMCs ought to
remember the exhortation of the apostle Paul: 'For God has not given
us a spirit of fear, but of power and of love and of a sound mind' (2
Timothy 1:7).

Spiritual impact

If then our faith is genuine, then our fruit must also be genuine. On one
level, it would be untrue to say that the spirituality of Black Christians
is superior to that of any other group. Different, yes! Superior, no!
Equally, there is no suggestion that Black Christians are more or less
honest, have a greater or lesser integrity, or love more or less than any
other group of Christians. To say otherwise is like buying into the
notion that Black men are a great deal 'better endowed' sexually than
other men. Nevertheless, there is something to be said about a spirituality which demands that God's children become more like Christ,
which insists on holy and righteous living, which affirms and demonstrates the value of all people. There is an attraction to a spirituality that
says, 'In the presence of God, something can be done about your situation, right here, right now!' There is an appeal to a lifestyle that priorit-
ises communication with God through prayer, fasting and reading his
word. There is a confidence to be gained when we are able to say, 'Look
what the Lord has done!'

If God no longer makes himself known, it is difficult to make him
known. The BMCs are in a season when God is making himself known

through this community. The onus therefore rests firmly on them to ensure that Black spirituality is not confined to the lives of their adherents. This spirituality must move beyond something to be admired, as though it were a spectator sport. Instead, it must be 'TTT' – transferable, transportable and transformational: transferable to others; transportable to wherever Black Christians happen to go; and transformational for the people, structure, institutions and communities who are impacted by it. Only then can the BMCs be confident that they are making a real spiritual impact.

Meeting the aspirations of our members

The National Health Service tells us that there are many patients in hospital who do not need to be there. For some, there is a difficulty in finding appropriate homes; others have acquired hospital-related illnesses and are therefore unable to leave. While I do not accept the frequently used description, 'The church is a hospital', some BMCs have allowed themselves to become just that. An overemphasis on meeting people's needs has led some constantly to create new needs to meet the hunger for perfection. In an indirect way, we have raised the threshold for what good health, prosperity, family life, happiness, peace, satisfaction, blessings and life's purpose should look like. While this is to be applauded, at some point leaders need to be directed back not only to the cross of Christ but to the crosses next to him. They need to be admonished that the preservation of the soul is more important than that of the body. Therefore, they must move on to preach and teach the whole counsel of God.

Having said that, it is important that Christians recognise that what has brought them to Christ may not sustain them in their walk with God. Many pastors cannot understand why some members, in whom they have dedicated so much time and effort, eventually leave their ministry. Often the reason is simple – those who are not sick do not need a physician. Meeting someone's need is not sufficient to retain their loyalty, as we well know from the story of the ten men with leprosy in Luke 17:11-19. The meeting of needs is often the platform to the next flight of stairs. Like Jesus, we should be sending some of the people on our counselling couches out for a reality check – to go and win a few souls for Christ, to do volunteer work in homeless shelters or refuges for battered wives, to do something that might cause them to readjust their perspective on life.

Now here is my big moment! Having committed treason with my view on Christians who are always needy, I will also add that, to my mind, there is another section of the church which has not seen growth and development for many years. They should no longer console themselves or be consoled with notions of holiness, falling standards, lack of discipline among the young or those who leave their church. These are excuses that cannot stand the test of time. Often their members are disillusioned, demotivated and demoralised. While some stay due to commitment, duty or responsibilities, others join the 'transfer growth market'. This in turn causes resentment and divisions.

If I had to invent a profession for myself it would be working with failing churches, helping them to make radical changes to turn themselves around. Every denomination should have a 'crack team' who are committed to church growth and development and who are able to offer consistent support to struggling pastors and churches. It is often the case that growing churches are struggling churches. This is because they have steep learning curves and must deal with issues they have never dealt with before. Struggling, therefore, is not about size but about effectiveness at any given point in time. For the BMCs to remain a dynamic church movement, they have to manage the expectations of their members and, at the same time, to grow in the areas that are of significance to their communities and members.

Inspiring a new generation

It is one thing to keep the current crop of Christians on song. However, there is always a new challenge around the corner. A church's ability to inspire another generation is almost always the litmus test of what will happen to it in the future. The Caribbean churches experienced this in the 1980s and early 1990s, when they lost a whole generation of young people. Their leadership were too preoccupied with keeping the pioneers and older members happy and on-side to notice that they needed new skills, language and interpretative approaches. Sadly, some still have not recognised this. In a profession where seniority, nepotism and preference predominate, it goes without saying that it is not the best man or woman who gets the job, but the best liked or the one least likely to rock the boat.

African churches need to learn the brutal lessons of the Caribbean churches if they are not to repeat the same mistakes. If we assume that their current crop of leaders have an average age of forty-two, this means that they will be around for at least another twenty-three years. Younger leaders, who are currently between the ages of twenty-five and thirty, cannot reasonably expect to become senior pastors until they are aged between forty-seven and fifty-three at the earliest. We therefore have to skip a generation to get another crop of young leaders. Lack of success and promotional prospects within certain strands of BMCs could lead to a 'brain drain' of credible potential leaders to other strands of the church, where the career path is more obvious. But it is the under twenty-fives that we must inspire. The old 'generation gap' is what we need to be cognisant of. The BMCs need to ditch their reticence on these issues to ensure that there is a generation to which they can pass the baton.

But there is another aspect of the inspiration of young people, and that is the establishment of a generous and radical youth provision. It is near impossible to continue the level of growth in the BMCs without addressing the issue of young people in the church. I have argued long and hard that the churches are failing in this area of ministry. That is why I spent a lot of time and effort raising the profile of children's work and youthwork, and ensuring that an ongoing provision is in place to train them. I have also taken the lead in developing a Certificate in Youthwork and Ministry course to enable youthworkers to gain a recognised Higher Education University qualification. This is the first youthwork course designed to meet the needs of the Black community in the UK. Thankfully, the church has responded in some measure to these initiatives, but this is not nearly enough to meet the demand and need. It was heartening to hear that the NTCOG, which has a good track record for youthwork, announced in 2003 that they were carrying out an independent review of their youthwork provision. For the first time, a denomination was going to make the changes necessary to meet this challenge. However, so far the process has delivered very little: the consultant's report was not discussed with the youthworkers across the denomination, and failed to deliver an open recruitment process. Instead, the same old processes prevailed. Suffice it to say that a lack of confidence and disappointment has ensued. No doubt this will make the task even harder for the incumbent National Youth Director.

The challenge to the BMCs is simple. If they have over one hundred adult members, there is no excuse for not employing a full-time youth worker. Furthermore, it would make more sense for churches who invest a significant amount of resources into evangelism and missions work to divert at least some of those resources into children's and youth work.

Might not these young people invite their peers if they felt they could bring them to something they were not ashamed of and which excited them? Once they caught the excitement, might not these friends in turn invite their parents and friends? The potential is there to produce a real harvest. Unless we abandon the habit of placing the most inexperienced Christians in charge of children, and the least inspiring to lead young people, this will remain the BMCs' Achilles heel.

Using public space

BMCs have an opportunity to be an powerful voice in the public domain, and it is an opportunity that cannot be ignored or neglected. The media is the marketplace in which ideas are shared and opinions expressed. If the BMCs' plans and convictions do not make the news, then it is unlikely they will capture the imagination of the masses. Whatever systems we put in place, the ongoing growth and the often nomadic existence of some churches means that they are only reachable through the media.

Still, there is a challenge beyond communicating among ourselves. The issue of who represents the true voice of the churches within the media is important. There are some issues that ought to fall within the remit of the BMCs. Black Christians should be at the forefront of the debates on immigration and asylum, on education and employment. We should be seeking to make an impact on the issues of justice, poverty, social exclusion, crime, and the judicial and prison systems – after all, one in every hundred Black people is in prison. We surely have much that is important to say about teenage pregnancy and lone-parenting. The political view has long been that it is Black, especially Caribbean, people who are responsible for the rise in teenage and single parents: but, as the wife of one overseer puts it, African Caribbeans tend to behave differently towards their children – they tend not to abort, give them up for adoption or send them to another country. It is this kind of simple clarification and challenging of perspectives that will make a difference.

Yet it is the unity of the BMCs that will catapult them to greater prominence. No single church, however large, can capture the headlines or put across a case like a collective of churches. This is where organisations like ACEA and EA could be of tremendous service. When ACEA announced that the BMCs were coming together in 2000 for Faith in the Future, it caught the imagination of the nation, and generated a rapid response from politicians. We were able to dictate what the headlines the following day were going to be. This is the church is at its best. Leaders of the BMCs must take hold of ACEA and make it into their servant. If it is to do the incredible and important task of being their eyes, mouth, hands and feet in society, it must be affirmed in public as well as in the pulpit, and church leaders must ensure that it is sufficiently resourced.

The BMCs will, however, fail to make an impact unless they establish credible institutions to operate alongside the churches. Both in Africa and the Caribbean, the missionary schools, hospitals and clinics that grew up alongside the churches have left an important legacy. Take education: the government wants to open at least 60 city academies by 2010, 30 of which are to be based in London. The equation is simple: if organisations provide sponsorship of £1 million, they can take over a failing school. If they provide £2 million, the government will provide the rest of the resources to build and run a new academy. It is time for both African and Caribbean pastors to re-examine the education debate. In the past it was looked upon as a Caribbean problem, but the evidence now shows that there has been a convergence in the failure of African and Caribbean pupils to do well at school. One educator, who was involved in producing guidelines on this issue for head teachers, remarked, 'I am prepared to compromise directly using the term "African pupils" so as to communicate effectively with head teachers.'

As I have highlighted earlier, every faith community, large or small, makes education a priority and ensures that there are adequate provisions for their children. Yet the most able BMCs are reluctant to consider forming alliances in order to create their own schools. They see the issue solely as a racial issue, when in reality it is about how the church goes about establishing the kingdom of God here on earth. It is about how Black Christians position themselves to influence the educational debate, today and tomorrow. It is about transferring godly values in a relatively value-free society, and providing environments where children's faith is nurtured and not devalued.

It is a fact that many of the senior leaders who ignore this reality are sending their own children to private schools or have made provisions for them to be educated in the place of their birth. My colleague Keith Davidson, Education Director of the Seventh-day Adventist Church (which runs eight schools), always admonishes churches that they have got their priorities wrong. Most of them are only interested in buying church buildings; but he argues, 'If you build a school, you can also worship in it.' I have encountered leaders prepared to spend over half a million pounds for premises that did not even have the space for a Sunday school, while others are desperately looking to spend millions on purpose-built premises. It does not seem to have occurred to them to consider investing in a school building, and making it a place fit for the provision of a good education and for worship. Unless and until the BMCs can begin the process of establishing schools in the major cities of the UK, their level of influence is bound to remain stagnant.

The Chairman of ACEA Executive Board, Nezlin Sterling,[2] has often said, 'I look forward to the day when BMCs could sponsor a Member of Parliament.' I pray that this day is fast approaching; but perhaps we should learn the lessons from the story of the chicken and the egg. Which came first? The farmer says, 'The chicken came before the egg, because that is how I bought it.' The theologian says, 'The chicken came before the egg, because God made all the living creatures, including the birds of the air, and told them to be fruitful and multiply.' But the little girl says, 'The egg came first, because I had an egg for breakfast and chicken and chips for lunch.' So you see, some things may be a matter of opinion, of perspective or of experience. They can be part of God's plan and purpose; or they could be one of Satan's snares. I hope that this book has helped you shape your own views, has challenged your perceptions and in some way has unveiled yet one more dimension of the kingdom of God.

Endnotes

1 Office of National Statistics, Census 2001.
2 Details correct at time of writing.

Appendix:
'Black, Black-led or What?'
by Arlington Trotman

First published in Joel Edwards (ed.), Let's Praise Him Again: An African Caribbean Perspective on Worship, *Kingsway, 1992.*

Whose identity?

There is increasing awareness in Britain of the disharmony between blacks and whites that prevents the black church community from taking its full place and exerting a greater influence within the wider church community. To a large degree the black church community has been placed in a second-class and marginal context, and at the heart of this situation lies the issue of race. Such awareness has developed not only among Britain's blacks, but also in the United States of America and the Caribbean. One of the more significant results of this protracted marginalisation, has been its particularly negative effect on the identity of Afro-Caribbean Christians, and the lack of appreciation of the spiritual challenge they represent. Worship within the so-called 'black-led' church, as it has come to be called, cannot be adequately clarified and accurately understood without a reappraisal of the factors that have moulded its identity.

It was in the 1950s and 1960s that large numbers of blacks from the Caribbean, including a significant Christian fraternity, were recruited to fill numerous job vacancies, mainly in the service industries of post-war Britain. The majority of these people naturally wished to preserve and uphold their profound commitment to God and worship within 'mainstream' churches, within whose Caribbean branches more than fifty per cent were full members. While many encountered widespread rejection on racial grounds, others were alienated by the nominal tendencies of the British church, particularly those used to the more fundamentalist and spiritual emphasis characteristic of the Caribbean expression of faith.

Significantly, sociologists have maintained that black people have not really escaped slavery, and race alone consequently 'determines their social, economic and political position'.[1] It also seems true that race alone has determined our religious – or more particularly, Christian – status, especially in view of the kind of rejection Caribbean Christians faced in Britain. The rejection of those who ultimately became the pioneers of the so-called 'black-led' church was apparently based solely on their black skin, which relegated their faith to an inferior status. This sense of inferiority/superiority in religion in general, and in the Christian faith in particular, appears (for black Christians, at least) to have much to do with the sociological and racial value-judgements that are made by both secular society and the church.

The superiority myth

It is now well documented that Europeans in the seventeenth and eighteenth centuries were fed with pseudo-scientific and racist myths about black people in order to justify slavery. The most disturbing and effective of these included questions about identity: were black people really human? In his *History of Jamaica* (1774) Edward Long declared:

> . . . *in* these acts they are libidinous and shameless as monkeys or baboons. The equally hot temperament of their women has given probability to the charge of their admitting these animals frequently to their embrace . . . In general; negroes are void of genius and seem almost incapable of making progress in civility or science . . . They are the vilest of humankind to which they have little more pretensions of resemblance than what arises from their exterior form.[2]

The same judgement is evident a century later in Charles Parham's comment about the 'disgusting Southern darkey camp meetings',[3] with which he disparagingly compared William Seymour's Azusa Street Revival of 1906. More recently, when Christians from the Caribbean attended 'mainstream' churches in Britain, they were asked by clergy not to return as 'your presence will unsettle our parishioners'. This comment implied that blacks were some sort of sub-human being.

This superiority myth has been fostered and perpetuated by the privileged rulers; by administrators of education, employment and housing, who all too frequently passed inferior services and accommodation to black people. Their social, political, economic and religious status as determined by race alone has rooted black people in a distinct 'caste' in Britain. Their tenacious rejection of the nonentity status, however, has led many out of the social, economic and religious wilderness. It must be with equal determination, at least within the scope of this present work, that the true identity of these groups of Christians be properly and permanently established as a significant step towards full participation and recognition in the life of the British church.

Where groups of people such as Caribbeans are alienated, especially on religious grounds, the consequence is invariably that they accept their alienation and form their own communities of faith. David Sheppard gives clear assent to this principle, commenting, 'It is a natural reaction of a group which feels shut out from the mainstream life in a country to strengthen its own community life; it is natural for churches to be focus points of such a community, as black churches are today.'[4] Caribbean Christians, however, were not simply forming new communities of faith; they were already members of recognised denominations, forced to develop apart from the 'mainstream' churches in this strange land. But the need to continue worshipping God was not merely a reaction to the superiority myth; of course other factors affected the development and growth of Caribbean Christian groups in Britain and have characterised our worship. We'll look at some of these in the course of this chapter.

The image and likeness of God

It is within the constitution of the human race to worship God, and the Christian, black or white, is presumably at ease in his worship of the Triune God. Humanity's creation in the image and likeness of God (Gen. 1:26–27) is a clear statement of its purpose. Human beings have also been given supremacy in the cosmos; and though we are an integral part of the natural order, we cannot find the true meaning and purpose for our existence in that context alone; our final destiny is not to be found in our dominion over the world, nor indeed in our power of reason, but ultimately in our positive response to God, through a personal relationship with him. This provides the framework within which we fully experience the true purpose of our existence. We were made to worship God, and that need must ultimately find fulfilment. Alienated Christians from the Caribbean, therefore, fulfilled an innate desire for worship by meeting in kitchens, bedrooms, living rooms, and, when numbers became too large, in school and church halls. Though they often encountered great reluctance from administrators and incumbent clergy when searching for this accommodation, it was from these vital, yet difficult and humble beginnings that the so-called 'black-led' church has come about. In view of these and other highly relevant considerations, the question of whether 'black-led' is an accurate and acceptable identification demands further investigation.

The new phenomenon

The phenomenon of the 'black-led' church has in the last thirty-five years been as staggering as its growth. Its pioneers were mainly simple but devout men and women who worshipped God with passion and sincerity. Such has been the rapidity of its growth during these years that 'The Growth of the Black-led Church in Britain' has become a much-used title for a multiplicity of discussions, essays, articles, books and other assorted papers in recent times, all seeking to understand and describe the nature of this brand of faith, and the factors affecting its increase and importance. It is interesting to note, however, that the growth rate of Afro-Caribbean churches between 1979 and 1989 was a mere four per cent.[5] Needless to say, it has not been with much prominence, except in a very few cases,[6] that the 'black-led' church itself has been engaged in this task of describing the phenomenon. In fact the research has mainly been by whites, whose discourses ranged from the purely socio-economic to historical and theological papers. Much of this work, of course, has to be assessed on the basis of the researcher's primary objective. Roswith Gerloff,[7] for example, has to be credited for her perspective to enhance and promote unity between black and white people. Paul Charman's *Reflections, Black and White Christians in the City*[8] sought most boldly to foster greater understanding about black people and their relatively misunderstood brand of faith – and thereby the promotion of Christian unity.

In the meantime, the black-led church fought consistently for survival and recognition as a significant presence in Britain. This process was greatly assisted by its acquisition of freehold property and organisation of structures, which have largely secured its future. It has established community care projects, ensuring that its elderly and children receive adequate care and education, and it is renowned for its high degree of free-spirited but largely orderly evangelical worship. The infectiousness of this mode of worship has been evident in other evangelical Christian groups, evident by their inclusion of musical instruments (including very 'noisy' drums), and hand-clapping in their heretofore 'quiet' style of worship.

The black-led church has now reached a watershed in its history; one that is noticeable in many respects. First, there is now a fresh desire to understand and describe the theological, historical and racio-cultural background of the black-led church; to face and question those traditions and theological nuances, as well as the misconceptions that have frequently been the cause of much unnecessary division and disunity. There has also been a new desire among black Christians to explain the positive social, moral and spiritual influences which brought cohesion, and contributed to their identify.

The identity described

An important aspect of this self-examination is the process by which identity has been conferred on these church groups by researchers and social scientists. Labels such as 'black', 'Pentecostal', 'black-led' and 'West Indian' are part of a vocabulary variously used to describe local churches in England whose leadership and membership are predominantly West Indian in origin. Only within the past twenty years have these terms come into the relevant literature, especially from the mid-to-late 1970s, and most recently by the Community Religions Project of the Department of Theology and Religious Studies at Leeds University. In this project, Vanessa Howard defined the term 'black-led', for example, as those churches 'which have black leadership and where membership is predominantly black'.[9] A number of research projects have since been published and the term 'black-led' is invariably favoured. In their work, both Roswith Gerloff and Paul Charman consistently use it throughout. In all examples of its use, this phrase has to all intents and purposes been *imposed* on the Christian community by researchers who sought to understand and describe. It is important from a black perspective, therefore, to discover to what extent these terms – 'black-led' in particular – have correctly described our Christian community. Even if only briefly, we need to look at some biological and sociological implications of the words used, and at their impact on the religious and cultural identity of black people in Britain. We can thus reach a better understanding of worship within our denominations.

Heritage and baggage

In one most notable respect the term 'black', used as a prefix or stand-ing alone, cannot be challenged or questioned as to its appropriateness; it describes people born with black skin. (This is true even if some Asians, who share the racial discrimination, also appropriate the term.) This unchangeable fact of course means that the whole race cannot change its skin pigmentation; it is the 'natural colouring' of that race. Given this undeniable circumstance, researchers were correct to reflect the colour in their terminology, though as we shall discover 'black' may not be satisfactorily used in the description of all these church groups.

A second observation is crucial. Since a person's blackness is irrever-sible, and since black people, it must be assumed, are completely content with their biological and created heritage (God said: 'Let us make man in our own image, after our likeness,' Gen.1:26–27, which includes all humanity), there is no logical or ethical reason for black people to try to justify our heritage by using defensive or polemic language given to us by others in an attempt to define our religious experience.

The demolition of racial barriers is quite clearly stated in St Paul's reflection on the specific purpose of the Incarnation and Resurrection when he said: 'There is neither Jew nor Greek, there is neither slave nor free man, there is neither male nor female; for you are all one in Christ Jesus' (Gal. 3:28, NASB). Christians have all entered into the unity of the body of Christ and ought to express that unity by the variety of gifts given to each. Together, these facts tend to make any distinction drawn on the basis of Christian religious or biological considerations com-pletely unnecessary, as it must do on racial grounds.

Not everyone, however, is discontent with the term 'black' in this par-ticular context. Iain MacRobert[10] regards it as indicative of a mode of worship characterised by rhythms and forms peculiar to African culture and heritage, which, of course, have been reflected in the American, Caribbean, and now British black Christian life and worship, and which constitute an essential aspect of our identity.

Even so, an assessment of the sociological implications of the term 'black' reveals the destructive and painful connotations all too often associated with 'blackness'. 'Black Friday', 'Black Monday', the 'black sheep of the family', and the general reflection of unhelpful or bad con-ditions like the 'black-list', 'blackmail' – all these convey ideas of wick-edness and gloom. Such associations affect the way in which things and people are perceived, and help to mould the beliefs and values of the perceiver. At the same time, infinitely more dangerous pseudo-scientific myths perpetuated during the eighteenth and nineteenth centuries have led to many discriminatory and racist attitudes against black people. Many of these are still current in a subtle but powerful way. Not only have these associations, myths and misconceptions informed individual attitudes, but they have also affected the policies of governments and institutions in the modern world, obviously loaded heavily against the black person.

Bishop David Sheppard fully acknowledged this fact when he cited Lord Simey's speech of 1966 in the House of Lords:

> ... our coloured fellow-citizens ... had been educated in our schools, spoke our common language . . . but because of their colour they were given unskilled jobs . . . the first to become unemployed in a slump, they had the worst accommodation, the worst social services and the worst neighbourhood to live in . . . May God help us if we lose equality of citizenship with people merely because of their colour.[11]

The situation of 1966 pertains today, not only to Liverpool, of which Sheppard wrote, but also to much of the rest of Britain and the Western world. 'The confinement of negroes to the lowest stratum is clearly a national condition,' says Leonard Reissman. 'Because of race alone the negro has been kept in the bottom economic class, in the bottom status group and in the most ineffectual power position.'[12]

These conditions have even led governments to legislate against black people, as in the South African apartheid state. Furthermore, whites have not only imposed this secondary or marginalised social status as chief controllers of economic and political power (for reasons too detailed to reflect here), but have created significant tension in the mind of the black person about his own identity; such white people are therefore less than qualified to determine that identity, as in the term 'black-led'. It would be complacent and wrong if this imposed identity were regarded as sacred and accurately reflective of the experience and ecclesiology of black Christians in Britain.

The important place our church has come to assume in a multi-racial, multi-denominational evangelical structure is evident, in particular, by the wide usage of the term 'black-led'. It becomes vital, therefore, for an accurate understanding of the growth, theology and ecclesiology of this branch of evangelical Christianity, and for its identity to be comprehensive and true, not only for white researchers alone, but also for black adherents. I turn now to consider specifically the other principal terms that are frequently used.

'The black church'

The first and most obvious term in use is 'black church'. This has encountered much resistance and repulsion because of its separatist and discriminatory overtones against other races. While the ethnic make-up of these churches is predominately (and in some cases exclusively) black, few, if any, would consciously discourage or discriminate against members of other racial groups. Use of the term 'black church' naturally invites criticism of this kind, and given that the term necessarily justifies the ethnic origin of the majority of its members in Britain, its heritage is rooted in the Incarnation and Resurrection of Jesus Christ, the precise source of salvation for whites and all others. On the other hand, 'black church', it may be argued, reaffirms the racial identity of its black adherents, and also asserts a peculiar social and moral cohesiveness that has been the inevitable result of being 'black' (and rejected) in a white society. The 'black church' has also come to be indicative of a religio-cultural tradition that is characteristically 'missionary' and 'Caribbean' in expression, and unhelpfully tends to preclude from its life those would-be black adherents born in Britain.

Much of the Christian influence and teaching in the Caribbean – the springboard for the 'black church' in Britain today – has been attributable to Southern white American missionaries. The main thrust of this missionary message was holiness as an invisible and inward work, and which visibly manifests itself outwardly in language, dress and social habits. Though the early teaching was less of the European doctrinal expository type, these Protestant missionaries started with the death, atonement and resurrection of Christ, together with eternal life for those committed to him. More particularly, many white missionaries constantly stressed the *outward* expression, often to the neglect of good biblical exegesis on the decisive *inward* work. For instance, in the 1860 General Conference of the Wesleyan Methodist Church (now the Wesleyan Holiness Church), it was stipulated that commitment to modest dress, no visits to places of amusement, no divorce or remarriage, no jewellery, limited recreation and no tobacco – described as 'a great evil and unbecoming to a Christian, a waste of the Lord's money, and a defilement of the body' – was necessary for conversion. Some in the Pilgrim Holiness Movement, which also emphasised abstinence from these things, went further in the General Assembly in 1938, when an unsuccessful proposal to ban the wedding ring was made. Its General Conference of 1955 voted it unconstitutional to receive a person into membership until he stopped wearing gold.

This disposition towards stress on the outward appearance (mainly of female members) as a vital mark of holiness prevails also within the Church of God of Prophecy and the New Testament Church of God; but these issues were common in their application and acceptance among Caribbean Christians as a whole. In addition many slaves and their descendants were taught to read from the Lord's Prayer and the Decalogue in the King James version of the Bible, hence a revered and almost inviolable appreciation of that version by many Christians, and a mode of speech in the very elderly which occasionally betrays the nature of their early education.

All these factors have influenced what has come to be called the 'black church', and while good ethics, high moral standards and modesty all have their authority in Scripture, the cultural baggage attracted and reinforced by this particular missionary emphasis has not always reflected the best course in Christian expression. In the colonial Caribbean, it has seriously restricted the education and training of the masses of eventual emigrants, out of whom many leaders and pastors emerged to pioneer and guide the church in Britain. The present leadership is largely of that generation of very devout early immigrants – many of them the 'fruit' of the efforts of those Holiness Movement white missionaries.

In addition, congregations referred to as the 'black church' are not exclusively comprised of black people. A number of the established denominations in Britain have white leadership at their American head-quarters, for example, the Wesleyan Holiness Church, the New Testament Church of God and the Church of God of Prophecy. Furthermore, a number of our churches have a few white members in Britain and white pastors in the USA. In this context, 'black church' refers specifically to the British experience, and recognition of two factors become important. First, it would be somewhat arrogant, to say the least, and certainly unscriptural, to ignore white membership in Britain regardless of the small numbers involved; and secondly, white people should be given every encouragement to become members of any denomination in the true biblical fashion of the unified church. Consequently, the descriptive wording that includes 'black' could work against the church's mandate to evangelise *all* people.

In spite of everything, a proportion of black Christians within 'black-led' churches would still affirm the use of 'black church', since by its use they are not only affirming their racial identity, but also some degree of pride in being black – even if only in reaction to white prejudice. On the other hand, many black Christians born in Britain would understandably prefer to disclaim the cultural identity that is in many cases distinctly Caribbean, if only because they have no first-hand knowledge or experience of it, especially of those elements interwoven with the prevailing conception of biblical holiness. While these second and third generation Caribbean descendants would also affirm and be proud of their *biological* and *cultural i*dentity, the idea of a 'black church' does not become an easy option for them.

'The black-led church', the 'Pentecostal' church

The most frequently used of the imposed terminology is 'black-led church'. This descriptive label was first used in the early 1970s research done by Roswith Gerloff.[13] It is infinitely more accurate and respectable, however, than the term 'sect', used by Malcolm JC Calley, who explains:

> By 'sects' I understand a religious group, within a more general religious tradition, which recruits by voluntary association . . . A 'church' on the other hand, does not depend on converts for the bulk of its members, but recruits naturally, the children of members becoming members as they grow up.[14]

True, Calley's research was done in the early stages of the development of these churches in Britain, and he could not be expected to have the benefit of hindsight of their growth today. To describe them as 'sects', however, he seemed to have ignored the fact that what largely differentiated them from their original Christian tradition was their transplantation into England via immigration rather than evangelisation. These groups, moreover, were formed into denominations well before their establishment in England.

It has already been noted that some regard 'black-led' as a politically emotive phrase with racial overtones. While its use aims to emphasise positively that the leadership is given by those mainly distinguished by ethnic origin, not all churches with predominantly black congregations are in fact 'black-led'. Some 'mainstream' churches in Britain with black communities engage black ministers, but these are not necessarily 'black-led' since their internal leadership is white. Even so, the cardinal doctrines of God and salvation are not expressed in a fundamentally different way from that of the 'black-led' church, except for the difference of the 'oneness'[15] emphasis in some. Furthermore, some churches with black congregations in the USA have white ministers, but largely black and white leadership in the UK, such as the United Pentecostal Church. The term 'black-led' is also thought by some black ministers to be deeply offensive; Malachi Ramsay has remarked that it is 'degrading and lacking in respect';[16] his is by no means an isolated view. The church whose members and British leaders are predominantly black may now wish to identify itself according to these historical and theological foundations, but also on the basis of its experience; it must avoid descriptions, however, that perpetuate the social, political, economic and cultural religious negatives that resound in the term 'black-led'. This term may imply independence from its American leadership. But for the church in Britain to seek full independence from its white American headquarters simply to justify the 'black-led' label is a foolish attempt to emphasise its racial heritage, which is anyway God-given. In any case, this phrase would not change the exclusivist and separatist connotations that work not only against its Christian identity, but also restrict the biblical concepts of mission and unity of the body, regardless of ethnic origin (Acts 15:1-11).

Again these churches are frequently referred to as 'black-led Pentecostal' churches, or 'West Indian Pentecostalism', or simply 'the Pentecostal church'. Here 'Pentecostal' and 'black' are used synonymously; but a number of difficulties arise here. To begin with, there are obvious examples of churches whose ministers and congregations are black, but not necessarily 'Pentecostal'. The Bibleway Church and Wesleyan Holiness Church are cases in point. The latter church's doctrinal position is fundamentally Methodist, though its style of worship may be quite similar to that of most Pentecostal churches. It is in the theology of the spiritual gifts that some difference is evident – the gift of tongues in particular. It is true, however, to say that the majority of churches whose congregations and pastors are mainly black are 'Pentecostal', with variations in style and theological emphasis. For 'Pentecostalism' in all of these terms is primarily distinguished by its regard for speaking in tongues as the initial evidence of baptism in the Holy Spirit, and as a work subsequent to conversion.

It would be much more precise if these churches were named according to their historical and theological foundations. The Holiness revivals of mid to late nineteenth century America gave birth to the majority of them, and while doctrinal emphasis changed, the cardinal beliefs have not varied. The doctrine of entire sanctification, for example, does not differ fundamentally from 'baptism with the Holy Spirit' – a subject too detailed to be dealt with here. It is sufficient merely to acknowledge that while many churches have the distinctiveness of being 'Pentecostal', the same churches are also happy to stress the necessity and importance of all spiritual gifts, and would not regard tongues as fundamental for faith, redemption, or future salvation, in the same way that they are constrained to accept the need for preaching, conversion and baptism by immersion.

The words 'West Indian' or 'Afro-Caribbean' church are also occasionally used. All the foregoing observations about cultural identity and evangelistic restriction equally apply here, and the needs of the increasing numbers of second and third generation descendants of this ethnic group cannot be ignored. Any treatise on worship within these churches of mainly Caribbean people has to recognise that, while many of these Christian groups have either purchased their own buildings or are sharing with other denominations, designations like 'West Indian' or 'Afro-Caribbean' are inadequate. Any original suitability in them has diminished as the church has developed.

The possibility of an adequate terminology?

The difficulties in the current terms cannot be overstated, but it seems equally problematic to construct an all-embracing and accurate description, especially given the large number of different denominations which have developed over the last thirty years. Indeed, is a label necessary at all now that these denominations have properly established themselves in Britain, sharing a common identity with others in Christ?

What is essential is that if there must be a descriptive term that identifies our churches for religious and cultural purposes, it will need to reflect that potentially enriching diversity, at least in the ethnic composition of the congregations, while at the same time contributing to the unity that all Christians share (see I Cor. 12:4–27; Eph. 2:11–22). The body of Christ has not been caste in colour, class or creed, but the Word was made flesh for all, and racial barriers were broken down in the Crucifixion and Resurrection.

Identification in the mainstream churches

The 'mainstream' denominations (Anglican, Catholics, Baptists, URC and Methodists) are identified primarily by theology and church tradition. Anglicanism, for example, is an Episcopal system, with a nationalistic title ('Church of England'). In the New Testament the Greek word *episcopos* means 'bishop' or 'overseer' and is applied pre-eminently to Christ (1 Pet. 2:25), and then to leaders of local congregations (Phil. 1:1). This term was used as a generic description of the office, its meaning defined in accordance with the qualifications demanded by the church (see 1 Tim. 3:1ff; Tit. 1:7). There appears to be little indication in Scripture of the rule of a single bishop, but the early church defenders Ignatius of Antioch and Ireneaus of Lyons[17] were the first to insist on a monarchical episcopacy – a system of one bishop over all other bishops. Scripture and the tradition of the church Fathers, therefore, seems central to the process of identification of this church, as well as the Roman Catholic Church.

The Baptist Church is identified by the theological position that defends adult baptism as the apostolic method of admitting members to church fellowship. The Methodist Church is so called because of a nickname attached to John Wesley and his colleagues at Oxford University who prayed, read Scripture and studied 'methodically'. Methodism was founded, however, on the biblical doctrine of justification by faith through grace, and stressed sanctification based on the exegesis of texts such as 1 Thessalonians 5:23.

Greek orthodoxy is so called not so much because of its doctrinal position, but because of the tradition.[18] The term 'orthodoxy' in Greek simply means 'the right opinion'. In Eastern Orthodoxy, however, 'classical tradition' developed through creeds and councils by the early church fathers as a defence of the church against heresy lies at the heart of its identity.

Clearly, then, the identification of the 'mainstream' church has emerged primarily from biblical interpretation built on analytical expositions of Scripture, or a defence of biblical faith, not by race or colour as in the term 'black-led'. (Quite noticeable, however, is the development of 'house churches', whose growth between 1979 and 1989 reached 144 percent[19] and who seem to have avoided the problem of a suitable name.)

The Holiness Movement

We have seen that the common theological root of the so-called 'black-led' church is in the Holiness Movement. This movement emphasised biblical holiness as separation *from* self to God. The Greek term *hagios* (holy) has a very strong sense of 'separation from' common use, and

'consecration to' a hallowed state (1 Thess. 3:13; 2 Cor. 7:1). The movement began in nineteenth century America when Methodism had lost
its emphasis on the Bible and sanctification, and it sought to restore
power to Christianity through a re-emphasis of these in the revivalist
camp meetings, mainly in the southern USA and in parts of New York
State and the Midwest. Sanctification and speaking in tongues were
considered by Wesley as signs of baptism with the Holy Spirit; he had
also made a distinction between both of these and the state of the ordinary Christian.

The Holiness Movement also stressed freedom from 'carnal-mindedness'
– for example, gambling, smoking tobacco, alcohol, swearing, adultery and
social dancing – and emphasised 'outward holiness'. In addition, female
decorum merited special attention: the body became fully clothed by
dresses with full or elbow length sleeves, hems below the knees, and no low
necks; covered heads, understood by many as the wearing of hats in worship
(some women will not enter a church without a hat or scarf on their heads);
unplaited hair (understood as non-straightened hair). But Holiness theology was essentially a combination of Methodism and the doctrine of
Christian perfection, and it differed from 'fundamentalism' in that it was
more oriented to ethics and spiritual life than to the defence of doctrinal
orthodoxy. The Pentecostal and Holiness Churches emerged from these
waves of revival, becoming separated only on the issues of tongues and
organisational structures.

Another concern is the distinction to be made between culture (in
Caribbean terms) and Christianity, though of course these are not
mutually exclusive. The churches in question have the very special
problem of a difficult mixture of 'American–Caribbean' culture with a
strong African content on one hand (ladies' dress codes, language,
innate rhythms, the unwritten liturgy, etc.), and on the other a different
attitude from those born in Britain to the same cultural elements,
which would be ignored to the church's peril. Yet, to address this situation adequately may entail abandoning use of the term 'Holiness' with
its connotation of spiritual superiority, since this use of it would at best
be artificial and at worst unscriptural.

'Holiness Church' would not call attention to race as 'black-led' does,
since there is no implication of ethnicity in the term; nor would it imply
any organisational structure based on a race. Churches with white leadership in the USA and an almost exclusively black leadership in Britain,
if the British churches were brought by independence or greater participation of talented and able black leaders to equality at all levels of lead-

ership and administration, would not be affected either doctrinally or historically by the duality, for example, of the names 'Holiness Church' (British) and the Church of God or Wesleyan Church (American).

New labels reflecting the theological reasons why our churches came into existence would eliminate the inaccuracies inherent in the terms 'Afro-Caribbean', 'Caribbean', 'West Indian', 'Pentecostal', 'black' or 'black-led' churches, but not at the expense of racial, religious or cultural identity, black or white. The Caribbean cultural elements would, with appropriate biblical studies, be identified and separated as voluntary or incidental, not essential to the biblical requirements for faith.

But the implications of omitting or subsuming 'Pentecostal' cannot easily be ignored. First, there is a long scriptural tradition attached to this title, and the idea of omitting it would only be accepted with great difficulty; second, the theological differences (tongues, foot-washing) associated with it may be blurred, at least in principle; and third, the instant connotations of the word 'Pentecostal' (indicating passionate and open worship with an unwritten liturgy) could disappear. But if the term 'Pentecostal' *were* dropped, the biblical ideas of cross-cultural evangelism and multi-racial fellowship could be better served, in addition to immediate identification of our churches with the wider evangelical tradition in Britain. The church, black, white or mixed must offer a new mode of life to *all* people; and that alternative is found only in its message of salvation by faith through grace available to all in Christ.

The phrase 'Holiness-Pentecostal Church', already in use by some writers, would, of course, provide an accurate alternative, because of the 'Holiness' origin and the 'Pentecostal' distinctiveness, even if the latter has its foundation in the former. Yet some Pentecostal movements (white churches) that do not immediately connote 'Pentecostalism' (as popularly understood) may lie outside this term and invite even greater confusion.

It is not too difficult to see the need for an all-embracing term of identification that would satisfy diversity, ecclesiology and theology, culture and spirituality in the kingdom of God. It seems clear that a non-nationalistic or non-racial title may be used with great effectiveness.

While this discussion seeks to raise the appropriate questions and to stimulate dialogue on this important issue, it is clear that there are no simple answers. What seems to be a highly attractive approach is the use of a name that identifies our churches both theologically and historically. This would necessarily involve some combination of the 'Holiness' and 'Pentecostal' labels.

It is within the context of this reappraisal and analysis of the imposed 'black-led' title that worship within churches of mainly black adherents originating or descending from the Caribbean can be best understood, since clarification of the peculiar features of our church community will contribute to an enlightened understanding of our worship, and advance the permanent establishment of the church's true identity.

Endnotes

1 Neil J Smelser (ed.), *Sociology: An Introduction*, Wiley, 1967, p241.
2 Tim Ward, 'Growth of the Black-led Churches in Britain' (unpublished article).
3 Vinson Synan, *The Holiness-Pentecostal Movement in the United States*, Eerdmans, 1971, p180.
4 David Sheppard, *Bias to the Poor*, Hodder and Stoughton, 1983.
5 Marc Europe, *English Church Census*, 1989.
6 Works by Black Christians include: Ira Brooks, *Another Gentleman to the Ministry*, Compeer Press; Philip Mohabir, *Building Bridges*, Hodder, 1988; and Anita Jackson, *Catching Both Sides of the Wind: Conversations with Five Black Pastors*, British Council of Churches, 1985.
7 Roswith Gerloff, *Partnership Between Black and White*, Methodist Home Mission, 1977.
8 Paul Charman, *Reflections, Black and White Christians in the City*, Zebra Project, 1979.
9 Vanessa Howard, *A Report on Afro-Caribbean Christianity in Britain*, Community Religions Project, Research Paper (NS 4), Department of Theology and Religious Studies, Leeds University, 1987.
10 Iain MacRobert, Lecture sponsored by ACEA's Youth Network, Birmingham, 1991.
11 Sheppard, p33.
12 Smelser, p240.
13 Gerloff, see above.
14 Malcolm J Calley, *God's People: West Indian Pentecostal Sects in England*, Oxford University Press, 1965, p2.
15 'Oneness' is a non-Trinitarian theological position that stresses singularity in the Godhead, eg baptism 'in the name of Jesus' only, rather than 'in the name of the Father and of the Son and of the Holy Spirit'.
16 *Faith in the City: A Call for Action by Church and Nation*, Report of the Archbishop of Canterbury's Commission on Urban Priority Areas, Church Information office, 1985, p 42.
17 Williston Walker, *A History of the Christian Church*, T&T Clark, 1976, p41, 2.
18 Carl E Braaten (ed.), *Perspectives on Nineteenth and Twentieth Century Protestant Theology*, SCM, 1967, p9.
19 Marc Europe, see above.